CW00422168

THE COMPLETE IDIOT'S GUIDE® TO

Microsoft®
Excel 2000

by Sherry Kinkoph

que®

A Division of Macmillan Computer Publishing
201 West 103rd Street, Indianapolis, Indiana 46290

The Complete Idiot's Guide to Microsoft® Excel 2000

International Standard Book Number: 0-7897-1868-5

Library of Congress Catalog Card Number: 98-87062

Printed in the United States of America

First Printing: *May 1999*

01   00   99   4   3   2   1

Trademarks

Executive Editor
Angela Wethington

Acquisitions Editor
Stephanie J. McComb

Development Editors
Becky Campbell
Valerie Perry

Managing Editor
Thomas F. Hayes

Project Editor
Tom Stevens

Copy Editor
Bart Reed

Technical Editor
Kyle Bryant

Illustrator
Judd Winick

Indexer
Greg Pearson

Proofreader
Mary Ellen Stephenson

Layout Technician
Eric S. Miller

Contents at a Glance

Contents

viii

Part 2: Putting Excel to Work — 105

Part 6: Nothing but Net 319

About the Author

Sherry Kinkoph has authored over 25 computer books for Macmillan Publishing over the past five years, including books for both adults and children. Her recent publications include *How to Use Microsoft Office 97, Easy Office 97 Small Business Edition,* and *Sams Teach Yourself Quicken Deluxe 99 in 10 Minutes.* You can email Sherry at skinkoph@inetdirect.net.

Dedication

To my camping comrades—Scott Farmer, Shawn Sechrest, Greg Loving, Teresa Howell, Stacey Federhart, Kelly Hughes, and Melissa Cannon—campfires just aren't the same without you.

Acknowledgments

Special thanks to Jamie Milazzo and Stephanie McComb for their excellent acquisitions work, Becky Campbell for putting her development expertise to such good work, Bart Reed for dotting the I's and crossing the T's, Tom Stevens for shepherding this book every step of the way and making sure it made it to the printer on time, and Kyle Bryant for checking the geeky technical stuff and making sure all the steps work as promised. Finally, extra special thanks to the production team for assembling this handy guide and making it all look so nice.

Tell Us What You Think!

As the reader of this book, *you* are our most important critic and commentator. We value your opinion and want to know what we're doing right, what we could do better, what areas you'd like to see us publish in, and any other words of wisdom you're willing to pass our way.

As Executive Editor for the General Desktop Applications team at Macmillan Computer Publishing, I welcome your comments. You can fax, email, or write me directly to let me know what you did or didn't like about this book—as well as what we can do to make our books stronger.

Please note that I cannot help you with technical problems related to the topic of this book, and that due to the high volume of mail I receive, I might not be able to reply to every message.

When you write, please be sure to include this book's title and author as well as your name and phone or fax number. I will carefully review your comments and share them with the author and editors who worked on the book.

Fax: 317-581-4666

Email: **office_que@mcp.com**

Mail: Executive Editor
          General Desktop Applications
          Macmillan Computer Publishing
          201 West 103rd Street
          Indianapolis, IN 46290 USA

Introduction

The New and Improved Excel 2000

Well, they've gone and done it again. They've changed Microsoft Excel. That's right, another version is out—Microsoft Excel 2000. Depending on your personality type, you may respond to this news in one of several ways:

- ➤ If you're a "the glass-is-half-full" kind of person, you're probably pretty excited about a new-and-improved version of Excel. You're also probably wondering what new bells and whistles the fine programmers at Microsoft have added to an already-great spreadsheet program.

- ➤ If you're a "the glass-is-half-empty" kind of person, you're probably thinking, "Great, now I've got to relearn the whole darn program," or "What if those darn Microsoft programmers decided to take away my favorite features?"

- ➤ On the other hand, some seasoned Excel fans may be looking forward to an upgrade—it's about time they improved this application.

- ➤ If you're a new user—yippee! You don't have any of the hang-ups already described. You're a clean slate just waiting to soak in all you can learn about this super program.

Regardless of your personality type or outlook, you hold in your hands a book that can make the transition easy, whether you're upgrading from an older version of Excel or learning the program for the very first time. *The Complete Idiot's Guide to Microsoft Excel 2000* shows you everything you need to know about using the program to get your job done, even if your job involves number juggling at home or bean counting at the office.

Why Do You Need This Book?

Why an *Idiot's Guide*? Of course, you're not an idiot, but learning a new software program can make you feel like one at times. Unless you have a degree in Geekology, spending all your time wading through a giant technical handbook detailing every aspect of how Excel works just isn't up there on your list of things to do today. You've got work to complete, you've got people to meet, you've got a life.

If you're looking for a book to help you quickly learn the ins and outs of Excel without drowsing off, this *Idiot's Guide* is for you. It's no secret that Microsoft Excel is one of the best-selling programs of all time, and if time is of the essence to you, then this book can help you master the program quickly, painlessly, and without a lot of technical babble. You learn all the newest features Excel has to offer, including how to use Excel's Internet features and turn your worksheets into Web pages.

How Do You Use This Book?

This guide doesn't have any rules. You don't have to read this book from cover to cover, unless that's what you really want to do. Each chapter presents a topic in easy-to-understand language and easy-to-follow steps. Just pick and choose the topics that interest you. We've broken the book into six parts:

➤ Part 1, "Basic Training," provides a brief introduction to Excel, including new features to look for and information on using the program's basic functions, such as opening and saving files, working with worksheets, and finding help.

➤ Part 2, "Putting Excel to Work," covers automating data entry, working with formulas and functions, and fixing formula problems.

➤ Part 3, "Worksheet Grooming," explains how to format your worksheet data to make it professional looking and presentable to others.

➤ Part 4, "Charting New Territory," instructs you on how to use Excel's charting tools to create charts and graphs.

➤ Part 5, "Building and Analyzing Databases," shows you how to use Excel as a database tool, including organizing and sorting data and performing what-if scenarios.

➤ Part 6, "Nothing but Net," covers using Excel on the Internet and in network environments, as well as integrating Excel with other applications.

In addition to these parts, you will find an appendix in the back of the book to help you learn Windows 98 (if you're a new convert). Plus, you can find a glossary in the back that covers all those geeky technical terms commonly associated with Excel.

When you encounter any keys, key combinations (two keyboard keys you must press simultaneously), buttons, or commands you're supposed to select, the information appears in color. Here are some examples:

Press **Enter** to continue.

Press **Ctrl+X** to cut the selected data.

Click **OK** to exit the dialog box.

Open the **File** menu and select **New**.

You also find numerous tip boxes scattered throughout each chapter to help you along the way.

Techno Talk

Look to these boxes to learn about advanced features or other geeky terms and concepts.

Check This Out

These tip boxes contain hints, shortcuts, and other useful information to help you get things done faster or easier.

New Excel 2000 Feature

If you're a seasoned Excel user, look to these tip boxes to identify new features you'll want to know about.

That's about all there is to know about using this book. You're now ready to jump in and start using Excel 2000.

Part 1

Basic Training

Need to attend a boot camp on spreadsheet basics? Then you've come to the right place. Drop and give me 50—50 worksheet cells, that is. This part of the book covers all the basic features you need to know about to feel comfortable using Excel 2000. By the end of this section, you'll be able to navigate a workbook without the aid of a compass. You'll learn how to enter all types of spreadsheet data into cells and manipulate worksheets like a seasoned drill sergeant. You'll know how to open, close, and save files in record time, even under the stress of combat situations—such as when your boss needs the latest sales figures in the next 10 seconds. You will also learn how to apply spreadsheet first aid for when you need help with Excel as well as find out how to customize Excel to suit your own work needs. Are you ready? Then fall out!

Chapter 1

Excel in a Nutshell

In This Chapter

➤ The lowdown on spreadsheet programs in general

➤ Find out how to start and exit Excel

➤ Learn how to navigate the program window and identify its many elements

➤ The scoop on Excel's newest features

Okay, enough small talk. Let's get down to business. If you need an overview of Excel or just want to see what's new and improved in this latest incarnation of the program, then this chapter's just for you. Start reading.

Spreadsheets: A Brief Retrospective

Before the advent of computer programs, spreadsheets were the bane of the office world, an endless printout of rows and columns on green-and-white striped ledger paper. Paper spreadsheets were used to record all manner of data, such as credit and debit numbers and product inventories. Many an accountant spent many an hour recording tidy little rows and columns of data and punching numbers into a calculator to spit out a result, which then had to be entered into an intersecting row and column on the ledger. Needless to say, erasers were big sellers back then, and you didn't dare record a spreadsheet in ink unless you were pretty darn sure the data wasn't going to change.

Spreadsheet

At its very heart, a *spreadsheet* is just one big table or chart with data spread out all over the page, hence the name.

When computer programs came along, the world of number juggling was revolutionized. No more tedious data entry and reentry, and no more bulky calculators hogging room on the desk. Best of all, no more eraser marks or crossed-out lines. The invention of the spreadsheet program allowed users to quickly enter data electronically and edit it as needed, as well as to perform complex calculations with nary a stray mark or miscalculation.

So, where does Excel fit into the picture? Microsoft Excel is one of the best-selling spreadsheet programs of all times (but you probably knew this already since you bought a copy). The beauty of a spreadsheet program such as Excel is that everything's built in—the rows and columns, formatting controls, and mathematical functions are all right there for you, ready to use.

Excel can turn anyone into an instant accountant. You don't have to be a math wizard, and you don't need an MBA—all you need are a spreadsheet program and a little instruction, and soon you'll be crunching numbers into complex formulas and calculations, balancing budgets, keeping statistics on your softball team—and doing other high-profile tasks.

Now that you know where spreadsheets come from, what can you do with Excel? I'm glad you asked. The following is a sampling of uses:

➤ Organize and calculate number data, such as your department's sales totals.

➤ Create a pie chart showing which department is bringing in the most revenue.

➤ Perform what-if scenarios to examine various interest rates on a car loan.

➤ Figure the depreciation of the car you just bought after you drove it off the lot.

➤ Track your child's Girl Scout cookie sales.

➤ Keep a mileage record of each trip you had to make in the new car to deliver the darn cookies.

➤ Generate a budget detailing your household income and expenses.

These are just a few scant suggestions—your mileage may vary, of course. In fact, when it comes to uses for Excel, you're limited only by your own imagination.

Starting and Exiting Excel

If you know how to start one Windows program, you know how to start them all. This is a pretty true statement whether you're using Windows 95 or Windows 98. Most programs start the same way—via the Start menu. To start Excel, follow these steps:

1. Click the **Start** button on the taskbar.

2. Click **Programs** to display the Programs menu.

3. Select **Microsoft Excel**. The following figure shows an example of a typical Programs menu.

Programs menu

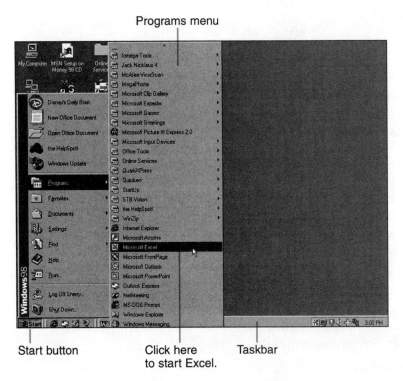

You can start Excel just like you do any other Windows-based program.

Start button   Click here   Taskbar
to start Excel.

Which Windows Are You Using?

Excel 2000 runs in Windows 95 or Windows 98. All of the figures in this book were created using Windows 98, so if you're using Windows 95, some onscreen items may look a bit different from what you see in this book.

How About a Shortcut Icon?

To speed up your procedure for starting Excel, consider adding a shortcut icon to the Windows desktop. That way, you can quickly open the program by double-clicking the icon. To add a shortcut icon, click the right mouse button (this is called right-clicking) over the Windows desktop and choose New, Shortcut. This opens the Create Shortcut dialog box. Click the Browse button and locate the folder where you chose to install Excel and select the Excel.exe file (you'll probably find it in your Program Files folder on your C drive, nestled inside Microsoft Office folder, then inside the Office folder), then click Open. Click Next and the dialog box displays a default name for the shortcut. You can use this name or type in another. Click Finish and the shortcut icon is placed on the desktop.

I realize you're not ready to exit just yet—heck, you just opened the program. However, take a moment and learn how to do so now. That way, you'll be ready when the time comes. To exit, use any of these methods:

➤ Open the File menu and choose Exit.

➤ Click the Close button (the one with an x in it) in the upper-right corner of the program window.

➤ Press ALT+F4 on the keyboard.

➤ Click the Control-menu icon (located in the upper-left corner of the program window) and select Close.

➤ Double-click the Control-menu icon.

If you haven't saved your work, you'll be prompted to do so before exiting. Click Yes to save your changes (you'll need to give the file a name), click No to exit without saving the changes, or click Cancel to forget about exiting and return to the program window.

Control-Menu Icon?

It's the tiny icon in the upper-left corner of the program window, to the left of the program title. When clicked once, this icon opens a menu of commands for controlling the program window, such as sizing or moving the window. The Control menu repeats the commands for minimizing, maximizing, and closing that are available as buttons in the upper-right corner of the program window. You can also double-click the Control-menu icon to exit Excel altogether.

Working with Program Window Elements

When you open Excel, the first thing you see is a big, blank worksheet just waiting for you to fill it with data. The following figure shows an example of such a sight.

Title bar   Formula bar   Menu bar   Toolbars

Program window controls

Excel's main screen includes a worksheet, toolbars, and more.

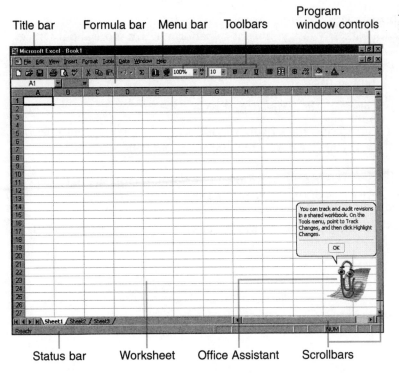

Status bar   Worksheet   Office Assistant   Scrollbars

The Excel program window contains many of the same features found in other Windows-based programs. For example, if you've used other programs, you're used to seeing a title bar, menu bar, toolbars, and scrollbars. Here's a brief rundown of the onscreen elements found in the Excel program window:

Title bar   Shows the program name and the name of the workbook you're currently using.

Menu bar   All of Excel's commands reside in the menu lists available on the menu bar. To display a menu, click its name. To select a command from the menu list, click the command name.

Toolbars   Excel displays two toolbars, by default, when you first start the program: the Standard and Formatting toolbars. Each houses a collection of common Excel tools and features you can quickly access with a click of a button.

Formula bar   Use this bar to enter and edit formulas for performing calculations on data in the worksheet cells. Learn more about using the Formula bar in Chapter 3, "Data Entry in a Dash," and in Part 2, "Putting Excel to Work."

Program window controls   These three buttons control the program window. Right below them, you'll notice three identical buttons. The second set of buttons are for controlling the active file, or workbook, window. The controls include the Minimize, Restore, and Close buttons.

Office Assistant   This animated feature (which is Clippit, by default) is ready to offer assistance with any task you want to perform. Learn more about Office Assistant in Chapter 5, "Help Me, Please!"

Worksheet   The Excel worksheet contains the rows and columns that form the grid in the program window. Much like a document page in a word processing file, a worksheet is simply a spreadsheet page.

Status bar   This bar keeps track of your worksheet status, such as number of pages. For example, if you're saving a file, the status bar will say so.

Scrollbars   Each worksheet has vertical and horizontal scrollbars that you can use to view different areas of the worksheet page.

The next few sections examine several of these onscreen elements in greater detail.

Repetition Is Rampant

Many of Excel's commands and features are duplicated. For example, buttons on the toolbars activate commands also found on the menu bar. Most users prefer clicking toolbar buttons over opening and selecting menu commands. However, if you're not too keen on alternate paths to the same commands or features, or maybe you're just an avid keyboard user who never intends to use the mouse to click anything, consider turning off the toolbars. This will free up more onscreen workspace. To do so, open the **View** command and select **Toolbars**. Deselect the toolbar you want to hide. Follow this same step to turn the toolbar back on.

Worksheets, Workbooks, Workthis, Workthat?

A preponderance of the prefix "work" exists in Excel, but don't be alarmed. There's not much work involved with sorting the terms out. In Excel, spreadsheets are called *worksheets* (you might want to memorize this for the quiz later). A worksheet is a page in a workbook where you can enter and store data, perform calculations, organize information, and carry out other such tasks. Worksheets are organized into *workbooks* (this will probably be on the quiz, too). An Excel workbook is a file much like a word processing document file—one file with multiple pages. By default, Excel opens a blank workbook and activates one worksheet, with two more waiting in the wings. Each worksheet in a workbook is represented by a tab at the bottom of the workbook window, as shown in the following figure. You simply click the tab to display the worksheet.

Each worksheet is comprised of columns and rows. These intersect to form the grid you see in the preceding figure. Each intersection is a box, called a *cell*. You learn more about using cells in Chapter 3 and more about using worksheets and workbooks in Chapter 4, "The Wonderful World of Worksheets." I just wanted to whet your appetite for now.

Each file you open in Excel is called a work-book. *A workbook is comprised of worksheets.*

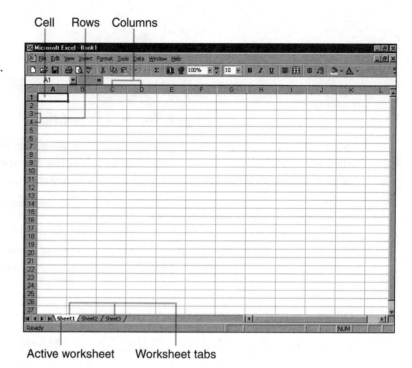

Cell   Rows   Columns

Active worksheet   Worksheet tabs

How Do I Move Around in Here?

You can move around the Excel program window using the mouse or the keyboard. As you move your mouse pointer around onscreen, it changes shape. Anytime you move your mouse pointer inside the worksheet area of the screen, the pointer becomes a giant plus sign, but it's still the same old mouse pointer you use to select and point at things. Anytime you move the mouse pointer outside the worksheet area, it becomes the old arrow-shaped pointer again.

To move around a worksheet, just click the cell in which you want to work. You can use the scrollbars to view different portions of the worksheet page. Click the scroll-bar's arrow buttons to move in the appropriate direction, or you can drag the scroll box to move your view in larger chunks. The following figure identifies the scrollbar's components.

Jumping Around with a Click

You can also click anywhere on the scrollbar to move to another page or area of the worksheet. For example, if you click below the scroll box on the vertical scrollbar, you view another screen full of worksheet cells.

Vertical scrollbar   Click the arrow buttons to move up or down.

Use Excel's scrollbars to help you view the worksheet page.

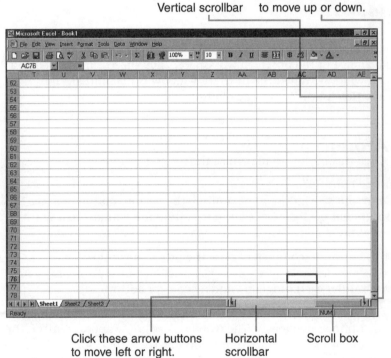

Click these arrow buttons to move left or right.   Horizontal scrollbar   Scroll box

Using the keyboard to move around the program window is a little more complicated. Lucky for you, I've included a handy chart of key combinations (see Table 1.1) you can use to zip around your worksheets.

Table 1.1 Moving Around the Screen with the Keyboard

Press	To Move
Left-arrow key	Left one cell
Right-arrow key	Right one cell
Up-arrow key	Up one cell
Down-arrow key	Down one cell
Home	To the beginning of the current row
End+[any arrow key]	To the end cell of the current row
Crtl+Home	To the first cell in the worksheet containing data
Ctrl+End	To the last cell in the last column and row containing data

Controlling Windows

Use Excel's program window controls (located at the far-right end of the title bar) to minimize, maximize, or close the program window. If your program window isn't already taking full advantage of the onscreen workspace, click the **Maximize** button to enlarge the program window. When the program window is maximized, the Restore button appears. Here's how to use each button:

Minimize Click this button to reduce the program window to a button on the taskbar. To open the window again, click its button on the taskbar.

Maximize Click this button to maximize the program window to its fullest size, which takes up the entire screen.

Restore If the program window is maximized, the Restore button replaces the Maximize button. Click the **Restore** button to restore the window to a slightly reduced size.

Close Click this button to completely close the program window.

The following figure identifies each program window control button.

In addition to the program window, you'll also see a workbook window containing three worksheets, as mentioned previously. The workbook window appears within the program window; basically, it's a window within a window (hey, they don't call this operating system *Windows* for nothing, you know). The workbook window also has three window control buttons. You'll find them at the far-right end of the menu bar, as shown in the previous figure. Use them to minimize, maximize, or close the workbook window.

Workbook window controls   Minimize   Restore   Close

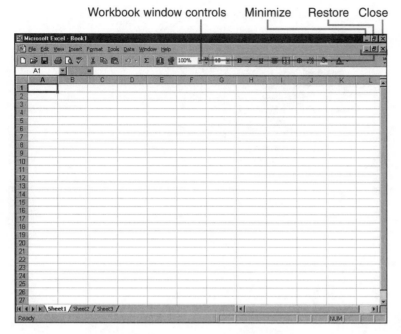

Use the window controls to change the window size.

What About Resizing Windows the Old-Fashioned Way?

You can also resize the Excel window using the window borders. Hover your mouse pointer over the border of the window until it takes the shape of a double-sided arrow; then hold down the left mouse button and drag the window border to resize it. If you click and drag a border, you'll resize that particular border. If you click and drag on a window corner, you'll resize the entire window.

Ordering from Menus

Microsoft has changed the way menus work in Excel 2000, as opposed to previous versions of Excel. The new Excel offers personalized menus that show only the controls you use the most (see the next two figures). Simply put, this means that a menu won't show every available command unless you tell it to; instead, it shows the commands you commonly work with. You can also customize how menus are displayed.

17

Excel's new personalized menus show only the commands you use the most.

Click here to display the entire menu.

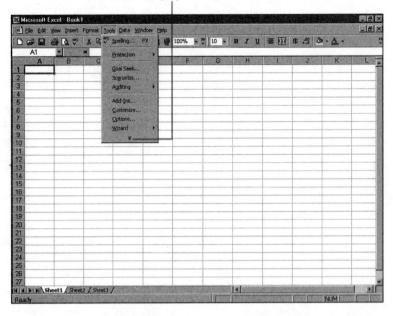

Here's the menu expanded to show all the available commands.

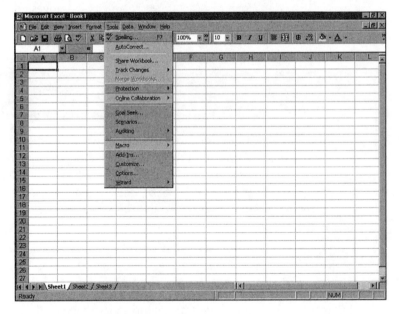

Here's how to work with the new personalized menus:

➤ To open a menu, click the menu name on the menu bar using the mouse. If you're an avid keyboard user, press the **ALT** key and the underlined letter of the menu name.

18

➤ To choose a command from a menu, simply click the command or press the command's selection letter (the underlined letter in the command name).

➤ To view all the commands on a menu, open the menu and wait a few seconds, or you can click the double-arrow icon at the bottom of the menu.

➤ A right-pointing arrow next to a menu command means a submenu can be viewed. Move your mouse pointer over the arrow to display the submenu. (Some submenus even have submenus to select commands from.)

New Excel 2000 Feature

Personalized menus are new to this version of Excel and can help tailor the way you use the program.

To customize your menus, open the **View** menu and select **Toolbars**, and then select **Customize**. From the Customize dialog box, click the **Options** tab to view the menu options (see the following figure). To turn off the personalized menu feature (which means the menus will no longer display just the commands you most recently used), deselect the **Menus Show Recently Used Commands First** check box. To reset the default set of visible commands, click the **Reset My Usage Data** button. Click **Close** to exit the dialog box and apply the changes.

Deselect this check box to turn off the option.

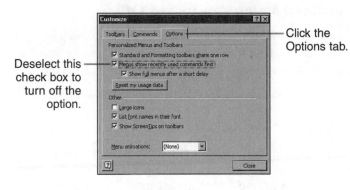

Click the Options tab.

You can customize your menus using the Customize dialog box.

Other Menu-Customizing Options

The Customize dialog box has other customizing options you can apply to menus. For example, deselect the **Show Full Menus After a Short Delay** check box if you want to see only the full menu by clicking the double arrow at the bottom of the menu. Use the **Menu Animations** drop-down list to select an animated style to apply. The style affects how your menus display—mind you, this is a very subtle effect. Feel free to experiment with these options!

My Personalized Menus Are Turned Off

I've turned off my personalized menus for the remainder of this book so you can see the full menu in any of the figures that show a menu. I just want you to know in case you notice that your menus look slightly different from mine.

Twiddling Your Toolbars

Excel's toolbars offer quick shortcuts to commonly used commands. Just click a button to activate the command or feature. By default, Excel opens with the Standard and Formatting toolbars displayed. Additional toolbars are available, and most will open when you begin using a feature related to a particular toolbar. If you ever want to know the name of a toolbar button, hover your mouse pointer over the button and a ScreenTip will appear with the button's name, as shown in the next figure.

To display or hide a toolbar, open the **View** menu and select **Toolbars**. This opens a submenu listing every available toolbar for the program. A check mark next to the toolbar name indicates the toolbar is already displayed. To hide a toolbar, deselect its check mark.

ScreenTip

ScreenTips readily identify the name of toolbar buttons.

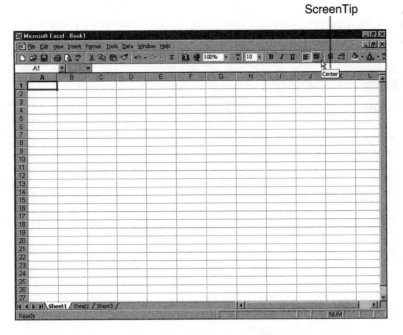

My Toolbars Are Gone!

If you open Excel one day and find your toolbars gone, don't panic. A previous user may have just turned them off. Open the **View** menu, select **Toolbars**, and then choose the toolbar you want to display again. If you share your computer with other users, you can expect to encounter situations like these. You might also find that they've reconfigured the Excel toolbars, adding or removing buttons. You can return any toolbar to its original state. To do so, click the **Add or Remove Buttons** drop-down arrow at the far right end of the toolbar, and then select **Reset Toolbar**.

If you've worked with previous versions of Excel, you may have noticed that the Standard and Formatting toolbars share a row onscreen in Excel 2000. In order to fit the toolbars side by side, both toolbars show only the buttons you most recently used (or are likely to use). This is the default setting, but you can change it if you want (learn how in Chapter 6, "Fine-Tuning Excel"). I've turned on the option for

21

displaying both toolbars fully (with all the default buttons showing) for the remainder of this book, just in case you're wondering why your Excel screen looks slightly different from mine.

What's New in Excel 2000?

If you're a brand-new Excel user, then everything about the program seems new to you. However, if you're a seasoned Excel user, you're probably curious about what's different in Excel 2000 as compared with earlier versions of Excel. This section's for you. Here's a list of improvements Microsoft has made to Excel 2000:

➤ **Personalized menus**   You've already seen what this improvement looks like (we covered it earlier in this chapter).

➤ **Personalized toolbars**   The makers of Excel are helping to conserve screen space by consolidating your default toolbars. Instead of each toolbar stretching out across the program window, the Standard and Formatting toolbars appear on a single row beneath the menu bar. Learn more about this new feature in Chapter 6.

➤ **Email button**   Speaking of toolbars, there's a new Email button you can click on the Standard toolbar to quickly send your workbook as a file attachment to an email message, or to turn a worksheet into an email message. Learn more about this feature in Chapter 23, "Integrating Excel with Other Applications."

➤ **Quicker file switching**   Microsoft has made it easier to switch between multiple files. Each open Excel file appears as a button on the taskbar, so you can quickly switch from one file to another. Learn more about using this feature in Chapter 2, "File Fundamentals."

➤ **Detect and Repair**   This new command has been added to the Help menu to assist you with program failures. When selected, this menu option checks over the noncritical program files. Learn how to use this feature in Chapter 5.

➤ **Euro currency**   Excel now supports the new Euro currency, for those of you using this currency in spreadsheet reports and calculations (see Chapter 11, "Formatting for Fun or Profit").

➤ **New Open dialog box features**   Now, when you open the Open dialog box, you'll see more files, different tools, and a Places Bar (a pane on the left side of the box that lets you quickly access commonly used folders, such as the My Documents folder). Learn more about this new dialog box in Chapter 2.

➤ **Collect and Paste**   You can now collect multiple items from multiple sources, place them in the Clipboard, and then paste them into your file (see Chapter 23).

➤ **Improved Office Assistant**   If you've used other Microsoft Office programs (such as Word, PowerPoint, and Access), as well as previous versions of Excel, you're probably familiar with the Office Assistant, an animated Help tool designed to assist you while using a program. The new Office Assistant feature is no longer confined to a box; instead, the animated feature appears free of confines and is ready to assist as always. (Learn more about this feature in Chapter 5.)

➤ **Improved clip art and graphics features**   Microsoft has improved the way the Clip Art Gallery works and has added some more shapes to the AutoShapes palette. (Learn more about these features in Chapters 13, "Getting Graphic," and 14, "Adding Borders and Backgrounds.")

That should be enough to keep you interested for now. You learn more about these and other new features throughout the rest of this book.

Worried About Year 2000 Compliance?

Don't fret; Excel 2000 has been carefully tested to Microsoft's Year 2000–compliance standard, which means nothing goofy will happen if you're using Excel 2000 when the year 2000 rolls around. As you've probably heard by now, when computers were first manufactured, programmers programmed them to read dates much as people do—for example, '98 for 1998. Unfortunately, when the calendar flips to the year 2000, '00 won't necessarily mean 2000; some computers will think it means 1900, which could really throw some things off. Thankfully, you won't experience that trouble with Excel 2000.

The Least You Need to Know

➤ Spreadsheet programs are perfect tools for organizing data, especially numerical data.

➤ The Excel program window looks and works a lot like any other Windows-based program, complete with a menu bar and toolbars.

➤ An Excel file is called a *workbook*, and each workbook is comprised of one or more *worksheets* (the sheets where you enter all the data).

➤ You can navigate worksheets with a mouse or keyboard, whichever you prefer.

➤ Excel 2000 has a lot of improvements, and you learn more about them in the pages to come.

Chapter 2

File Fundamentals

In This Chapter

➤ Opening and closing files

➤ All about saving files

➤ Opening and viewing two or more files at once

➤ Using the Open dialog box to delete or rename files, and search for files (it's a very versatile dialog box)

Files are fundamental to the world of computers. Without them, the computer world stops revolving (it also stops revolving when the power goes out, but that's a whole other topic). Files hold within them the little bits and bytes of data that you entered and tell a program how to present that information. Files store your letters, memos, email messages, reports, game scores, and most importantly, your worksheets.

Files are where it's at when it comes to data storage. For that reason, you'll find that a great many computer tasks focus on working with files (for example, saving files, opening files, closing files, using two or more files at once, swapping data between files, starting new files, deleting old files, finding files you misplaced, and so on).

Excel wouldn't be the spreadsheet program that it is without files, so here's a chapter explaining how to work with Excel files.

Opening and Closing Files

If you're going to work with files, you're going to have to know how to get in and out of them. Whether it's a new file or an existing file, the action of opening and closing is part of using the file. The nice thing about learning such tasks is that once you know how to do them in one program, these skills carry over to other programs.

If you already know how to perform such tasks, it's still a good idea to read this section, because it covers how to use the new and improved Open dialog box in Excel 2000.

A Word About Folder Hierarchy

If you're new to the structure of files, folders, and drives, you may not be aware that a hierarchy is involved when it comes to your computer's hard disk drive. Files are stored in folders, some folders are stored in other folders, and so on until you trace back to the drive letter that holds all your folders. Therefore, when you're saving your files into folders and retrieving them again, you often have to look through folders to find the files again. To take a look at your own computer's folder hierarchy, use Windows Explorer.

Starting New Files

When you open Excel, a brand-spanking-new file appears onscreen ready for you to use. However, you can open a new file whenever you want. To start a new file, use either of these methods:

➤ Click the **New** button on the Standard toolbar.

➤ Open the **File** menu and select **New**; then double-click the **Workbook** icon in the **General** tab of the New dialog box.

Using Templates

If you've got templates installed, you can start a new file based on an Excel template (a ready-made, preformatted file you can use as a base for making your own files). Look through the various tabs in the New dialog box to see the available templates and then double-click the one you want to open. If you didn't install Excel's templates, revisit the installation appendix at the back of this book to learn how.

Opening Existing Files

If you've already created and saved some workbooks (you learn all about saving files in the next section), you'll want to open them again so you can work on them some more. To open an existing file, start by opening the Open dialog box. Use one of these methods:

➤ Click the **Open** button on the Standard toolbar. This opens the Open dialog box, as shown in the following figure.

➤ Open the **File** menu and select **Open**. Again, you see the dialog box shown in the following figure.

New Open Dialog Box

The Open dialog box has some major changes from previous versions of Excel. For example, the Places bar lists icons representing your most commonly used folders. Clicking one of the folders listed is a lot faster than using the Look In drop-down box. Take a moment and familiarize yourself with the new elements and how they work.

Use the Open dialog box to select the file you want to open.

Folders · Click this drop-down arrow to switch drives or folders · Toolbar

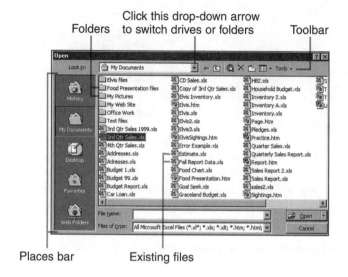

Places bar · Existing files

The Open dialog box looks very different from that of previous versions of Excel. Take a look at the various elements you'll encounter:

Look In drop-down list Click the drop-down arrow to display a list of drives and folders. Use this list to change which folder or drive is displayed in the list box.

Open toolbar Located at the top of the dialog box, this toolbar has buttons for changing folders, deleting files, changing how the list box displays the files, and more. Table 2.1 details each of the buttons and how they are used.

List box The wide open area of the dialog box lists all the files found in the selected folder or drive.

Places bar Use this bar to access commonly used folders. For example, click the History folder to see a list of the last 20 to 50 files you used.

Open button Click the arrow on this button to display a drop-down list of options for how you want to open the selected file.

Let's start by going over the steps for opening a file; then we'll go over how to use the nitty-gritty elements in the dialog box.

To open a file from the Open dialog box, follow these steps:

1. Locate the folder or drive where the file is stored. Use the **Look In** drop-down list to change drives or folders, or you can click a folder on the **Places** bar.

2. Select the file you want to open from the list box.

3. Click the **Open** button or double-click the file icon.

28

The new Places bar displays five commonly used folders. To display a folder's contents, simply click the folder on the Places bar. Here's a rundown of what these folders contain:

➤ The **History** folder lists the last 20 to 50 files you used, whether they were Excel files or other program files.

➤ The **My Documents** folder is typically the default folder where your files are stored.

➤ The **Desktop** icon displays all the folders or files found on your Windows Desktop.

➤ The **Favorites** folder lists shortcuts to all your favorite Web sites (if you chose to save them to this folder).

➤ The **Web Folders** folder lists all your Web-related folders and HTML files you store on a Web server, such as one your corporate intranet utilizes.

The Open dialog box toolbar has buttons that can help you manage files. Table 2.1 details these buttons and how they are used.

Table 2.1   The Open Dialog Box's Toolbar Buttons

Button	Function
⇐	Use this button like the Back button in a Web browser; it returns you to the previous "screen" (in this case, the previous list of folders and files in the list box).
⬆	Click this button to move up a level in the folder hierarchy.
🔍	Click this button to open your browser program to search the Web for files (you'll need an Internet connection to do this).
✕	Click this button to delete the selected file in the list box.
📁	Click this button to start a new folder.
▦	Use the **View** drop-down list to change how your files and folders are listed in the list box: List (default), Details, Properties, and Preview. The Details view lets you see details about the file, such as the file size and date it was created. The Preview view lets you preview what's in the file before selecting it.
Tools ▾	Click the **Tools** drop-down list to display additional tools you can use, such as Find and Rename.

Finally, another new element to look at in the Open dialog box is the Open command button. A simple click on the button opens the file as usual, but a click on the drop-down arrow reveals a list of other options, as shown in the next figure. Here's a rundown of your options:

Open   Opens the file as normal.

Open Read-Only   Opens the file as a read-only file, which means you can't make any changes to the file (hence the name *read-only*).

Open as Copy   Opens a duplicate copy of the file you select using the prefix **Copy of** as part of the filename (such as **Copy of Sales Report**). You can then save the file with your changes using a more descriptive name.

Open in Browser   Opens the file (if it's in an HTML file format) in your browser window.

You now have four differ-ent choices of how to open a file.

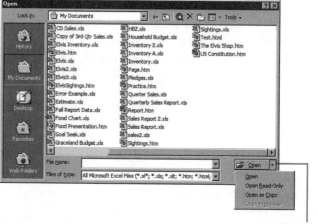

Click here.

Renaming Files in the Open Dialog Box

You can easily rename a file listed in the Open dialog box. Right–click the file and select **Rename** from the shortcut list. This places a cursor in the file-name and highlights the entire name. Now you can edit the existing name or enter a new one as needed.

Closing Files

To close a file you no longer want onscreen, use either of these methods:

➤ Click the **Close** (x) button in the workbook window controls (located beneath the program window controls).

➤ Open the **File** menu and select **Close**.

If you haven't saved your work yet, you are prompted to do so before closing the file. You learn more about saving files in the next section.

Saving Files

After spending all those hours building the perfect worksheet, you'll probably want to save it so you can work on it again or pass it along to someone else. When you save an Excel workbook for the first time, you need to assign the file a name (something to help you easily remember it so you can find it again). You can use up to 255 characters, including letters and numbers (and spaces), in a filename. However, my advice is not to get too carried away. The old adage "less is more" applies here. If you keep your filenames short and to the point, you'll have an easier time finding them later.

When you work on a new file, Excel assigns the file a default name of *Book 1*. You may have noticed it already; it's displayed in the title bar. If you open another file, that file is then named *Book 2*. You get the idea, right? Most users prefer to assign more recognizable names to their files. For example, if you've created a worksheet detailing your department's third-quarter sales, you might name the file *3rd Qtr Sales*.

When you save a file for the first time, you use the Save As dialog box, as shown in the next figure. This dialog box looks hauntingly familiar, doesn't it? With a few minor differences, this box is nearly the same as the Open dialog box you learned about previously. It contains the Places bar with the most popular folders, the toolbar, and the list box—wow, déjà vu. You'll be happy to know that this dialog box works like the Open dialog box. For a refresher on how to use the Places bar or the toolbar buttons, go back to the previous section.

Assigning names isn't the only thing involved with saving files. You can also save files in another file format. Every file you create has a particular format, which indicates the source program the file was created in; Excel files, for example, are typically saved as `.xls` spreadsheet files.

The file format is represented by a file extension that appears after the filename, separated by a dot. A file named `Sales.xls` is clearly an Excel file. A file you create in Word (`Report.doc`, for example) uses another format that identifies it as a document file.

Use the Save dialog box to save the file and give it a name.

List box

Click here to change the folder or drive.

Toolbar

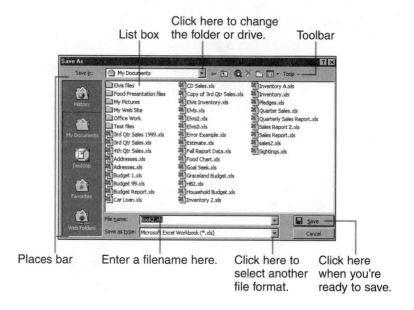

Places bar

Enter a filename here.

Click here to select another file format.

Click here when you're ready to save.

Techno Talk

File Format

A file is saved with codes that tell the program how to display the file, called the *file format*. Most file formats are identified by file extensions that give a clue as to which source program was used to create the file. To open the file in another program, you usually need to save the file as a different file format—which automatically gives it a different extension—so that another program can display the file properly.

This means you can take an Excel workbook file and save it in a Lotus 1-2-3 file format so that your friend who uses Lotus 1-2-3 can open and view the file. Pretty cool, huh? Does your work colleague use an older version of Excel? No problem, you can save your file in an older Excel file format so he, too, can work with the workbook.

Default File Formats

Keep in mind that Excel will save your workbooks in the default file format, which happens to be the Microsoft Excel 2000 file format. If you attempt to share a workbook that you've saved in this format with someone who uses an older version of Excel, that person won't be able to open the file. However, if the entire department uses an older version of the program, why be the odd man out? You can change the default file format. To do so, open the **Tools** menu and select **Options**. In the Options dialog box, select the **Transition** tab and use the **Save Excel Files As** drop-down list to choose another format. Click **OK**. Now, the next time you save a file, it's saved automatically in the format you selected.

Saving a New File

Follow these steps to save a file for the very first time:

1. Click the **Save** button on the Standard toolbar or open the **File** menu and select **Save**. This opens the Save As dialog box shown earlier.
2. To save the file in a particular folder or drive, use the **Save In** drop-down list to select the folder or drive, or you can select a folder from the **Places bar**.
3. Click inside the **File Name** text box and enter a name for the file.
4. To save the file as a different file format, click the **Save as Type** drop-down arrow and choose a format.
5. When you're finally ready to save the file, click the **Save** button.

After assigning a name and saving the file for the first time, you won't have to go through this procedure again for any subsequent saves (unless you want to give the file a new name).

Saving an Existing File

To save an existing file (that is, a file you've already saved at least once), just click the **Save** button on the Standard toolbar. No dialog box will open. The file is automatically saved using the same settings you chose the first time you saved it.

However, what if you want to save your changes as a new file and keep the original intact? Or, what if you want to assign the file to another folder or format? To do so, follow these steps:

1. Open the **File** menu and select **Save As** to open the Save As dialog box as shown in the next figure.

Use the Save As dialog box to save an existing file under a new name, file type, or location.

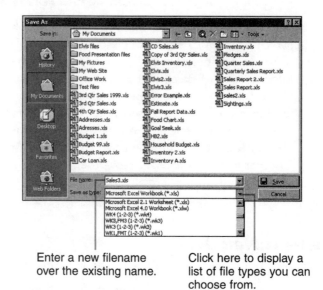

Enter a new filename over the existing name.

Click here to display a list of file types you can choose from.

2. Enter a new filename.
3. If needed, assign a new folder or file format.
4. Click **Save**.

That's it. You've created a new file, but left the original as it was.

Quick File Switching

This is new to Excel 2000; you can now switch between open files via the taskbar as well as the Windows menu.

Working with Multiple Files

You can open as many workbooks as you like, or at least as many as your computer's memory can work with. Why open multiple files? Because you can.

Let's say you need to check your worksheet figures against those compiled by your colleague. You can open your file and hers and then compare the two. Maybe you're compiling a list of products in one worksheet and need to confer with a list of product prices in another worksheet. If you open them both, you can switch between them, or you can even view them at the same time.

Switching Between Open Files

In older versions of Excel, all open files could be accessed through the Window menu. This is still the case, but now each file also appears as a button on the Windows taskbar on the desktop, making switching between files faster and easier.

Can't See the Taskbar?

If your Windows taskbar isn't visible onscreen, press **Ctrl+Esc** to view it.

You may already be used to switching between open programs using the taskbar (you just click the button representing the program you want to view). Use this same method to switch between open files. The figure below shows a taskbar with two Excel files open. To switch from one to the other, all you have to do is click the button representing the file you want to view.

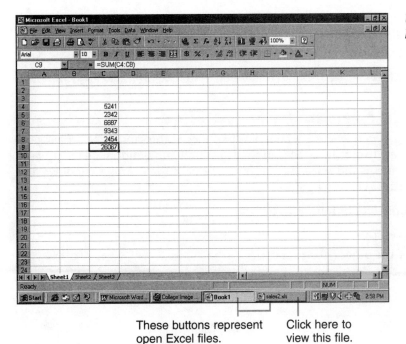

Use the taskbar to switch between open Excel files.

These buttons represent open Excel files.

Click here to view this file.

You can also switch between two open files using Excel's Window menu. The next figure shows the Window menu displaying the same two open files shown in the previous figure. To switch between them, simply click the file you want to view. The active file (the one you're currently viewing) always appears with a check mark next to it.

You can also use the Window menu to switch between open files.

Too Many Is Too Bad

Not to bum you out or anything, but if you have too many open files, it slows your computer down. It's a good idea to close files you're no longer using to free up computer memory. After all, more memory means more power.

Viewing Multiple Files at the Same Time

Alrighty then, let's get wild and crazy and view two files at the same time. Think you can handle it? To view two or more files in the Excel program window *simultaneously*, open the **Window** menu and select **Arrange**. This opens the Arrange Windows dialog box, shown in the following figure.

You can view multiple files in four different ways:

➤ Side by side (Vertical)

➤ One on top of the other (Horizontal)

➤ Spread out like a mosaic (Tiled)

➤ Stacked on top of each other in a neat pile (Cascade)

Use the Arrange Windows dialog box to decide how you want to view multiple windows.

Choose your view and click **OK**. Presto-chango! The program window displays the open files. The next figure shows two open files, side by side.

Active file

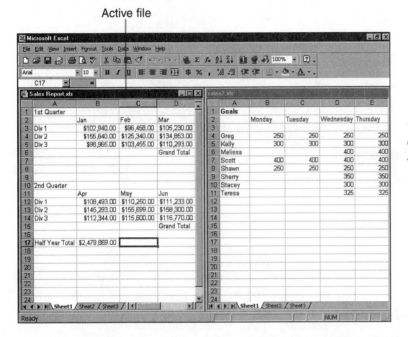

Two—count 'em—two open files onscreen at the same time!

The active file's title bar is always highlighted. To make another file active, just click it.

The Old Drag-and-Drop Method

You can move data between open files you're viewing simultaneously—simply select the data, drag it to the other file, and drop it in place. To copy the data instead of moving it, hold down the Ctrl key while dragging.

When you're finished viewing the files simultaneously, you can return them to their original states using the Maximize button.

Deleting Files

  If you're sure you don't need an Excel file, you can delete it from your computer's hard disk drive. To do so from the Excel program window, open the Open dialog box—that is, click the **Open** button or display the **File** menu and select **Open**. Locate and select the file you want to delete; then click the **Delete** button on the Open dialog box toolbar. It's gone.

Warning!

Excel won't let you delete a workbook file you currently have open. If you do want to delete a file you're working on, be sure to close it first.

Okay, it's not really gone. It has just been removed to your Windows Recycle Bin (unless you're working in a network environment, then the file is truly gone). You have to delete it again from the Recycle Bin to finally banish the file from your system. (I suppose you want me to tell you how to do this, too?) Return to your Windows Desktop (minimize the Excel program window as you learned in the first chapter), right-click the **Recycle Bin** icon, and choose **Empty Recycle Bin** from the resulting pop-up menu. Now the file is really, really gone.

Finding Files

Here's yet another thing the Open dialog box is good for—finding files. To use this feature, open the Open dialog box (again) by clicking the **Open** button or display the **File** menu and select **Open**. Click the **Tools** button on the Open dialog box toolbar and select **Find** from the list. This opens the Find dialog box shown in the next figure.

To search for a particular Excel file, start by selecting the drive you want to search. Click the **Look In** drop-down arrow and select the drive. Click the **Search Subfolders** check box to include any subfolders in the search.

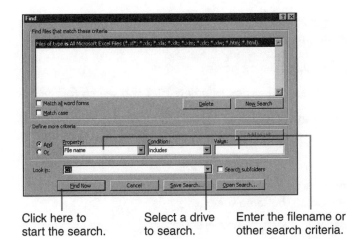

The Find dialog box can help you search for a file.

Click here to   Select a drive   Enter the filename or
start the search.   to search.   other search criteria.

By default, the **Property** box already has **File Name** selected. Leave it if you want to search for a specific filename (click the drop-down arrow to select another search criterion, such as **Contents** or **Last Modified**). Click inside the **Value** text box and enter the filename you're looking for (if you can remember the name). Click **Find Now** to start the search. A prompt box appears; click **Yes** to continue. After a moment, the Open dialog box displays any files matching the criteria you entered (see the next figure).

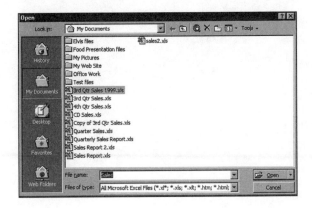

Search results will appear in the list box of the Open dialog box. In this example, I conducted a search for all the files with "Sales" as part of the filename.

The Least You Need to Know

➤ To open a file, use the Open dialog box.

➤ You can also use the Open dialog box to delete files and search for files.

➤ You can save a file in another folder or another file format.

➤ You can create a new file out of an existing file by using the Save As command.

➤ You can open more than one file at a time and switch between them, or you can view them onscreen at the same time.

Data Entry in a Dash

In This Chapter

➤ Learn what kinds of data you can enter into a spreadsheet

➤ Rules for entering numbers, dates, and times

➤ Fixing your typing errors with AutoCorrect

➤ All about AutoFill and fast data entry

It's Chapter 3 already and it's about time I showed you how to start entering data into your spreadsheet. We've got a lot of ground to cover, so let's not waste any time. There are several kinds of data you can use and several ways to enter this data. In this chapter, you learn the ground rules for working with the various data types.

The key to using data is to first figure out what kind of worksheet you want to build. What do you want to do with your worksheet? Here are a few examples to consider:

➤ A workbook that catalogs your Elvis memorabilia collection would probably hold text data that describes each item, dates that tell when you purchased each item, and maybe even number data that tells how much you paid for each item.

➤ Let's say you work for a profitable company that sells Elvis memorabilia. You might create a workbook that tracks your company's sales figures and the data would focus on numbers and dates.

➤ A workbook that not only tracks your company's sales figures but then also projects future sales would include number data and formulas.

Beginning to see any trends here? Naturally, you can create any kind of worksheet you want—whether it's as simple as a grocery list or as complex as an accounting balance sheet. The data you enter, however, determines how you use the worksheet. Want to learn more? Then what are you waiting for? Dig in.

Dealing with Data

Pop quiz: What kinds of data can you put into a worksheet (you did study for this quiz, didn't you?) The answer: text, numbers, dates, time, and formulas are all forms of data. For the sake of simplicity, data can be divided into the following three categories:

Labels   Any kind of text data or data you enter to identify a row or column is considered a *label*. For example, if you type the word *February* into a cell, Excel won't be able to perform a mathematical function with it—it's just a word.

Values   Numerical data is referred to as a *value*. Excel can calculate value entries. For example, if you type in the value *1024*, Excel can do something with it, such as multiply or add. Value entries can include numbers, dates, and times.

Formulas   A *formula* is an entry that tells Excel to perform calculations on the values in a cell or group of cells.

Say you've created a budget worksheet. In this type of worksheet, you might include a worksheet title, column labels for each month, and row labels for each expense category. All these entries would be text (labels). Within the columns for each month, you might enter the expenses for that category. These entries would be numbers (values). For each month, you might want to calculate the total expenses. These entries would be formulas. The following figure shows an example of such a worksheet under construction.

Excel usually knows which data category you're using and guesses at what you're going to do with it. For that reason, you'll notice that Excel displays different data types in different positions in your worksheet cells. Plain old text always lines up to the left of the cell it's in, and numbers always line up to the right of the cell. Subtle, eh? Check out the next figure to see an example of each data type used in a worksheet.

Formula bar   Formula

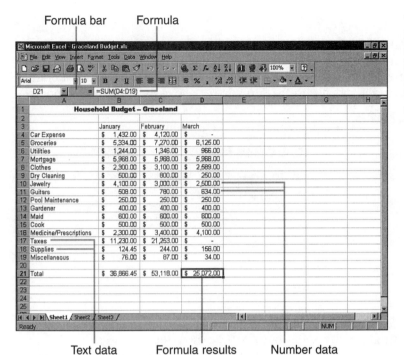

The data you enter into Excel can be broken down into three categories: labels (text), values (numbers, dates, and times), and formulas (calculations).

Text data   Formula results appear in the cell.   Number data

Using Numbers as Labels

There will be times when you want number data to be treated as text data. For example, perhaps you're building a workbook database of addresses. When recording addresses, you'll probably include zip codes. When you type in a zip code, Excel will assume you're entering a value and treat it as such. To make Excel treat the entry as a label instead, precede the entry with a single quote mark, such as '90210. The single quote mark is an alignment prefix that tells Excel to treat the following characters as text and to left-align them in the cell. Learn more about aligning data in Chapter 11, "Formatting for Fun or Profit."

Entering Data

To begin entering data into your worksheet, click the cell in which you want to place the data. When you select a cell, it's surrounded by a bold line called a *selector*, as shown in the next figure. When you start typing data in a selected cell, the data immediately appears in that cell and also in the Formula bar above the worksheet window.

When you enter data into a cell, it also appears in the Formula bar.

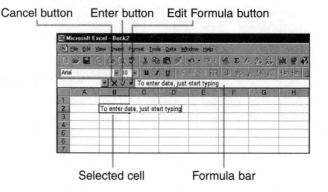

Cancel button   Enter button   Edit Formula button

Selected cell   Formula bar

Three buttons appear in the Formula bar as you enter data. The left button is the **Cancel** button. It's easy to identify because it has a red X in it. You can click it to cancel your entry. The middle button with the green check mark is the **Enter** button. You can click it to confirm that you want to enter the data into the cell (this is the same as pressing **Enter** on the keyboard). The third button with the equal sign is the **Edit Formula** button. I'll tell you what this button does in Chapter 9, "Functions: Fast Formulas for Fast Results."

There's no right or wrong way to enter cell data. You can do so directly in the cell, use the Formula bar, or employ a combination of both methods. The fastest method is to just start typing and keep typing.

When you finish typing in data, press **Enter** or click the **Enter** button on the Formula bar. You can also click in the next cell in which you want to enter data.

If your text is too lengthy to fit into the cell's column width, it might appear to be cut off, particularly if you proceed to enter text into the adjacent cell to the right (see the following figure). Don't worry—the text is still there; you just can't see it all. To see the data in its entirety, click the cell again. However, if you don't like seeing part of your data drop out of sight, widen the column. Open the **Format** menu and select **Column, AutoFit Selection**. (You learn more about formatting in Chapter 12, "Rearranging Your Worksheet Data.")

The Enter Dilemma

For most users, pressing **Enter** after creating an entry is a habit. By default, when you press **Enter**, Excel moves to the next cell directly below the cell into which you just entered data. This is great if that's the next cell you want to use, but if it's not, you might find yourself a little frustrated when you want to continue entering data without having to figure out which cell you're in. You can easily change the direction the **Enter** key takes by changing the settings in the Options dialog box. Open the **Tools** menu and select **Options**; then click the **Edit** tab. Make sure the **Move Selection After Enter** check box is selected; then click the **Direction** drop-down arrow and choose a new direction. For example, if you want Excel to take you to the next cell to the right when you press **Enter**, choose **Right** from the drop-down list. Click **OK** to exit the dialog box and activate the new settings.

Where did all the text go?

The data in this cell appears cut off, but it's still there.

Are Your Numbers Valid?

Entering text data is fairly straightforward, but entering numeric data is a bit more complicated. Some rules are involved with entering numeric data.

Valid numbers include the following:

➤ The numeric characters 0–9

➤ Any of these special characters: . + - ( ) , $ %

The first rule is pretty obvious, but what's with the special characters? Why is a percentage sign recognized as numeric data? Good question. It's because you use special characters to write mathematical problems, equations, formulas, and so on. When you enter numeric values, you can include commas, decimal points, dollar signs, percentage signs, and parentheses.

Entering Fractions

To enter a fraction, type the integer, a space, then the fraction, such as 2³/₄. If you leave out the space, Excel assumes the value is a text entry. If you want to enter only the fractional part, such as ³/₄, you must type a zero, a space, and then the fraction (0 ³/₄); otherwise, Excel assumes the value is a date (4-Mar).

Formatting Data

Learn all about making your data look good with formatting controls in Chapter 12, including how to add formatting to numbers using commas and dollar signs.

If you enter a number that's too long to fit in the cell, you might see number signs (#) similar to what's shown in the next figure. As cautioned before, don't panic. This simply means the number is too long to fit in the cell. You can widen the column to fix this. Open the **Format** menu, select **Column, AutoFit Selection** from the submenu.

Thankfully, Excel's default setting is to automatically resize your column if the number doesn't fit, so you probably won't encounter this problem in everyday use.

Excel lets you know your number entry is too big to fit in the cell by displaying a series of number signs.

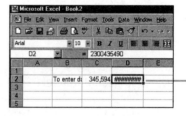

This means the number is too long to fit in the cell.

Entering Dates and Times

What about dates and times? Another good question. Dates and times are considered data, too, and you have a variety of ways to enter them. They're considered values because you can perform calculations on them. For example, you could have Excel calculate the number of days until Christmas.

To use any date or time values in your spreadsheet, type them in the format you want to see them displayed. Table 3.1 shows some typical date and time formats. When you enter a date using one of the formats shown, Excel converts the date into a number that represents how many days it falls after January 1, 1900. (Don't ask me why it does this, I didn't invent spreadsheets!) However, you'll never see this mysterious number. Excel always displays a normal date onscreen and uses the converted number in any calculations. Confusing? Goofy? It's both, … but I thought you ought to know about this fact, just in case there really is a test later.

Table 3.1   Valid Formats for Dates and Times

Format	Example
MM/DD/YY	9/9/99 or 09/09/98
MMM-YY	Aug-99
DD-MMM-YY	16-Sep-98
DD-MMM	29-Mar
HH:MM	16:50
HH:MM:SS	9:22:55
HH:MM AM/PM	6:45 PM
HH:MM:SS AM/PM	10:15:25 AM
MM/DD/YY HH:MM	11/5/98 12:15
HH:MM MM/DD/YY	11:05 8/22/99

You can use either dashes or slashes with your dates. You don't have to worry about capitalization; Excel ignores capitalization when it comes to dates. You can also edit the existing formats for dates. For example, you can spell out the entire month's name.

Unless you type AM or PM, Excel assumes that you're using a 24-hour military clock. Therefore, Excel interprets 8:20 as AM (not PM) unless you type 8:20 PM. If you want to say 8:20 PM without adding the PM, add 12 to the number so that it reads 20:20. Unless you've served in the military, this isn't always easy to remember.

Quick Date and Time

To quickly enter the current date in a cell, press **Ctrl+;**. To enter the current time, press **Ctrl+Shift+:**. Excel will fill in the date or time from your computer clock, so make sure you've set that accurately. (Set your computer's time by opening the **Start** menu and choosing **Settings**, **Control Panel** and then double-clicking the **Date/Time** icon.)

Editing Data

Editing data in a worksheet is easy. Double-click the cell or press **F2**, move the cursor to the place you want to edit, and make your changes. You can also click inside the Formula bar and make edits from there. Edit your worksheet entries just like you edit data in other programs. You can select data and type over it to add new data, insert data in the midst of existing data, and delete data. Use the **Backspace** and **Delete** keys to remove characters and make corrections.

To undo any immediate mistakes, click the **Undo** button on the Standard toolbar immediately after performing the action you want to undo, or you can open the **Edit** menu and select **Undo**. If you change your mind about the Undo operation, click the **Redo** button or open the **Edit** menu and select **Redo**. This will redo the action again.

You can choose to undo or redo multiple actions. Next to the Undo and Redo buttons on the Standard toolbar are tiny drop-down arrows you can click to display a list of all the actions for the current session (see the following figure). Your most recent actions appear at the top of the list. Select an action from the list by clicking it; Excel then undoes (or redoes) that action as well as all the actions listed above it. For example, if you select the third action from the top of the list, Excel will also undo the first and second actions.

Click here to display the list.

The list displays all your worksheet actions for the current session.

Deletion Choices

To delete cell contents, select the cell, open the **Edit** menu, and then choose **Clear**. From the submenu that appears, select the command that best describes what you want removed from the cell. Choose **All** to clear everything in the cell, choose **Formats** to clear all the formatting that's been applied to the cell, choose **Contents** to remove the data but leave the formatting, or choose **Comments** to clear any cell comments attached to the cell.

Speeding Up Data Entry

Nothing beats a good shortcut, and when it comes to data entry, Excel has several you can use. For example, if you find yourself entering repetitive data or a data series, such as the days of the month or week, you can use Excel's automated fill features to automatically finish entering the information for you. Another example is Excel's

AutoCorrect feature, which automatically corrects your typing mistakes as you type. It's like having your old English teacher sitting right inside your computer checking over your work.

Have No Fear, AutoCorrect Is Here

To keep your entries accurate, Excel's AutoCorrect feature is turned on by default. AutoCorrect recognizes commonly misspelled words and automatically corrects them as you type. For example, if you type "adn," AutoCorrect automatically changes the spelling to "and" as soon as you press the spacebar or the **Enter** key. Try it yourself. I'm not kidding—stop what you're doing and try it in your own Excel worksheet. Pretty cool, eh?

AutoCorrect Not On?

No sweat, just open the **Tools** menu, select **AutoCorrect**, then click the **Replace Text as You Type** option. Click **OK** to exit and apply.

AutoCorrect comes with a fairly long list of commonly misspelled words, but you can add your own entries to the list.

You can also use the AutoCorrect feature to expand abbreviations you repeatedly type. For example, perhaps your company name is really long—Mister Milton's Mighty Muffin Makers, for instance. You probably grow very weary of typing this in every time you need to refer to the company name. Well, why not turn it into an AutoCorrect entry; then, instead of typing in the complete name each time, you can simply type in the assigned abbreviation (such as MM). AutoCorrect expands the entry for you.

To add a new entry to AutoCorrect's list or to add an abbreviation for a word or phrase, follow these steps:

1. Open the **Tools** menu and choose **AutoCorrect**. This opens the AutoCorrect dialog box, as shown in the following figure.

2. Click inside the **Replace** text box and enter the misspelling. If you're adding an abbreviation, enter it in the text box instead.

3. Click inside the **With** text box and type in the correct spelling for the word. If you're adding an entry for a long word or phrase, enter the entire word or phrase.

4. Click the **Add** button. The entry is added to the list box.

5. Click **OK** to exit the dialog box.

The next time you type the misspelling or abbreviation, AutoCorrect comes to the rescue.

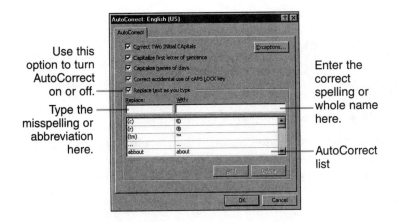

Use the AutoCorrect dialog box to add your own entries to the list.

Use this option to turn AutoCorrect on or off.

Type the misspelling or abbreviation here.

Enter the correct spelling or whole name here.

AutoCorrect list

You may have noticed a slew of other options in the AutoCorrect dialog box. You can turn these options on or off as needed. Here's a rundown of what they do:

Correct Two Initial Capitals   If you have a tendency to hold down the **Shift** key while capitalizing a word, sometimes you end up capitalizing more than the first letter. With this option on, AutoCorrect makes sure only the first letter is capitalized.

Capitalize First Letter of Sentence   To make sure every sentence starts with a capital letter, turn this option on.

Capitalize Names of Days   Like to see the days of the week capitalized? Select this option.

Correct Accidental Use of Caps Lock Key   Here's a handy option. If you've accidentally left the Caps Lock key on, this option corrects the problem for you.

Replace Text as You Type   This option turns the AutoCorrect feature on or off.

If you ever want to remove an entry from the AutoCorrect list, just open the dialog box back up, select the entry from the list box, and click the **Delete** button.

If you don't have an AutoCorrect option turned off, such as **Correct Two Initial Capitals**, and AutoCorrect fixes the text as you type, you can always go back and retype the occurrence. It will stay put the second time you type it in.

How About the Spell Checker?

Yes, Excel comes with a spell check feature you can use to help you with spelling problems, too. To use this feature, open the **Tools** menu and select **Spelling**, or you can click the **Spelling** button on the Standard toolbar.

Fill 'Er up with AutoFill

Now I'm going to show you an amazing shortcut that really speeds up your data entry—Excel's AutoFill feature. This little feature lets you quickly enter a data series into your worksheet cells or duplicate the same data as many times as necessary.

What's a data series? It's any series of related information, such as the days of the week, number sequences, months, and so on. For example, you can use AutoFill to fill in a series of months (January, February, March, and so on) across several columns in your worksheet, a series of days (Monday, Tuesday, Wednesday, and so on), or even a series of formulas. All you have to do is enter the first value and then let AutoFill handle the rest.

If you're using a series of dates, all you have to type is the one date to start the series. If you're using a number sequence, you need to enter two variables (such as 1, 2 or 5, 10) to start the fill series in order to establish the sequence. Before you get too confused, take a look at Table 3.2 for some examples.

Table 3.2   Fill Series Examples

You Type	AutoFill Inserts
Qtr 1	Qtr 2, Qtr 3, Qtr 4
Sales 1	Sales 2, Sales 3, Sales 4
Mon	Tue, Wed, Thur
Jan	Feb, Mar, Apr
1, 2	3, 4, 5, 6
5, 10	15, 20, 25, 30
1997	1998, 1999, 2000

The easiest way to create a data series is to use the fill handle of the cell border. When you select a cell or range of cells, the lower-right corner of the selected cell(s) shows a tiny square, known as the *fill handle* (see the next figure). When you place the cursor over the fill handle, it turns into a black plus sign that you can then click and drag. Use the fill handle to drag a fill series across adjacent cells.

You can create the following types of series using the fill handle:

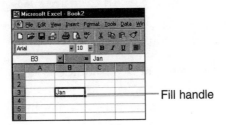

What's a Range?

A *range* is simply a group of related cells. You can learn more about using ranges in worksheets in Chapter 8, "Concocting Formulas."

➤ If you simply want to copy the same entry into other cells, type the entry once, select the cell, and then drag the fill handle with the mouse to fill the adjacent cells with the same data.

➤ If you want to enter a month (Jan, Feb, Mar) or weekday (Mon, Tue, Wed) series, type the first entry and then drag the fill handle to fill adjacent cells with the complete series.

➤ If you want to use a number series, you must remember to type the first two entries in order to tell Excel how to present the series. For example, if you type 5 and 10 into the first two cells, select the cells, and then drag the fill handle to complete the series, Excel enters 15, 20, and so on in the adjacent cells.

Use the fill handle to drag a fill series across the worksheet.

Ready to try it yourself? Use these steps:

1. Type the first entry in the first cell. (If you want to use a number series, enter the first two values in the first two cells.)

2. Select the cell or cells containing the entry or entries.

3. Position your mouse pointer over the fill handle in the lower-right corner of the selected cell(s). The handle was pointed out for you in the previous figure.

4. Click and hold the mouse pointer over the fill handle; then drag across the cells you want to fill. You can drag in any direction. An outline appears as you drag, and a ScreenTip displays the value of the cell the pointer is currently over.

5. Release the mouse button. AutoFill completes the series, as shown in the following figure.

Drag the fill handle over the cells you want to fill, and AutoFill automatically fills in the data.

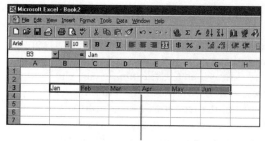

The series is filled in.

If you need to create a different kind of series or assign additional series options, use the Series dialog box, shown in the next figure. This dialog box lets you create a fill series with specific start and stop values. Follow these steps to customize your AutoFill:

1. Select the first cell of the fill series and enter the starting data.

2. Select the adjacent cells you want to fill.

3. Open the **Edit** menu and select **Fill**, then select **Series**. This opens the Series dialog box (see the following figure).

Use the Series dialog box to specify a specific start and stop value for the series.

4. From the **Series In** options, select how you want the series filled—by rows or columns.

5. From the **Type** options, select the type of series you want to create:

   Linear   Adds the step value you define in step 6 to the series start value you entered in step 1.

   Growth   Multiplies the step value you define in step 6 to the series start value defined in step 1.

   Date   Enables the Date Unit options for establishing a series of dates.

   AutoFill   Excel creates automatic data series for you based on your start entry in step 1 (for example, Qtr 1, Qtr 2, Qtr 3, or Part 1, Part 2, Part 3, and so on). Skip to step 8 to finish using the Series dialog box.

6. If you chose the **Linear, Growth,** or **Date** series types, use the **Step Value** box to enter the amount by which the series changes from cell to cell. In the **Stop Value** box, enter the last value you want filled in the series. (Use this option only if you think you've highlighted too many cells for the series in step 1).

7. If you chose the **Date** series type, select a data unit to apply under the Date Unit options.

8. Click **OK** to exit the dialog box. Excel fills in the data series and type you specified.

Using AutoComplete

If you're like most spreadsheet users, you probably spend a lot of time entering repetitive data, such as entering the same text labels over and over again. You can use Excel's AutoComplete feature to simplify such tedious procedures. Follow these steps to check it out:

1. Type the labels in the first few cells of the column.

2. When you're ready to enter a duplicate label in another cell, right-click the empty cell.

3. Choose **Pick from List** from the shortcut menu that appears. A list of previously typed words appears beneath your cell (see the following figure).

4. Choose the word you want from the list. Excel automatically inserts it in the cell.

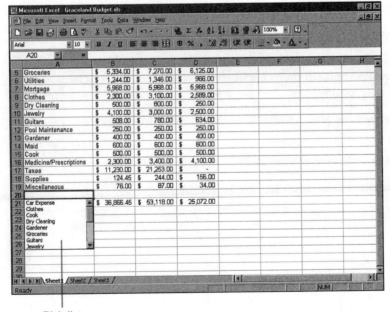

Use AutoComplete to help with repetitious entries.

Pick list

AutoComplete in Action

You might notice the AutoComplete feature kicking in while you enter text. If you repeat the first few letters of a previous entry, AutoComplete guesses that you're typing repeat information and finishes your word for you. If it's not the correct word, however, just keep typing and ignore AutoComplete.

The Least You Need to Know

➤ Data you enter into a worksheet falls into one of three categories: labels, values, and formulas.

➤ Text entries are considered labels because you can't perform calculations on them.

➤ Values include numbers, dates, and times—any data you can perform calculations on.

➤ Formulas are calculations; learn more about them in Chapter 9, "Functions: Fast Formulas for Fast Results."

➤ Speed up data entry using the AutoFill feature; it quickly fills adjacent cells with data.

➤ Excel's AutoCorrect feature fixes your spelling mistakes as you type.

➤ AutoComplete automatically offers to help you enter repetitious data.

Chapter 4

The Wonderful World of Worksheets

In This Chapter

➤ How to address a cell

➤ Tips and tricks for navigating worksheets

➤ How to rename sheets

➤ Steps for adding, deleting, copying, and moving worksheets

➤ How to assign passwords to your workbooks and worksheets

Up until this point, you've had a cursory introduction to the world of worksheets. Now it's time to expand your horizons. Where did those worksheets come from? What makes them tick? How do they survive? You'll find answers to these and other fascinating questions as we look at the ever-changing world of worksheets.

Before you mistake this chapter for a fascinating Discovery Channel program, there really is more to worksheets than meets the eye. I'm not kidding. For example, did you know you can give each worksheet in a workbook a name? Or, how about this— you can assign passwords to your workbooks. Did you know that every cell in a worksheet has an address? There really is a lot you can learn about worksheets, as you're about to find out.

Let's recap what you've learned about workbooks and worksheets thus far in our exploration of Excel:

➤ Every file you create in Excel is called a *workbook*.

➤ A workbook is comprised of one or more *worksheets* (also called *sheets* for short).

➤ By default, Excel opens a blank workbook every time you start the program. This workbook contains three blank worksheets.

➤ Each worksheet is comprised of columns and rows that intersect to form *cells*.

➤ Each worksheet is represented by a tab at the bottom of the program window.

Now, let's take a more detailed look at the world of workbooks and worksheets, starting with an examination of the worksheet structure.

Understanding Worksheet Structure

Each worksheet is comprised of 256 columns and 65,536 rows. Wow! Just glancing at the worksheet, you wouldn't think it had so much space, but it does. We're talking prime real estate here, all at your fingertips. Depending on how you use the worksheet, however, you may not necessarily need all that space; most users don't. (Don't worry; the unused cells won't print out on your paper hard copies.)

With so much space available in a single worksheet, you can easily get lost in the vast forest of worksheet cells. The first thing you need to know about using worksheets is how to read cell names, also known as *addresses* or *references*. Each cell in the worksheet grid has an address based on which row and column it's in.

Excel labels columns with letters and rows with numbers. Cell names always reference the column letter first, then the row number. For example, the cell in the top-left corner of the worksheet is A1 (see the following figure). The cell to the right is B1.

Every cell in the work-sheet grid has an address.

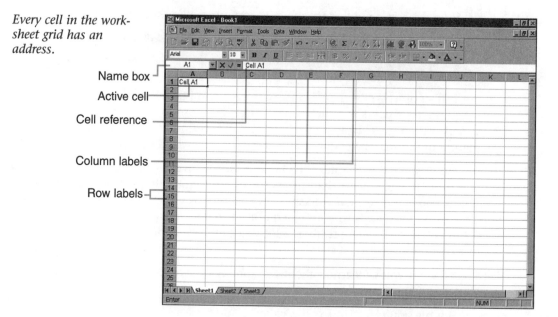

If you become confused about which cell you're currently in, look at the reference area at the far-left end of the Formula bar. This is called the **Name** box (see the previous figure). The **Name** box is kind of like a "you are here" marker; it will always show you which cell you're currently using.

You learn more about using cell references later in this book. For example, you learn how to use them in formulas (Chapter 8, "Concocting Formulas") and ranges (Chapter 7, "Working the Wide Open Ranges"). At least now you know what a cell reference is—the cell's particular address in the worksheet grid.

Reference Box

If you've worked with other spreadsheet programs in the past, the box identifying the active cell may have been called a *reference box*. This is the same as the **Name** box in Excel.

Navigating Worksheets

As you learned in Chapter 1, "Excel in a Nutshell," you can move around the worksheet grid in various ways. Here's a recap:

➤ Click the cell you want to work in. (Does it get any simpler than this?) The active cell is surrounded by a highlighted border, sometimes referred to as a *selector*.

➤ Use the scrollbars to change your viewing area of a worksheet.

➤ If you prefer navigating strictly with the keyboard, use the keyboard arrow keys to move from cell to cell. (Check out the other shortcut keys you can use on the inside front and back covers of this book.)

Quick Scroll

If you're using the Microsoft IntelliMouse (the mouse with the scroll wheel between the buttons), you can scroll around your worksheet by using the center wheel button. To pan a worksheet, hold down the wheel button and drag in the direction you want to go.

You still have a couple more ways to navigate your worksheets: You can use the Go To command and the worksheet scroll arrows. These methods are discussed in the following sections.

Using the Go To Command

For the larger worksheets you create, use the Go To command to locate the cell you want to work with, as shown in the following steps:

1. Open the **Edit** menu and select **Go To** (or press **F5** on the keyboard). This opens the **Go To** dialog box (see the following figure).

Use the Go To dialog box to quickly move to any cell in the worksheet.

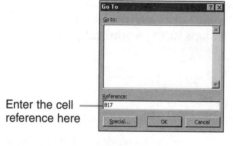

Enter the cell reference here

I Can't See My Cell!

If you've scrolled your view and can no longer see the active cell, press **Ctrl+backspace** on the keyboard to quickly display the active cell.

2. Enter the cell reference you want to go to in the **Reference** text box.

3. Click **OK** or press **Enter**. Excel whisks you away to that particular cell. (If only we could get to real-life destinations this quickly.)

The Go To dialog box keeps track of the previous locations you entered. To revisit a cell, open the dialog box and double-click the cell reference listed in the Go To list box.

Using the Worksheet Scroll Arrows

To work with a particular sheet, just click its tab at the bottom of the workbook window. To the left of the sheet tabs are worksheet scroll arrow buttons (see the following figure). You can use these buttons to move from sheet to sheet, too, which is particularly helpful when you're working with more than three sheets at a time (you learn how to add sheets later in this chapter).

Using the Go To Special Command

If you click the Special button in the Go To dialog box, the Go To Special dialog box opens. It contains a list of options that you can use to go to or highlight cells containing certain contents. For example, you can choose to highlight all the cells containing formulas or locate a cell with a comment.

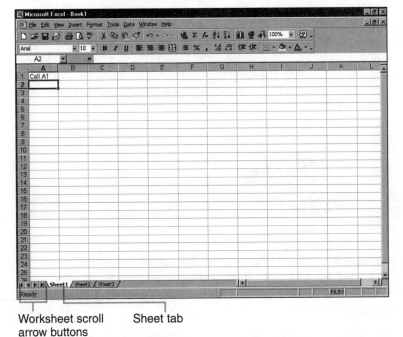

Use worksheet scroll arrows to move from sheet to sheet.

Worksheet scroll   Sheet tab
arrow buttons

If you add additional sheets to the workbook, things can get a little crowded down by the sheet tabs, making it difficult to read the tab names. Use the worksheet scroll arrow buttons to help you move from sheet to sheet. Table 4.1 explains how to use each worksheet scroll arrow button.

61

Table 4.1 Worksheet Scroll Arrows

Button	Purpose
	Scroll to the first sheet in the workbook
	Scroll to the previous sheet
	Scroll to the next sheet
	Scroll to the last sheet in the workbook

Splitting Sheets

Now, here's a little trick to help you speed up navigation between open workbooks. Consider viewing several portions of the same file at the same time. Yes, you can do that. For example, if you're working with an exceptionally long worksheet, you might find yourself scrolling endlessly from one end to another, up and down, and side to side. (It makes me dizzy thinking about it.) Instead of scrolling around, you can divide the window into two or four parts. Each part of the window, called a *pane*, lets you view portions of the worksheet.

Techno Talk

Pane

The term pane is bandied about quite frequently in the computer world. Quite simply, it means a section of the window or viewing area. In Excel, you can split a worksheet into two viewing panes. On the Web, many longer pages are split into smaller panes.

Perhaps you have a large spreadsheet you're working with (pretend, just to humor me). Each column in the spreadsheet has a column heading describing the data found in that particular column and each row lists data for each column. For example, an inventory spreadsheet might have column headings for Product Name, Product ID, Quantity on Hand, Quantity on Order, and so on. Each row in the inventory would have cell entries for each of the columns described. Perhaps the inventory list is several pages long (you're still playing along with me, right?). If you scroll down a bit in the Excel window, you lose sight of the column headings you entered at the top of the spreadsheet. To refer to them again, you must scroll back up to the top. Argh!

But, hey, if you split the window into panes, the top portion can show the column headings, and you can scroll down the database in the second pane without losing track of which column contains which data. Is that cool, or what? Wait until you see what it looks like.

To divide a workbook window into panes, follow these steps:

1. Open the workbook and worksheet you want to split into panes.

2. Select a cell directly below and to the right of where you want to split the window. Depending on which cell you select, the window can be divided horizontally, vertically, or both.

    To split the window horizontally, click a cell in column A below where you want the split to occur.

    To split the window vertically, click in the first row in the column to the right of where you want the split to occur.

3. Open the **Window** menu and select **Split**. The worksheet is immediately split into two panes (see the next figure).

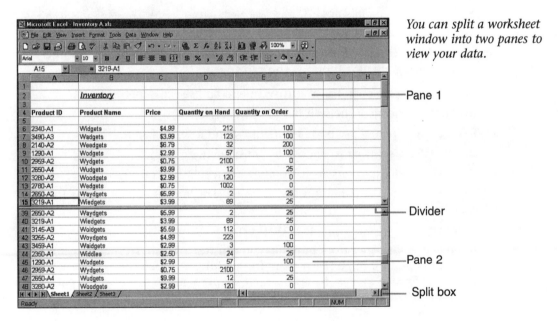

You can split a worksheet window into two panes to view your data.

You can also split a worksheet window by using the split boxes on the scrollbars. (The previous and following figures show where split boxes are located.) They're very tiny and hard to see. To use a split box, hover your mouse pointer over the box, hold down the mouse button, and drag the split box across the screen. A split bar (a gray divider line) moves with the mouse. Release the mouse button where you want the split to occur. The window is now divided into two panes. The following figure shows a vertical split.

Here's an example of a vertical split.

Split box ──

Pane 1 ──

Pane 2 ──

Microsoft Excel - Inventory A.xls

File Edit View Insert Format Tools Data Window Help

A15   =   3219-A1

	B		D	E	F	G	H	I	J	K
2	*Inventory*									
4	Product Name		Quantity on Hand	Quantity on Order						
5										
6	Widgets		212	100						
7	Wadgets		123	100						
8	Weedgets		32	200						
9	Wodgets		57	100						
10	Wydgets		2100	0						
11	Wudgets		12	25						
12	Woodgets		120	0						
13	Wedgets		1002	0						
14	Waydgets		2	25						
15	Wiedgets		89	25						
16	Woidgets		112	0						
17	Woydgets		223	0						
18	Waidgets		3	100						
19	Widdles		24	25						
20	Widgets		212	100						
21	Wadgets		123	100						
22	Weedgets		32	200						
23	Wodgets		57	100						
24	Wydgets		2100	0						
25	Wudgets		12	25						

Sheet

Ready   NUM

After you've split a window into panes, use the scrollbars to scroll your view in each pane. The following are more options you can try:

➤ To remove a split, open the **Window** menu and select **Remove Split**.

➤ To resize a pane, drag the split bar (divider) onscreen.

➤ To create four panes, use both a horizontal and a vertical split.

➤ Double-click a split bar to remove a split quickly.

➤ To quickly add a split onscreen, double-click a split box on the scrollbar.

➤ To move around the panes quickly, press **F6**. This moves you clockwise from pane to pane.

➤ To move counterclockwise, press **Shift+F6**.

➤ To prevent your panes from moving, you can freeze them. Not literally, mind you (although that might keep them fresher longer). Open the **Window** menu and select **Freeze Panes**. Now you can't scroll them. To unfreeze the panes, open the **Window** menu and select **Unfreeze Panes**.

Freezing Without a Split

You don't have to use split panes to freeze a part of your worksheet. Just click directly below where you want the "freeze" to occur, and then select **Window, Freeze Panes**. This freezes the rows directly above the active cell.

That's everything you need to know about navigating worksheets. Ready to move on? Good, so am I.

Naming Sheets

By default, Excel assigns very nondescript names to the sheet tabs representing each worksheet: Sheet 1, Sheet 2, Sheet 3, and so on. You have the option of giving each sheet its own distinct name. For example, you may have filled one sheet with your company's entire inventory listing and another sheet with calculations of the total value of the items in stock. You might name the first sheet Inventory and the second Total Value. The distinct names immediately tell you what's on each sheet.

To rename a worksheet, use these steps:

1. Right-click the sheet tab of the sheet you want to rename.
2. A shortcut menu pops up onscreen, as shown in the next figure. Select the **Rename** command.
3. The sheet's tab is highlighted. Type in a new name for the sheet (you can use up to 31 characters).
4. Press **Enter** when you're finished. Excel displays the new name on the worksheet tab (see the following figure).

*Use the shortcut menu to select the **Rename** command.*

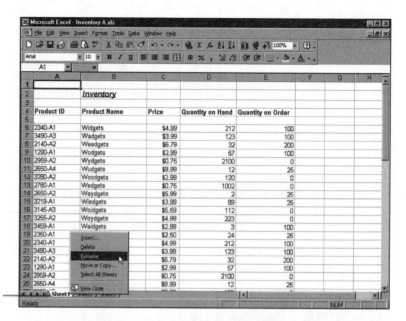

Right-click here. ⎯⎯

Ta-da! The new name appears on the tab.

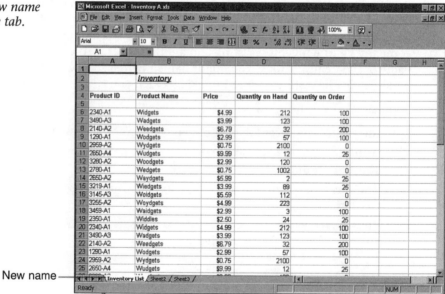

New name⎯⎯

Adding and Deleting Sheets

Need another sheet to work with? Perhaps you want to remove the extras you don't need? Adding and deleting worksheets in your workbook file is easy. To add a sheet, follow these steps:

1. Click the worksheet tab that appears in front of where you want to insert a new sheet.

2. Open the **Insert** menu and select **Worksheet**.

3. Excel inserts the new sheet and gives it a default name.

Another way to add a sheet is to use the shortcut menu. Right-click the sheet tab and select **Insert** from the shortcut menu. In the Insert dialog box that appears, as shown in the next figure, select the **Worksheet** icon from the **General** tab and click **OK**. The sheet is added to the workbook.

Quick Rename

For an even faster way of renaming a sheet, double-click the sheet tab and type in a new name. Then press **Enter**. You bypass selecting the Rename command with this method.

Quick Insert

To quickly add a new sheet by using the keyboard, just press **Shift+F11**.

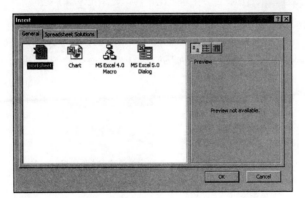

Use the Insert dialog box to add sheets to your workbook.

Adding Sheets at the End

To add a sheet after the last sheet in your workbook or before the first sheet, insert a new sheet anywhere; then drag the sheet tab to the beginning or end of the list of sheet tabs.

When you delete a sheet, you're deleting all the data contained within the sheet, too. To delete a worksheet, use these steps:

1. Select the sheet you want to delete.

2. Open the **Edit** menu and select **Delete Sheet** (you can also right-click the sheet tab and choose **Delete** from the shortcut menu).

3. You're prompted to confirm the deletion, as shown in the following figure. Click **OK**, and Excel deletes the worksheet.

As an added safety measure, Excel asks you to confirm the deletion before actually deleting any data.

Moving and Copying Sheets

Need to rearrange your worksheets? No problem. Select the worksheet you want to move and then drag its tab to a new location among the other sheet tabs. For example, to move Sheet 1 to the back of the stack, drag its tab to the end of the tab display. The drag-and-drop method is perfect for reordering your sheets.

You can also use the **Move or Copy Sheet** command. You'll find this command on the **Edit** menu or on the shortcut menu that appears when you right-click a sheet tab. When selected, the command opens the **Move or Copy** dialog box, shown in the next figure.

You can move or copy sheets in your workbook by using the aptly named Move or Copy dialog box.

To move the worksheet to a different workbook altogether, select the workbook's name from the **To Book** drop-down list. In the **Before Sheet** list box, choose the worksheet you want to place the selected sheet before; then click **OK**. To copy the selected worksheet instead of moving it, do the same but click the **Create a Copy** check box before clicking **OK**.

To copy several worksheets to another file, click the first tab in the group of sheets you want copied, press and hold down the **Shift** key, and then click the last tab in the group. If the sheets aren't in sequential order, click the first tab, press and hold the **Ctrl** key, and then click the tab of each remaining sheet you want to select. You can now open the **Move or Copy** dialog box and perform the move or copy action.

Protecting Worksheets

Here's an interesting topic: worksheet protection. What is it, why use it, and why does it sound so dangerous? Some users enter a great deal of sensitive data into worksheets—data that shouldn't be read or accessed by anyone else (for example, employee salary information and other types of confidential data). Other users end up sharing workbook files with colleagues and need to protect the original data from any changes or updates. If you're in either of these proverbial boats, you can assign passwords to protect your workbook data.

Hiding Columns and Rows

Another way to protect sensitive data is to hide it. You can learn all about hiding columns and rows in Chapter 12, "Rearranging Your Worksheet Data."

Assigning Passwords with the Save As Dialog Box

When you assign a password to a workbook, this prevents another user from opening the file without the proper password. Use these steps to assign a password to a workbook file via the Save As dialog box:

1. Open the file you want to protect.

2. Open the **File** menu and select **Save As**. This opens the Save As dialog box, as shown in the following figure.

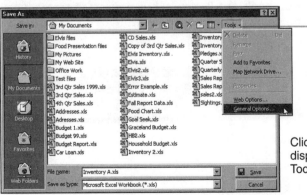

Use the Save As dialog box to get to General Options so you can protect a worksheet from prying eyes or accidental modifications.

Click here to display the Tools list.

3. Click the **Tools** drop-down arrow on the toolbar and then select **General Options**. This opens the Save Options dialog box, shown in the following figure.

*Enter a password in the **Password to Open** text box.*

It's Case Sensitive!

The password you enter is *case sensitive*, which means if you use uppercase and lowercase letters, you'll have to remember exactly what you typed when you enter the password later to open the file.

4. To assign a password to the workbook file, click inside the **Password to Open** text box and enter a password. You can use up to 15 characters, including text, numbers, spaces, and symbols.

5. Press **Enter**. The **Confirm Password** dialog box appears, as shown in the next figure. Reenter the password exactly as you typed it before. Click **OK**.

6. Click **OK** to exit the dialog box; then click **Save** to save the file and assign the password.

Confirm your password by typing it again.

The next time you want to open the file, you'll need to enter the password. When you attempt to open the workbook, the Password box appears onscreen, similar to the one shown in the following figure. Click inside the **Password** text box and type in your password; then click **OK** or press **Enter**.

To open the workbook, you must first enter the correct password.

Write It Down!

If you do assign a password to a workbook, be sure to write it down somewhere. If you lose it, you won't be able to access the file again, and even Microsoft's technical support team won't be able to help you.

Creating Read-Only Files

To allow other users to view the workbook file but not allow them to make changes to the data, consider assigning the file read-only status. You can use this option without password-protecting the file. Mark the **Read-Only Recommended** check box in the **Save Options** dialog box. When this option is assigned, the person viewing the file can open it and read its contents but cannot make changes. (Note that any changes made can be saved as a *new* file, but the original data remains intact.)

Using the Protection Commands

Another way you can assign passwords to workbooks is to use the Protection tools. Open the **Tools** menu and select **Protection**, then select **Protect Workbook**. This opens the **Protect Workbook** dialog box, shown in the next figure. From this dialog box, you can choose to protect the workbook structure, which means the sheets contained in the workbook can't be moved, deleted, added to, hidden, or renamed. You can also choose to protect the workbook's windows from being hidden, closed, or resized. In other words, users won't be able to change the way the actual spreadsheet window appears and they won't be able to resize or close the window in any way.

71

The Protect Workbook dialog box offers two options for protecting the workbook data.

Like the password command used with the Save As dialog box, you must enter and confirm the password assigned with the **Protect Workbook** dialog box.

When you open the file at a later time, you won't be able to make any changes to the workbook structure or window sizes (depending on the options you assigned). To restore the file so you can make changes again, open the **Tools** menu and select **Unprotect Workbook**.

You can also assign a password to a single sheet in the workbook. To do so, open the **Tools** menu and select **Protection**, and then select **Protect Sheet**. This opens the Protect Sheet dialog box, shown in the following figure. Not only can you assign a password to the sheet you're currently using, but you can also choose to protect its contents (prevent any changes being made to cells); objects (prevent any changes being made to worksheet objects, such as clip art); and scenarios (prevent changes to worksheet scenarios—speculations you make about your data to see how changes affect the outcome).

The Protect Sheet dialog box offers options for protecting individual worksheets in a workbook.

Protecting Shared Workbooks

If you and your colleagues plan on using Excel's Track Changes feature, you can use the **Protect and Share Workbook** command to set a password that prevents the removal of this feature. Open the **Tools** menu and select **Protection**, then **Protect and Share Workbook** to assign the password.

So, let's summarize the protection options available with Excel:

➤ If you want complete file protection, assign a password to your Excel file. This protects the file from ever being opened by anyone else (unless you tell them the password).

➤ If you want to share your workbook, but protect it from any changes to its structure or appearance, use the Protect Workbook option.

➤ If you're sharing workbooks and want to protect a single sheet, rather than the whole workbook, use the Protect Sheet option.

You can certainly use a mix of these options if you want, but the more passwords you have to remember, the more likely you are to forget one or lose one. (To truly be secure, or if you're truly paranoid, it's best to assign different passwords and change them regularly.)

The Least You Need to Know

➤ Every cell in a worksheet has an address, also called a *cell reference*.

➤ You can rename sheet tabs to help you identify their contents.

➤ Use the worksheet scroll arrow buttons to view different sheets.

➤ Use the Go To command to quickly locate any cell on the worksheet.

➤ If you've got a big worksheet, you can split your view of this sheet into panes to make it easier to read the data in different parts of the sheet.

➤ You can add and delete sheets as needed, as well as move them from one workbook to another.

➤ To protect your data, assign a password to your workbook file.

Help Me, Please!

At some point while working with Excel, you're going to find yourself in a jam. It doesn't matter how experienced or inexperienced you are, something will come up. Your dilemma may be about a new feature you're trying to use, a question about an Excel topic, or anything else you might need help with. Before you panic, fire off the flare gun, and grab the life preserver, try Excel's help features.

Excel has several different help options you can pursue when you're in a jam, and now is as good a time as any to learn the best route to take in times of trouble. Walk—don't run—to the nearest section, and remember, this is only a drill.

Using the Office Assistant

Hey, there's nothing wrong with asking for help. Everybody needs a little help from time to time, and that's exactly the sentiment behind the Office Assistant. Perhaps you've encountered this character already. I say *character* because Clippit, the animated paper clip, is the character that the Excel programmers have preselected as your helpful Office Assistant. (I've pointed out Clippit for you in the next figure.)

Help is immediately available in the form of the Office Assistant.

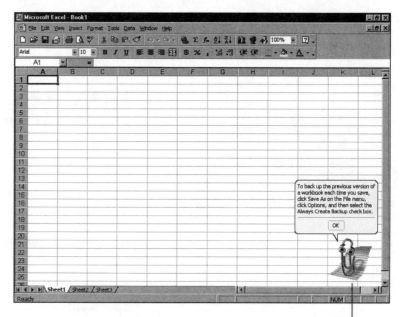

Clippit, the Office Assistant

The Office Assistant appears automatically to offer you help whenever it thinks you need it. Clippit appears as soon as you open Excel for the very first time. However, you don't have to settle for the animated paper clip (although he is very nice and blends in with your other desk accessories). You can elect to use other animated characters as your Office Assistant, and I'll tell you how to change characters later in this section. In the meantime, let's deal with Clippit, because he's the default selection.

New Excel 2000 Feature

The new and improved Office Assistant is more animated than previous versions, and best of all, it's no longer contained in a little box. Office Assistant, regardless of which character you choose, can operate outside the confinements of the help bubble window.

Displaying the Office Assistant

The Office Assistant is an interactive help tool that can readily assist you with any questions you may have while using Excel. It can also help you out while you're performing tasks. To summon help at any time, use any of these methods:

➤ Press **F1** on the keyboard.

➤ Open the **Help** menu and select **Microsoft Excel Help**.

➤ Click the **Microsoft Excel Help** button on the Standard toolbar.

➤ If the Office Assistant already appears active onscreen, click the character.

 When you ask for help (or when Excel thinks you need help), the Office Assistant displays a message balloon, which is just a dialog box in disguise. You can type in a question, conduct a search, or view tips about the feature you're using (see the next figure). You can also customize the appearance of the animated feature and make changes to the help options.

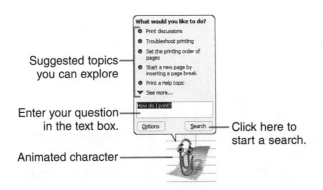

Suggested topics you can explore

Enter your question in the text box.

Animated character

Click here to start a search.

The message balloon offers topics and tips, as well as letting you ask your own questions.

Office Assistant offers you links (much like those found on Web pages) to the Microsoft Excel Help database. In addition to these links, which you can click to display more information, you can also click buttons (such as the **Search** button or the **Options** button). The message balloon operates like a regular dialog box—it just looks a little different.

Asking a Question

To ask the Office Assistant a question, click inside the text box and type in your question. Then click the **Search** button or press **Enter**. Don't worry about capitalization or punctuation—in fact, you don't even have to type in a complete question. You can type in a single word, such as **formatting** or **print**, and Office Assistant will attempt to find related topics.

As soon as you start the search, Office Assistant looks through its Help database and responds with a list of possible topics. Depending on the topic you're looking up, the list may include more topics than can fit in the message balloon. In this case, click the **See More** link.

It Appears Without Being Asked!

The Office Assistant will appear automatically when you attempt a new Excel task. If you want help with the task or want to proceed without the Office Assistant onscreen, select the appropriate option in the Office Assistant message balloon.

Viewing a Topic

To view a particular topic, click its link. This opens a Help window that details topic information (see the next figure). The Help window may appear anchored on the right or left side of the screen, or it may appear as a free-floating window. Depending on the topic you looked up, the Help window has several options you can pursue:

➤ Click the underlined text to view more information; underlined words or sentences are links to additional help information.

➤ Click double-arrow icons to display related help topics.

➤ Some Help windows display more text than others; use the scrollbar to view the text.

➤ Click a graphic to open an additional Help window to read more information about the topic.

➤ Click the **Show Me** button to see a demo of how a feature works.

➤ Use the buttons at the top of the window to navigate Help topics.

➤ Use the Help window's **Maximize** or **Minimize** buttons to change the window's size.

➤ To close the Help window, click the window's **Close** button.

Table 5.1 explains how to use the buttons at the top of the Help window.

Click a topic to open a Help window.   Help window   *An example of a typical Help window.*

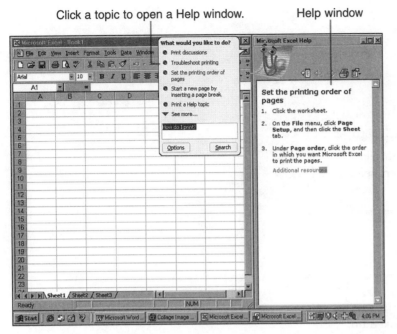

Table 5.1   Help Window Buttons

Button	Name	Function
	Show	Opens the Help tabs
	Back	Returns to the previous Help topic
	Forward	Moves to the next Help topic
	Print	Opens the Print dialog box
	Options	Displays a list of Help options

Using the Help Tabs

The Help tabs, shown in the following figure, let you delve into the Help topics database on your own terms. You can employ three different methods to glean information from the Help database:

➤ Look up specific words by using the **Index** tab.

➤ Browse the various topics by using the **Contents** tab.

➤ Continue entering questions by using the **Answer Wizard** tab.

Regardless of which method you use, they all tap into the same Help database, so select a method that suits your own quizzical nature.

79

Use the Help tabs to search through the Help database by topic, specific terms, or by questions you enter.

Help tabs

Topic Categories

Specific topics

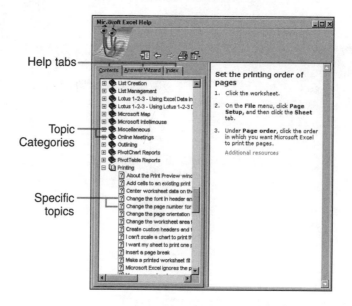

To view the Help tabs, click the **Show** button at the top of the Help window.

To browse various Help topics, click the **Contents** tab (see the previous figure), and scroll through the list until you see the topic category you want to check out. Then, double-click the book icon to the left of the category. The previous figure shows the Printing category opened with related topics represented by page icons with a question mark on them. To view a particular topic, click the topic. As soon as you click a topic, its information appears in the right pane of the Help window.

To look up a specific term, click the **Index** tab, shown in the next figure. Here you can enter a word to look up or scroll through the alphabetical listing. The bottom list box displays related matches. To view a match, click the topic and the right pane displays the information.

Use the Index tab to look up specific terms in the Help database.

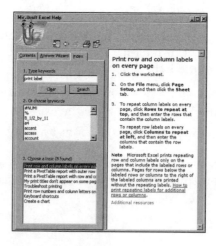

The Answer Wizard tab works just like the Office Assistant message balloon. You type in a question and click the Search button (see the following figure) and a list of topics appears. Click a topic to view its help information.

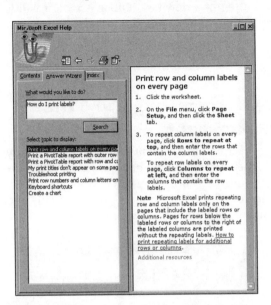

Use the Answer Wizard tab to enter specific questions to look up in the database.

Navigating to the Help Tabs Without Office Assistant

To open the Help window without going through the Office Assistant message balloon, you can set up Help to open the Help window by using the **F1** key only. To do this, click the **Options** button in the Office Assistant balloon, and then click the **Options** tab. Deselect the **Respond to F1 key** check box and click **OK**. The next time you want to open the Help window, press **F1** on your keyboard. This bypasses the Office Assistant.

Closing the Office Assistant

To exit the Office Assistant message balloon dialog box at any time, click anywhere outside the balloon. This closes the balloon, but the Office Assistant character remains onscreen. If you're a new user, you might want to keep the character

Printing Topics

You can print a topic at any time. Click the **Print** button at the top of the Help window. This opens the Print dialog box. Click **OK** to print the topic.

onscreen in case you need help with something as you work. It stays off to the side so it won't interfere with your spreadsheet. Of course, anytime you attempt a new task, Office Assistant will jump into action again and offer to help.

To hide the character completely, open the **Help** menu and select **Hide the Office Assistant**.

Customizing the Office Assistant

Okay, so maybe you don't like Clippit or you think he's acting like he had too much coffee. You're not stuck with him. You can choose another character. Click the **Options** button in the Office Assistant message balloon. This opens the Office Assistant dialog box, shown in the following figure.

Use the Office Assistant dialog box to change animated characters.

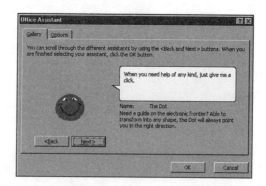

To change characters, click the **Gallery** tab and then use the **Back** and **Next** buttons to view each available character. Each character you view does its little animation routine, presenting a sales pitch to persuade you to pick it. You'll find an Einstein wannabe, a robot, an animated dot, the Office logo, a morphing globe, a cartoon cat and dog, and Clippit. When you find the character you want, click **OK**. (If the new character proves too annoying, you can always return to this dialog box and choose another character.)

Click the **Options** tab in the Office Assistant dialog box to view some other help options you can turn on or off (see the next figure). As you can see, many of the Office Assistant's tasks are selected by default. For example, the **Move When in the Way** check box is selected, which means the Office Assistant will automatically move out of the way as you work.

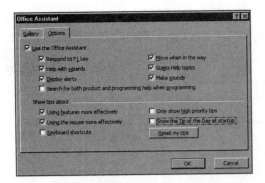

Use the Options tab to change how the Office Assistant behaves.

You can turn any of the options on or off to suit your needs and work style. Perhaps you don't want Office Assistant popping up any old time it thinks you need help; if so, deselect the **Guess Help Topics** check box. Rather not hear the Office Assistant sounds? Deselect the **Make Sounds** check box. You get the drift, right?

The lower portion of the Options tab offers selections for controlling how tips are displayed in Office Assistant. These, too, can be turned on or off. For example, new users might like the Tip of the Day feature, which shows a tip each time you open Excel. Click the **Show the Tip of the Day at Startup** check box to use this feature.

Click **OK** to exit the Office Assistant dialog box.

Using the What's This? Feature

Here's a feature new users are sure to appreciate. You can find out what an onscreen item does by opening the What's This? feature. To use this feature, open the **Help** menu and select **What's This?** (or press **Shift+F1** on the keyboard). As soon as you do, the mouse pointer changes to the shape of a question mark. Click the onscreen item or command you want to know more about, and a description box appears detailing that item and how it's used (see the following figure).

To close the description box, press **Esc** or click anywhere outside the box.

Some dialog boxes you encounter include a **What's This?** icon located in the upper-right corner, next to the close button. To learn more about a particular element or option within the dialog box, select the **What's This?** icon and then click the element you want to know more about. A description box appears that explains how the option is used.

Right-Click It!

In some Excel dialog boxes, you can right-click to display the **What's This?** command. Click the command and then point-and-click the dialog box element you need help with.

Use the What's This?
feature to learn about
onscreen elements.

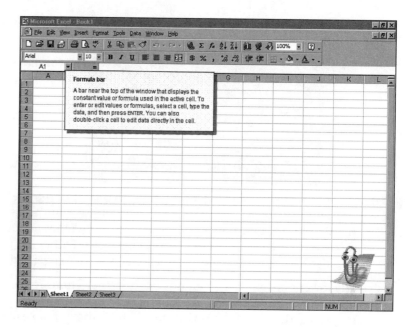

Using Lotus 1-2-3 Help

Are you a former 1-2-3 user? (You didn't think Excel was the only spreadsheet program out there, did you?) If you are, the makers of Microsoft Excel have made the transition of learning a new spreadsheet program easier than ever. Be aware that some differences exist between the two programs (for example, Excel calculates certain formulas and functions differently than 1-2-3). For a complete list of differences, open the **Help** menu and select **Lotus 1-2-3 Help**. This displays the **Help for Lotus 1-2-3 Users** dialog box, shown in the next figure.

Use the Help for Lotus
1-2-3 Users dialog box
if you're switching
from Lotus 1-2-3 to
Microsoft Excel.

Select the 1-2-3 command
you want help with.

Select the Instructions option
to view text-based instructions.

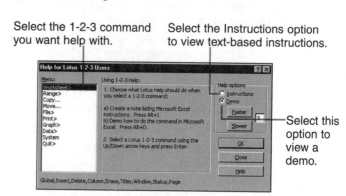

Select this
option to
view a
demo.

To learn more about Lotus 1-2-3 Help, click the **Help** button in the dialog box. This opens a Help window containing related topics, such as the differences between the two programs, equivalent spreadsheet terminology, and tips for converting 1-2-3 worksheets into Excel worksheets.

To see step-by-step instructions of how to perform a 1-2-3 task in Excel, follow these steps:

1. Click the **Instructions** option in the **Help for Lotus 1-2-3 Users** dialog box.

2. In the list box, double-click the 1-2-3 command. Commands in the list that are followed by a greater than sign (>) reveal submenus that contain additional command choices. Double-click the submenu commands until you reach the command instructions you want.

3. The Excel window displays a help box, shown in the next figure, listing the instructions you need to follow to carry out the command in Excel.

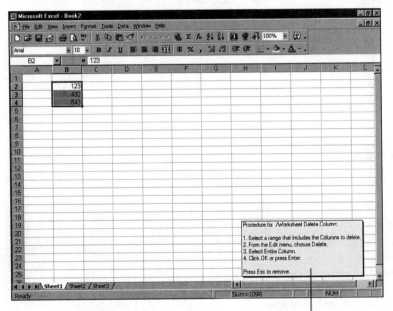

Lotus 1-2-3 Help appears as a text box in the Excel window.

Lotus 1-2-3 Help

You can keep the help box onscreen as long as you need it. To close the box, press **Esc** (Lotus 1-2-3 help won't go away when you click outside the help box).

In addition to text-based help, Lotus 1-2-3 Help also features demos you can play to learn how to perform 1-2-3 tasks in Excel. From the **Help for Lotus 1-2-3 Users** dialog box, select the **Demo** option; then double-click the 1-2-3 command from the list box and keep double-clicking until you locate the exact command you want help with. With the command highlighted in the list box, click **OK**. The next box that appears

Speed It Up or Slow It Down

Use the **Faster** and **Slower** buttons in the **Help for Lotus 1-2-3 Users** dialog box to determine how quickly the demo plays. To slow things down, click the **Slower** button and replay the demo.

85

onscreen lets you enter the spreadsheet data to use in the demonstration. For example, if you choose **Range, Name, Create** from the list box and click **OK**, a box similar to the one shown in the next figure appears. Type in or select any spreadsheet data you want help with and then click **OK**. Lotus 1-2-3 Help starts a prerecorded demo that shows you how to perform the task in Excel.

Enter the spreadsheet data you want to see used in the demonstration.

Enter the data to demonstrate on...   ...then click OK

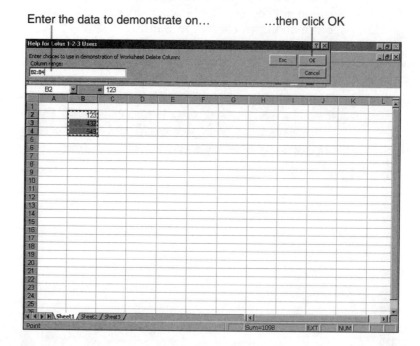

Finding Excel Help on the Web

As if you haven't learned enough ways to find help with Excel, here's another route you can take: You can log on to the Internet from Excel and find help on the Web. Of course, you'll need an Internet connection in order to do this, as well as a Web browser such as Internet Explorer.

To find help on the Internet, open the **Help** menu and select **Office on the Web**. This immediately opens your Web browser and a connection dialog box for connecting to your Internet account (if you're not already logged on). Next, click **Connect**. A Web page opens that displays various links to help sources on the Microsoft Web site (see the following figure). To follow a link, simply click it.

To exit the browser, click the **Close** button and then log off your Internet account.

You'll Need an Internet Account

You can access Microsoft's Help Web pages only if your computer system is set up to connect to the Internet. You'll need a modem and an Internet account with a service provider (a company that lets you use its connection for a small fee) or another source (maybe you have a direct connection to the Internet at your workplace). You'll also need a Web browser program, such as Internet Explorer. If you've got these three things, you can use the Microsoft Help Web pages.

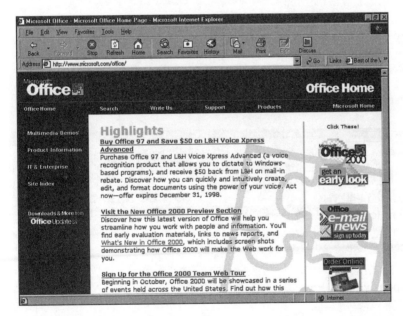

You'll find all kinds of links to help and other information on the Microsoft Web site.

Another route to Excel help on the Web is through the Office Assistant message balloon. If you enter a question and Office Assistant doesn't display the topic you're looking for, click the **None of the above, look for more help on the Web** link. This opens the Help window, as shown in the next figure, where you can enter additional topic information and visit the Microsoft Web site. The keyword you previously entered in the message balloon appears in the Help window. To enter additional keywords, click inside the empty text box and type them. When you're ready to search the Microsoft site, click the **Send and go to the Web** button.

You can also jump onto the Web to look up topics by using Excel's Help window.

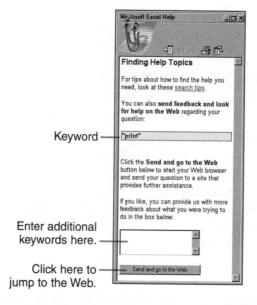

Keyword —

Enter additional keywords here. —

Click here to — jump to the Web.

The Web browser opens (if you're logged on to the Internet) and displays a list of search results matching your keyword, as shown in the next figure. The links displayed are articles containing the keyword you entered in the Office Assistant message balloon or Help window. To follow a link, click it. To conduct another search, use the search tools located on the left side of the Web page.

The resulting Web page displays links you can follow to related topics.

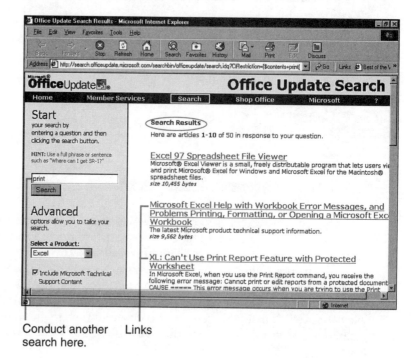

Conduct another   Links
search here.

Conducting a Web Search

To search the Microsoft Web site by using the site's search tools, enter a keyword into the search text box and click the Search button. To search for information related to a particular product, choose the product from the Select a Product drop-down list before starting the search.

Detect and Repair

Excel has a new feature on the Help menu that can assist you with technical difficulties you're experiencing in running the application. Open the Help menu and select Detect and Repair. This opens the Detect and Repair dialog box. Click the Start button, and the feature attempts to find and fix errors in the application itself. The process can take a few minutes; however, if you're experiencing problems with the application, this just might clear them up.

If All Else Fails

You can always call up the Microsoft technical support people. Open the Help menu, select About Microsoft Excel, and then click the Tech Support button in the About Microsoft Excel dialog box. This opens another dialog box with information about contacting Microsoft.

The Least You Need to Know

➤ Use the Office Assistant feature for help with Excel topics and new features.

➤ Use the What's This? feature to find help with onscreen elements and options in dialog boxes.

➤ If you're upgrading from Lotus 1-2-3, you can find plenty of information to help you make the transition to Excel.

➤ For additional help, check out the Microsoft Web site. You can log on and view Web pages without closing the Excel program window.

Chapter 6

Fine-Tuning Excel

In This Chapter

➤ Learn how to add and remove buttons on your toolbars

➤ Create your own tailor-made toolbar from scratch

➤ Tips for customizing your menus

➤ Find out how to use the Options dialog box to customize how Excel looks and works

---

This is your last chapter in basic training boot camp. If you can survive this chapter, you're well on your way to full Excel expertise. Not everybody takes time to learn how to customize the program to meet their needs, but I strongly encourage you not to bypass this important aspect of your Excel education. For instance, wouldn't you like to know why the Excel programmers have combined the default Standard and Formatting toolbars to share a single row? Want to find out how to make your own toolbars? Perhaps you've always wanted to move your menus around?

Customizing Excel Toolbars

In the new-and-improved Excel, the two default toolbars (Standard and Formatting) share the same row. (See the following figure.) If you're a veteran Excel user, I'm sure you've picked up on this fact as soon as you started Excel 2000. In previous versions of the program, the Standard and Formatting toolbars were located directly below the menu bar (the Standard toolbar on top, and the Formatting toolbar right below it) and took up all the horizontal space from one side of the window to the other.

Remember that? Of course, if you really liked the old way these toolbars were displayed, you can change it back. Read on.

The Standard and Formatting toolbars both appear onscreen, side-by-side.

Standard toolbar   Formatting toolbar

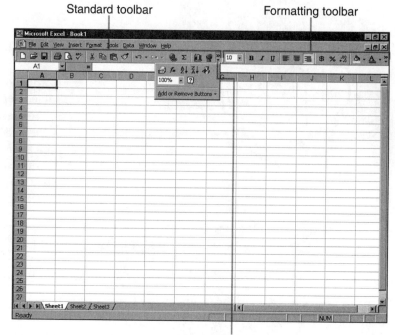

More Buttons button

So, why the big change? Flexibility is the answer. With the toolbars sharing the same row, you can now see more of the worksheet. Also, only the buttons representing the features you work with the most are displayed. As you learned in Chapter 1, "Excel in a Nutshell," not enough room exists to show every toolbar button. Simply click the **More Buttons** button to see the buttons you haven't used recently. The preceding figure points out the Standard toolbar's More Buttons button (try saying that three times fast).

The figures you see from here on out show both the Standard and Formatting toolbars displayed in full. Just remember, you can turn your own default toolbars on or off to suit your own work needs.

Floating Versus Anchored

Some of the toolbars you open in Excel are floating toolbars. This means they float out over the worksheet area and can be moved by dragging them around. Other toolbars are anchored at the edge of the spreadsheet, such as the Standard and Formatting toolbars or the Drawing toolbar. However, you can anchor any floating toolbar to any edge of the work area and float any previously anchored toolbar as you please.

Viewing Toolbars

Although you see only the two default toolbars when you first open Excel, more than half a dozen other toolbars are available. Depending on which task you're performing, the other toolbars open themselves from time to time. Naturally, you wouldn't want to see all of the Excel toolbars at once (you wouldn't have room for a worksheet), but you can turn them on or off as needed. To quickly display a toolbar, right-click a blank area of any toolbar currently onscreen. This opens a shortcut menu that lists all the toolbars. Those with check marks next to them are already displayed. Click a toolbar name to select or deselect it.

For example, traditionally, the Chart toolbar is a floating toolbar (see the next figure).

The floating Chart toolbar   Close button

Excel toolbars can either float or be anchored to an edge of the program window.

Drawing toolbar

These toolbars are anchored along the edges of the program window.

To move a floating toolbar, drag its title bar. To anchor it, double-click its title bar. As soon as you do, it's anchored in place along with the Standard and Formatting toolbars at the top of the spreadsheet window (it's added below the default toolbars).

To turn it into a floating toolbar again, hover your mouse pointer over a space in the toolbar; then click and drag it out onto the worksheet area (see the next figure). You can do the same with any anchored toolbar; locate an empty spot between buttons, hold down the left mouse button, and drag the toolbar away from the edge of the window.

Use the drag-and-drop method to move toolbars around onscreen.

Click and drag here to free the toolbar from its anchored position.   Anchored Chart toolbar

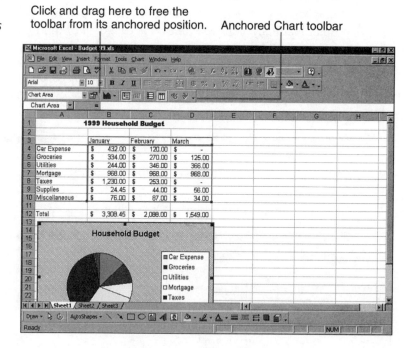

Mind you, freeing your toolbars from their moorings isn't always a good idea. Floating toolbars take up space in your worksheet viewing area, and it's a pain to keep moving them out of the way all the time. Besides, you don't want a flotilla of toolbars crowding out your view of the worksheet data, do you?

To close an anchored toolbar, open the **View** menu, select **Toolbars**, and then deselect the toolbar from the list. To close a floating toolbar, you can use the same method, or you can simply click the tiny **Close** (**X**) button located on the upper-right corner of the floating toolbar's title bar.

Separating the Default Toolbars

If you're not too keen on seeing your beloved Standard and Formatting toolbars crammed together in one area, you can revert to the tried-and-true display of yesteryear—

but just remember, you're going to lose worksheet viewing space. To change the toolbar display, follow these steps:

1. Open the **View** menu, select **Toolbars**, and then select **Customize**, or open the **Tools** menu and select **Customize**. Both these methods open the **Customize** dialog box, as shown in the following figure.

2. On the **Options** tab, deselect the **Standard and Formatting Toolbars Share One Row** check box.

3. Click **OK**. Now you've got two full toolbars stacked onscreen.

New Excel 2000 Feature

The Quick Customize method described in the next section is new to Excel 2000. It lets you quickly turn on or off the buttons you want included on the toolbars.

Use the Customize dialog box to change how toolbars are displayed.

Need Larger Icons?

The Options tab has a setting for using larger icons on your toolbars. Click the **Large Icons** check box to increase the size of the icons. If you select this option, be warned—we're talking super-size large, not just slightly bigger. This option makes the buttons so large that the toolbars take up half the screen.

Adding and Removing Buttons

After using Excel for a while, you may find that you don't use all the buttons on the toolbars. For example, you might want to lose some of the formatting buttons on the Formatting toolbar. It's easy to customize a toolbar to suit your work needs.

Let's start by using the Quick Customize method on the Standard or Formatting toolbars:

1. Click the **More Buttons** button on the toolbar you want to change, and then click **Add or Remove Buttons** (see the following figure).

2. A list of buttons appears. Those with check marks next to them are currently being displayed and are part of the toolbar. Those without check marks are not accessible from the toolbar. To turn a button on or off, select it (or deselect it) in the list.

Can I Get the Default Buttons Back?

If you get too carried away changing buttons, you can always restore the default set. Click the **More Buttons** button on the toolbar and then click **Add or Remove Buttons**, and then click **Reset Toolbar**.

Use the More Buttons button to quickly turn toolbar buttons on or off.

Click here to display the list.

These toolbar buttons are on.

These buttons are off.

3. To exit the list, press **Esc** or click anywhere outside the list.

You can follow these steps for any toolbar; every anchored toolbar has a **More Buttons** button.

Creating Your Own Toolbar

Now, how about learning to tailor-make your own toolbar by using the Customize dialog box? This method lets you create and name your own toolbar as well as include only the buttons you want. To create a toolbar that fits the way you work, follow these steps:

1. Open **Tools** menu and select **Customize**. You can also click the **More Buttons** button on any toolbar, click **Add or Remove Buttons**, and then click **Customize**. Either of these methods opens the Customize dialog box shown in the following figure.

Use the Customize dialog box to create your own customized toolbars.

Using Customization Mode

Any time you open the Customize dialog box, Excel is set to *customization mode*, which means you can make changes to existing toolbars and menus. If you try clicking a toolbar button or menu command in this mode, the command is not activated. Instead, it's selected for editing.

2. Click the **Toolbars** tab (if it isn't already displayed) and then click the **New** button. This opens the New Toolbar dialog box (see the next figure).

In the New Toolbar dialog box, you can type a name for your homemade toolbar.

3. Type a name for the toolbar and click **OK**.

4. An empty toolbar appears onscreen (you may have to drag the Customize dialog box out of the way to see it). Now click the **Commands** tab in the Customize dialog box (see the following figure).

An empty floating toolbar awaits you, ready to hold any toolbar button you want.

Click here to display all the available commands.   My new empty toolbar

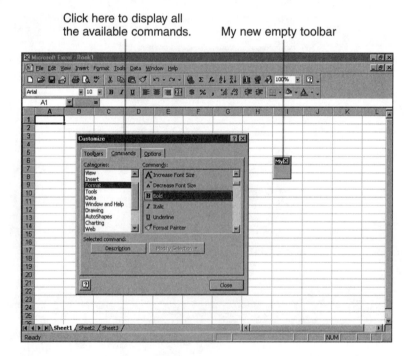

5. Here's the fun part. Look through the **Categories** list box and locate the commands you want to include on your toolbar. Select a category to view its commands.

6. When you find a command you want to include, drag it from the **Commands** list box onto your floating toolbar. Release the mouse button and a new button is added, as shown in the next figure.

What's This Command Do?

While examining commands to add to your toolbar, use the **Description** button to help you determine what a command does. Select the command from the **Commands** list box and then click the **Description** button to see a brief description of the selected command.

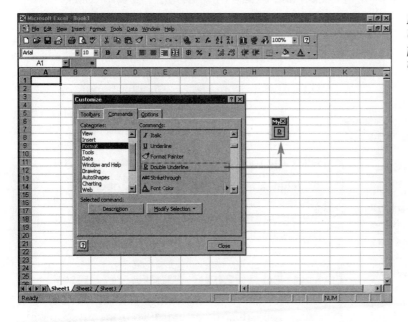

I dragged the Double Underline command from the list box to the toolbar.

7. Continue dragging commands to your toolbar until you have the ones you want. If you make a mistake, drag the icon off the toolbar and release the mouse button. Go ahead, try it.

8. When finished, click **Close** to exit the Customize dialog box.

I Need Some Space!

To give your toolbars some space between buttons or space between a series of related buttons, you can insert a *group line*. A group line is a vertical line used to separate groups of buttons. The Customize dialog box must be open in order to insert group lines. Right-click to the left of where you want to insert a group line; then select **Begin a Group** from the pop-up menu. To remove a group line, right-click it and deselect the **Begin a Group** command.

No More ScreenTips

If you're feeling fairly comfortable with your knowledge of each tool-bar button, you can turn off the **Show ScreenTips on Toolbars** option in the Customize dialog box. Select **View, Toolbars, Customize**; then click the **Options** tab to find the check box.

You can use the drag-and-drop technique to remove buttons from your toolbars in a flash, but the Customize dialog box must be open to do this.

To restore a toolbar to its default state, open the Customize dialog box again, click the **Toolbars** tab, select the toolbar, and then click the **Reset** button.

To delete a toolbar you've created, open the **Toolbars** tab in the Customize dialog box, select the toolbar from the list box, and then click the **Delete** button.

Customizing Excel Menus

Toolbars aren't the only things you can customize in Excel. You can also customize your menus. You can drag commands around from menu to menu, or you can rearrange their order on the default menu. The designers of Excel can't possibly predict the needs of every user, so they've allowed for a great deal of flexibility in Excel's customization features. You can even create your own menus to suit your own work needs. What freedom!

To change a menu, revisit the Customize dialog box again. Yes, you use the same commands and tools to change menus that you use to change toolbars. Open the **Tools** menu and select **Customize**. Now you're in Customization mode, which means you can edit menus and toolbars to your heart's content. Open the menu you want to edit. You can drag commands you don't want right off the menu. That's right, just drag 'em off—select the command, hold down the left mouse button, and drag the command right off the menu. When you release the mouse button, the command is gone.

To add commands, click the **Commands** tab in the Customize dialog box and use the **Categories** list box to select a command group. Locate the exact command you want to add in the **Commands** list and drag it onto the menu, dropping it where you want it inserted. You can also drag commands from one menu to another.

To create a brand-new menu, scroll down the **Categories** list in the Customize dialog box and select the **New Menu** item (see the following figure). From the Commands list box, drag the New Menu item to the Excel menu bar and drop it where you want it to appear. Now you can start adding commands to it; click the menu to open it and then drag commands from the **Command** tab in the Customize dialog box onto the menu.

Drag the New Menu *item onto your Excel menu bar to create your own menu.*

To rename the menu, right-click it and type a new name in the **Name** text box (see the next figure). Use the **Begin a Group** command in the shortcut menu to add a group line to your menu to separate commands. To exit Customization mode after creating and completing your new menu, click **Close** to close the Customize dialog box.

More Menu Customization Options

Click the **Options** tab in the Customize dialog box to display a few more menu options that you can control. For example, select the **Menus Show Recently Used Commands First** option if you want the menus set to Personalize mode.

Give your menu a mean-ingful name by using this shortcut menu.

Right-click here.   Type a name here.

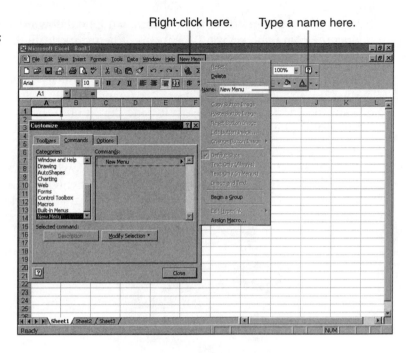

To delete a menu you've created, open the Customize dialog box to switch to Customization mode; then drag the menu off the menu bar. That's all there is to it.

Customizing How Excel Works

You simply have oodles of customizing options you can apply—too many to cover in this chapter. However, I'll happily point out some of the more commonly used options. The starting point for customizing how Excel looks and works is the Options dialog box (see the following figure). To display this box, open the **Tools** menu and select **Options**.

You find most of Excel's customizing options in the Options dialog box.

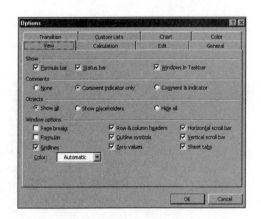

You have eight different tabs of options you can change. Each one focuses on a particular category of options. Here's a brief rundown of what you find on each tab and a few practical suggestions for using some of the options you find:

➤ **View** Use the options on this tab to control Excel's onscreen elements. For example, you can free up more space to see your worksheet by turning off the Formula bar, status bar, and the two scrollbars.

To turn off the gridlines in your worksheet, deselect the **Gridlines** check box on the **View** tab.

➤ **Calculation** This tab has options for controlling how Excel calculates and recalculates worksheet values.

➤ **Edit** You find options for controlling Excel's editing features here. For example, you can choose to turn off editing directly in the cell and perform only editing tasks in the Formula bar.

To set a fixed decimal point for the numbers you enter into your worksheet, click the **Fixed Decimal** check box on the **Edit** tab and designate the number of decimal points you want to use.

If you prefer to do all your editing in the Formula bar rather than in individual cells, deselect the **Edit directly in cell** check box.

➤ **General** This tab houses a mishmash of control settings that don't fall under a particular category. Here are a few useful options you can change:

Excel keeps track of the last four files you worked with and lists them at the bottom of the **File** menu. You can increase the number of files by incrementing the number in the **Recently Used File List** box on the **General** tab.

By default, Excel saves all the files you create in the My Documents folder (unless you specify otherwise at the time of saving). To choose another default folder, enter a new folder location in the **Default File Location** text box.

Also, by default, Excel opens new workbooks with three worksheets. You can increase or decrease this number by using the **Sheets in New Workbook** box.

Don't like the default font and font size used in your worksheets? Change them by entering new settings in the **Standard Font** and **Size** boxes.

➤ **Transition** If you're making the switch from another spreadsheet program to Excel, you'll find options on this tab that can help you make the transition more smoothly.

➤ **Custom Lists** The options on this tab control how lists are used with Excel's AutoFill command. (You learned about using AutoFill in Chapter 3, "Data Entry in a Dash.") You can add new custom lists or delete old ones from this tab.

To add a new custom list, enter the list in the list box, pressing **Enter** to separate each series item, and then click the **Add** button.

To delete a list, select it from the **Custom lists** box, and then click the **Delete** button. Confirm the deletion by clicking **OK.**

103

➤ **Chart**   Use the options on this tab to set parameters for the charts you create in Excel. (Learn more about creating charts in Part 4, "Charting New Territory.")

➤ **Color**   Use this tab to specify which colors Excel lists in its color palettes. The colors set here are the ones available in the other Excel features that use colors, such as the drawing tools.

Be sure to try out the various options you find in the Options dialog box for yourself and see whether any improve the way you use Excel.

The Least You Need to Know

➤ You can change which buttons actually appear or don't appear on the Excel toolbars.

➤ You can design your own toolbar and fill it with your favorite buttons.

➤ Why stop at toolbars? You can also customize Excel's menus as well as make your own.

➤ For other customizing options, check out the Options dialog box. It's filled with all kinds of options for changing how Excel looks and works.

Part 2

Putting Excel to Work

Ready to take this baby out for a spin to see what she can do? The real power of Excel is its calculation capabilities. Excel's formulas and functions can manipulate your data in ways you never dreamed possible. This is where the real fun is, too. You can perform simple or complex mathematical functions, project future scenarios, or perform other number-crunching tasks without having to become an overnight math wizard. In fact, number juggling has never been easier than with Excel 2000.

In this part of the book, you learn how to build formulas in Excel and work with functions, ranges, and Excel's auditing tools for finding worksheet problems. You don't have to be an accountant (or a mechanic) to appreciate the power under Excel's hood; just slip into the driver's seat and check it out for yourself.

Chapter 7

Working the Wide-Open Ranges

In This Chapter

➤ Learn how to select ranges with the mouse or the keyboard

➤ Find out how to give your ranges distinct names

➤ Learn how to work with sheet-level ranges

Ever have a longing to ride the wide-open range, to feel the wind in your hair and see the vast Western prairie sprawled across the horizon before you? Well, I can't help you with that, other than recommend a good travel agent, but I can tell you how to roam the vast open ranges of your Excel worksheet. Like the romantic vision of the Wild West of yesteryear, your worksheet is unexplored territory just waiting for you to move a herd of data through. In this chapter, you learn all about Excel ranges and how they're used to round up data.

What's a Range?

One way you can organize and work with Excel data is to use ranges. Sadly enough, Excel ranges have nothing to do with cowboys, cattle, or land. An Excel *range* is a rectangular group of related cells (or even a single cell) that you can connect in a column, a row, or a combination of columns and rows, or even an entire worksheet. Why would you want to do this? Because you can use ranges for a variety of worksheet tasks. Let me give you a few examples:

➤ You can select a range of cells and format them all in one fell swoop.

➤ You can use a range to print only a selected group of cells.

➤ You can lasso a range to copy or move the data all at once.

➤ Far and away the most useful way to use ranges is in formulas. Instead of referring to every individual cell reference, you can use a range to refer to the whole group of cells you want to calculate.

Ranges are very useful in Excel, so you'd better take time to learn how they work.

Selecting Ranges

How are your dragging skills? You know, where you press and hold down the left mouse button and drag it across the screen to select items? You're going to fine-tune these skills when selecting ranges in Excel.

Techno Talk

Range

A single cell or block of cells identified by a name or a reference. You can use a range in a formula instead of entering each cell reference.

As you've already learned, you can select any cell in Excel with a simple click. To select more than one cell, however, you must use the click-and-drag technique. To select a range with the mouse, follow these steps:

1. Click the first cell in the range you want to select.

2. Hold down the left mouse button and drag across all the cells you want to include in the range.

3. The range appears highlighted onscreen, as shown in the following figure. When you've selected the range you want, release the mouse button.

Now you're ready to format, name, copy, or move the selected range.

What about keyboard users? How do you select a range by using only the keyboard? Hey, I wouldn't leave you guys out. Here's the keyboard method for selecting a range:

1. Move to the first cell of the range you want to select.

2. Hold down the **Shift** key and use the arrow keys to highlight all the cells you want to include in the range.

To deselect a range, click anywhere outside the range or press any keyboard arrow key.

When you select a range, it's referred to by its specific anchor points: the upper-left corner and the lower-right corner. In most instances, a range involves more than one cell; therefore, the range reference separates the anchor points with a colon. For example, range A1:B3 would include cells A1, A2, A3, B1, B2, B3.

Select All
button Selected range

When you select a range of cells in Excel, they're highlighted onscreen.

Selecting Multiple Ranges

If you need to select more than one range in a worksheet, select the first range and then hold down the **Ctrl** key and select the next range. If you're using the keyboard, press **Shift+F8**, press **Shift**, and then select another range, pressing **Shift+F8** between selections.

You can use some shortcuts when selecting ranges. Take a look at Table 7.1 to see what they are.

109

Table 7.1   Range Selection Shortcuts

To Select	Mouse Shortcut	Keyboard Shortcut
Column	Click the column letter	Press **Ctrl+Spacebar**
Row	Click the row number	Press **Shift+Spacebar**
Entire sheet	Click the Select All button (the blank spot above the row numbers, to the left of the column letters; refer to the preceding figure)	Press **Ctrl+Shift+Spacebar**

Branding Your Ranges

Excel's default range names don't readily identify a range's contents. To easily identify your data, you can give a specific range name to a single cell or a large group of cells. It's much easier to refer to your data by a name than with a meaningless cell address. For example, a range named Sales_Totals is a lot easier to decipher than B2:F1. The formula =INCOME-EXPENSE is easier to understand than =B8:B24-C8:C24. Giving ranges recognizable names will make your formulas more logical and easier to follow.

Range names appear in the **Name** box at the top of your worksheet, to the left of the Formula bar (see the next figure). When you have at least one defined range name in a worksheet, you can click the **Name** drop-down arrow to see a list of range names to make your selection from. You can also use the Go To command to quickly move to and select a named range.

Range Rules

Before you get too excited about naming ranges all over your worksheet, you need to know a few rules first. Pay attention; these are important:

➤ Range names must start with a letter or an underscore (_). After that, you can use any character, including punctuation and other special keyboard symbols, except a hyphen or space.

➤ You can use uppercase and lowercase letters with range names.

➤ Don't use spaces; use an underscore (_) or a period (.) instead. Spaces aren't allowed in range names (don't ask me why).

To further illustrate, let me show you some examples of invalid and valid range names:

Invalid Names	Valid Names
Sales Totals	Sales_Totals
Year-End Totals	Year_End_Totals
1999	YR1999
#items	_#items
Qtr 1	Qtr1

Name box

Click the drop-down arrow to
display a list of range names.

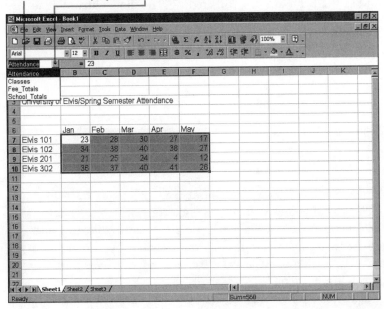

The Name drop-down list displays assigned range names.

Naming with the Define Name Dialog Box

Let's start naming ranges. Have you got a range in your worksheet worthy of a name? If so, follow these steps:

1. Select the range you want to name.

2. Open the **Insert** menu and select **Name** and then **Define**. This opens the Define Name dialog box, shown in the next figure.

3. Click inside the **Names in workbook** text box and type in the range name you want to use. Notice that Excel proposes a range name for you based on the text found in the row or column of the selected range, and it also replaces any spaces with underscores. If you don't like the proposed name, just type your own over the existing name.

Use the Define Name dialog box to give a meaningful name to a range.

Enter a range name here.

Existing range names

Collapse Dialog button

4. Check the **Refers To** box to make sure it's referencing the correct cells for the range. If it isn't, click the **Collapse Dialog** button (refer to the previous figure) at the far-right end of the Refers To box; this reduces the dialog box to a bar so you can see your worksheet. Then select the correct cells in the worksheet. To reopen the full dialog box, click the **Collapse Dialog** button again.

Collapse It

The Collapse Dialog button is common throughout Excel. It's a quick way of getting the dialog box out of your way so you can see the data on the worksheet. When you select the button, it reduces the dialog box to a floating bar on the worksheet window. You can drag this bar out of your way, too, if necessary. Just click and drag its title bar. Click the **Expand Dialog** button to restore the box to its full size again.

When Do I Use Range Names?

Just hang on. You learn all about using range names in formulas in Chapter 8, "Concocting Formulas." You learn about formatting ranges in Chapter 11, "Formatting for Fun or Profit."

5. Click **OK** to exit the dialog box.

Check the new range name in the **Name** box (see the following figure). Repeat these steps to name as many ranges as you like in your worksheet.

Naming on-the-Fly

Is the Define Name dialog box not fast enough for you? There's a quicker way to assign a range name. You can do so directly in the **Name** box (see the figure on page 114). Have a go at naming a range by using these steps:

1. Select the range you want to name.
2. Click inside the **Name** box and start typing in a name, as shown in the following figure.
3. Press **Enter** when you're finished.

The range name is added to the list and assigned to the selected cells.

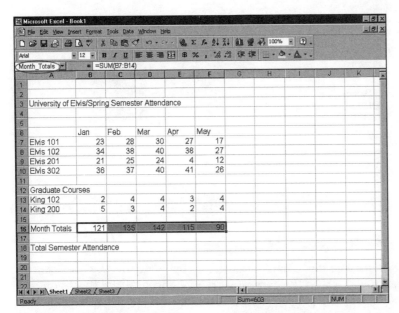

The range name now appears in the Name box.

Using the Go To Command

Got a big worksheet with lots of range names? It's easy to locate the range you want by using the Go To command. Press **Ctrl+G** to quickly summon the **Go To** box; then click the range name in the **Go To** list and press **Enter** (or click **OK**). The Go To list keeps a list of all the range names used in the current workbook.

You can also enter a range name directly into the Name box.

Click here and type in a name.

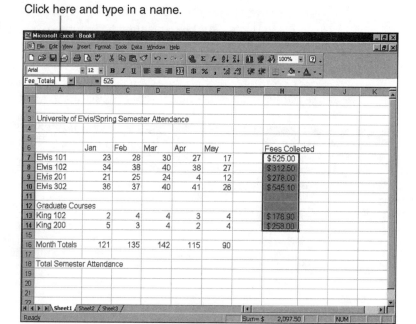

Working with Multilevel Ranges

Here's an interesting point: The range names you create by using the **Define Name** dialog box apply to all the sheets in the current workbook, not just the sheet you're actively using. For example, perhaps you've created a range on Sheet 1 named Sales_Totals. If you switch to Sheet 2 and display the **Name** drop-down list, the range name Sales_Totals appears. If you select Sales_Totals from the list, Sheet 1 becomes active again with the Sales_Totals range highlighted. For this reason, you cannot use the same range name in another worksheet in the same workbook.

You can create sheet-level names to define related ranges across worksheets. For example, perhaps you have a worksheet for each quarter's sales, and all four worksheets need a range named Sales_Totals. What do you do then? You create sheet-level range names. When naming such ranges, you must precede the range name with the name of the sheet followed by an exclamation mark—for example, Sheet2!Sales_Totals or Sheet3!Sales_Totals. (Substitute your own sheet names where applicable.) This method lets you use the same range name but defines it for each sheet. If you want to refer to a sheet-level range from another sheet, be sure to include the entire sheet name.

The Least You Need to Know

➤ You can use ranges to keep your Excel data organized.

➤ You can perform formatting feats on many cells at once if you simply select the range you want to use.

➤ You can assign names to your ranges to help you remember what types of data they hold.

➤ The number one rule in range naming: The name must begin with a letter or an underscore.

➤ The number two rule: No spaces allowed in range names. You can use an underscore or period to represent spaces between words in range names.

Concocting Formulas

Formulas are the key to your Excel chemistry set. In fact, Excel would be a very bland program indeed without them. In this chapter, I show you everything you need to know to create your own Excel formulas and put them to work. Before we begin concocting formulas, make sure you've got your lab coat on, get out those protective goggles, and, oh, better grab that fire extinguisher. The formulas you'll be working with can be extremely reactive and dangerous. Are you ready?

What's a Formula?

If you've never worked with a spreadsheet program before, let me introduce you to *formulas*. Workbooks use formulas to perform calculations on the data you enter. With formulas, you can perform addition, subtraction, multiplication, and division by using the values in various cells. As it turns out, you don't have to handle any noxious chemicals, so technically you don't really need your lab coat and goggles after all (unless you just feel better wearing them).

Formula

A calculation or set of calculations that can be performed on worksheet values to produce a result.

Formula Rule Number One

Every formula in Excel must begin with an equal sign (=). It's the law.

Every formula in Excel must start with an equal sign; that's rule number one. Without an equal sign, Excel doesn't recognize the data as a formula but only as a regular cell entry.

Aside from the equal sign, formulas generally consist of one or more cell addresses or values and a mathematical operator, such as + (addition), – (subtraction), * (multiplication), or / (division). For example, if you want to determine the average of values in cells A5, B5, and C5, you would use the following formula:

$$=(A5+B5+C5)/3$$

Take a look at the following figure. It shows the formula I just described in action. Notice that the cell where I chose to insert the formula shows the results of the formula, and the formula itself appears in the Formula bar at the top of the worksheet.

At first glance, this formula probably looks a bit intimidating, particularly if you're more of a right-brain, creative type of person. Don't worry. I'll explain it all in the sections that follow.

Type a formula in the cell where you want the resulting value to appear.

Formula bar   Formula   Formula result

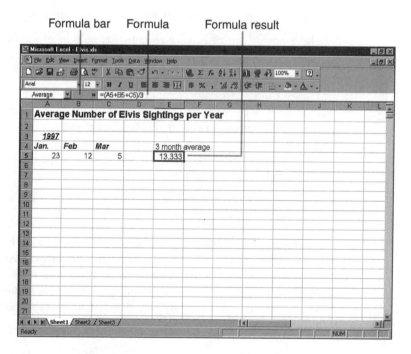

Get Your Operators in Order

I've already mentioned several of the mathematical operators Excel uses in formulas. For example, to add the value in cell A4 to the value in cell B4, you need to build a formula that includes an operator for adding the two cells, which happens to be a plus sign (+). Your formula would look like this:

    =A4+B4

Table 8.1 lists the various operators you can use in Excel formulas.

Table 8.1   Formula Operators

Operator	Operation
+	Addition
–	Subtraction or negation
*	Multiplication
/	Division
%	Percentage
^	Exponentiation
=	Equal to
<	Less than
<=	Less than or equal to
>	Greater than
>=	Greater than or equal to
<>	Not equal to

Dealing with Operator Precedence

Now for formula rule number two—*operator precedence*. Excel performs a series of operations from left to right in the following order, which gives some operators precedence over others:

First	All operations enclosed in parentheses
Second	Exponential equations
Third	Multiplication and division
Fourth	Addition and subtraction

Help!

If you ever get into a jam while building formulas, don't forget you can tap into Excel's extensive Help system for assistance. To learn more about finding help in Excel, turn to Chapter 5, "Help Me, Please!"

Operator Precedence

The order in which Excel performs calculations in a formula is based on the operators.

When in Doubt

If you do happen to forget the order of precedence, just enclose the formula in parentheses anyway. It won't hurt anything if you do, even if the parentheses turn out to be unnecessary.

Formula Rule Number Two

Excel always performs operations following the order of precedence; anything in parentheses first, followed by exponential equations, multiplication and division, and then addition and subtraction.

When you're creating equations, the order of operations determines the results. For example, if you want to determine the average of the values in cells A1, B1, and C1, and you enter the equation =A1+B1+C1/3, you'll get the wrong answer. Why? Anyone? (Please raise your hands.) Excel will divide the value in cell C1 by 3 and add that result to A1+B1. That's because division takes precedence over addition, according to the laws of operator precedence.

So how do you determine the average of cells *A1*, *B1*, and *C1*? Anyone? (Come on, someone take a guess.) Give up? You have to group your values in parentheses. In the previous equation, you want to total the values in cells A1 through C1 first. To do this, you must enclose the group of values in parentheses: =(A1+B1+C1)/3. This way, Excel knows how to handle the formula. It tackles anything in parentheses first and then follows the remaining order of operator precedence.

Using Reference Operators

As if regular old operators weren't enough, you can also use Excel's reference operators to control how a formula groups cells and ranges to perform calculations. Reference operators allow you to combine named ranges, including absolute and relative cell references (you learn more about absolute and relative references later in this chapter). Not only do reference operators let you join cells and treat them as a whole, they also let you refer to a common area where ranges intersect. Before your eyes glaze over, read on; all will become clear in a minute.

For example, perhaps your formula needs to refer to range C3:C20 and to cell D12. To instruct Excel to evaluate all the data contained in these references, use a reference operator, in this case a comma (,). The formula would look like this:

=SUM(C3:C20,D12)

Table 8.2 explains each of the reference operators and how they are used.

Table 8.2   Reference Operators

Operator	Example	Performs
:	=SUM(C3:D12)	Range operator. Evaluates the reference as a single reference, including all the cells in the range from both corners in the reference.
,	=SUM(C3:C20,D12)	Union operator. Evaluates the two references as a single reference.
[space]	=SUM(C3:C20 C10:D15)	Intersect operator. Evaluates the cells common to both references.
[space]	=SUM(Totals Sales)	Intersect operator. Evaluates the intersecting cell(s) of the column labeled Totals and the row labeled Sales.

What's SUM?

SUM is one of the most widely used functions in the world. It's used to sum up values in your worksheets. You can learn all about functions in Chapter 9, "Functions: Fast Formulas for Fast Results," so stay tuned.

Using Comparative Operators

In addition to arithmetic and reference operators, you can use comparative operators in your Excel formulas. This type of operator lets you compare values and evaluate results. For example, suppose you have an inventory worksheet in which you want to easily see the levels of in-stock products at a glance. You can insert a formula that shows you if the stock is above or below acceptable levels. Perhaps you want cell D21 to show you if the contents of column D fall above or below a certain level. To do so, you might enter a formula such as this:

=SUM(D6:D18)<D20

Range Recap

Remember, when referencing a range of cells, such as C3 through C20, use a colon to separate the range anchors in this way: C3:C20.

121

If the value is less than the level established in cell D20, Excel displays a True result in cell D21. If the value is greater than the contents of cell D20, the result is False. The next figure shows this very formula in action.

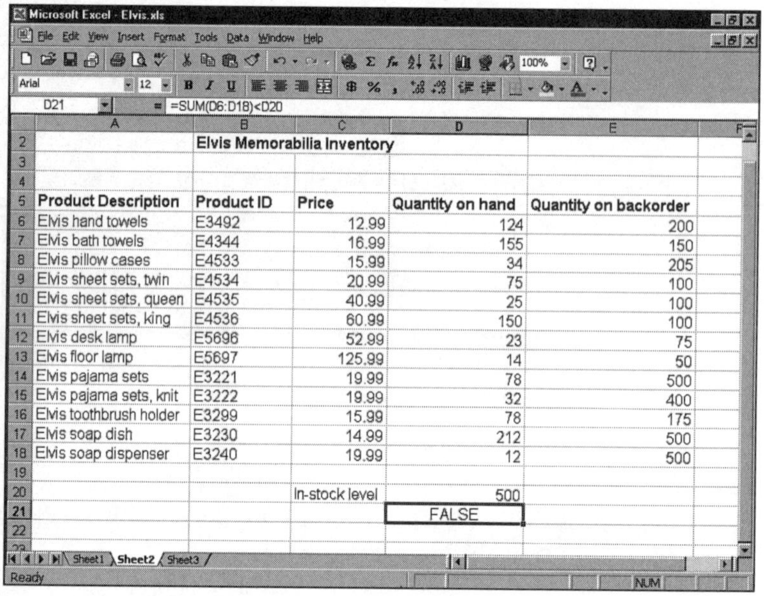

	Elvis Memorabilia Inventory			
Product Description	Product ID	Price	Quantity on hand	Quantity on backorder
Elvis hand towels	E3492	12.99	124	200
Elvis bath towels	E4344	16.99	155	150
Elvis pillow cases	E4533	15.99	34	205
Elvis sheet sets, twin	E4534	20.99	75	100
Elvis sheet sets, queen	E4535	40.99	25	100
Elvis sheet sets, king	E4536	60.99	150	100
Elvis desk lamp	E5696	52.99	23	75
Elvis floor lamp	E5697	125.99	14	50
Elvis pajama sets	E3221	19.99	78	500
Elvis pajama sets, knit	E3222	19.99	32	400
Elvis toothbrush holder	E3299	15.99	78	175
Elvis soap dish	E3230	14.99	212	500
Elvis soap dispenser	E3240	19.99	12	500
		In-stock level	500	
			FALSE	

Use comparative operators to compare data.

Table 8.3 lists each of the comparative operators used in Excel.

Table 8.3 Comparative Operators

Operator	Type
=	Equal to
<	Less than
<=	Less than or equal to
>	Greater than
>=	Greater than or equal to
<>	Not equal to

Entering Formulas

Enough about operators. Let's get down to business by entering some formulas. The real thrill of using a worksheet is seeing how quickly you can create a formula by pointing to the values, or *arguments*, you want to use and adding the appropriate operators. You don't have to worry that the calculation is incorrect; Excel won't make a mistake. Also, you can change any of the values included in the formula, and Excel will update the formula automatically. Pretty cool, eh?

You can enter formulas in two ways. You can enter a formula directly into a cell or you can use the Formula bar. Follow these steps:

1. Select the cell that you want to contain the formula and then type in an equal sign (=). This tells Excel that you're about to enter a formula (see the following figure).

The equal sign appears in the Formula bar.

Don't forget; you must enter an equal sign to start a formula.

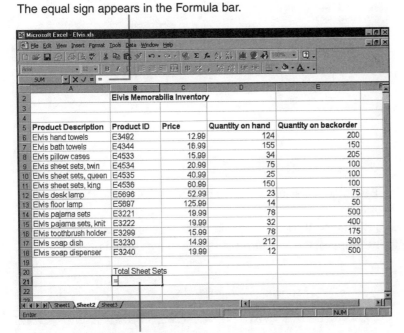

It also appears in the cell.

2. Select the first cell or range you want to include in the formula; simply click the cell or select the range on the worksheet itself. (You can also type in the cell reference if you don't like pointing and clicking all over the worksheet.) The cell reference you select appears in the active cell and in the Formula bar, as shown in the following figure.

3. Type in an operator, such as the plus sign (+).

4. Click the next cell or range you want included in the formula. Continue typing operators and selecting cells until you complete the formula.

5. When you finish the formula, click the **Enter** button on the Formula bar or press **Enter** on the keyboard.

Select the cells you want to use in the formula and then enter operators where needed.

Use operators to build your formula.

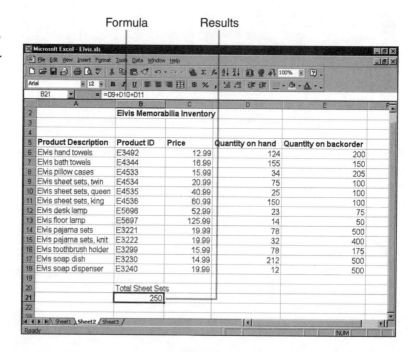

Each time you select a cell in the worksheet, it's added to the formula.

6. The cell now contains the results of the formula. To see the formula itself, select the cell again. The formula appears in the Formula bar, as shown in the next figure.

The formula appears in the Formula bar and the results appear in the cell.

Formula   Results

I Have an Error Message!

If you happen to get an error message after typing a formula, such as #DIV/0!, stop and double-check things. Make sure you used the correct cells. Also, make sure you didn't attempt to divide by zero. For more tips on sorting out formula errors, check out Chapter 10, "Fixing Formula Problems."

The easiest way to place cell references in your formula is to simply click the appropriate cell in the worksheet. For example, if you're building a formula that adds cells C3 and C4, instead of typing the cell addresses into the formula, click the cells in the worksheet and then insert an operator where necessary. Start by typing an equal sign and then click cell C3. Type an operator, such as a plus sign, and then click cell C4. To finish, press **Enter**.

Cancel That!

☒ To cancel a formula while in the middle of building it, just click the **Cancel** button on the Formula bar. You can also press **Esc**. A formula isn't calculated until you press **Enter** or click the **Enter** button on the Formula bar, so you can cancel it before it's completed.

Another way to enter formulas is to use the Formula palette. First, select the cell to contain the formula and then click the **Edit Formula** button (the button with an equal sign) on the Formula bar. This opens the Formula palette, as shown in the next figure. An equal sign is automatically inserted for you. Begin entering the cells you want to use in the formula and the operators necessary to perform the calculations. Notice that the Formula palette keeps track of the results. After you complete the entire formula, click **OK**. The formula now appears in the Formula bar and the results in the worksheet cell.

Use the Formula palette to assemble formulas and keep track of the results.

Edit Formula button

The Formula palette keeps track of the formula results.

Formula palette

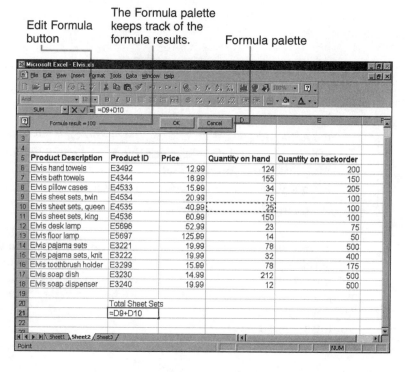

Where's My Cell?

If the cell you want to include in the formula doesn't appear in your current view of the worksheet, use the navigation keys, the scrollbars, or the Go To command to locate the cell.

You can edit a formula at any time. Select the cell containing the formula, click in the Formula bar, and then make the necessary changes. You can use the mouse to select new cell references to include in the formula. Use the **Backspace** and **Delete** keys to edit formula values and operators. Press **Enter** or click the **Enter** button, and Excel calculates the new results.

When you're editing formulas, cell references become color coded. Each cell reference appears in a different color, and the matching cell in the worksheet takes on the same color. This helps you identify the cells you're working with.

Absolute Versus Relative Cell Addresses

To make it easy for you to move and copy formulas, Excel uses a concept known as *relative addressing*. Oddly enough, this has nothing to do with cousins, nieces, nephews, or other familial ties. With relative addressing, Excel treats the cells you include in formulas as relative locations instead of set locations. This is a little tricky to comprehend if you're a new Excel user, so let me give you an example. Let's say you've filled the first three cells in column A with the following data:

A1   50

A2   100

A3   =A1+A2

When you create the formula in cell A3, Excel doesn't think, "Go to A1 and grab the value 50." Instead, it identifies the first cell in the formula as two above the current cell.

Relative Addressing

A reference that changes based on the formula's location. By default, every reference is a relative reference, unless you specify otherwise.

Basically, Excel thinks this: "Go up two cells, get the value, go up one cell, get the value, and then add the two." Now, if you move or copy the formula, the same set of instructions work again, but in a new location. If you copy the formula to cell B3, the formula becomes =B1+B2. If you copy the formula to cell C3, the formula becomes =C1+C2. The location of the cells is relative, get it?

This type of referencing saves you from having to create the same formula over and over again. You can just copy and paste it, and it will work the same in its new location.

So what do you do when you want the formula to refer to a specific cell no matter where it's moved or copied to? That's easy—you use an absolute cell address. For example, suppose you have several columns of pricing information that refer to one discount rate in cell A1. When you create a formula based on the rate, you always want it to refer to cell A1; you don't want the reference to adjust. In this case, you use an absolute cell reference. This type of reference stays put—in other words, it doesn't change just because the formula might move to another cell.

Absolute references always have a dollar sign ($) before the part that's absolute. Absolutely, I'm not kidding. Take a look at this example:

    =$A$1+A2

The cell reference to cell A1 in this formula is absolute. See the dollar signs in front of the column and row labels? In some instances, you might want to use a mixed reference in a formula. Mixed references contain both absolute and relative cell addresses. For example, you might want the row reference to stay fixed and the column to be relative. The reference $C6, for instance, keeps the column

Absolute Addressing

A reference that doesn't change even if you move or copy it. Absolute references are preceded with dollar signs.

from changing, but the row is relative. If the reference is written as C$6, the column is relative and the row is absolute.

To enter absolute or mixed references, follow these steps:

1. Select the cell that will contain the formula and type an equal sign (=).

2. Click the cell reference you want to include in the formula as an absolute reference.

3. Press **F4** on the keyboard. Excel enters dollar signs ($) before each part of the cell reference. The following figure shows an example.

When you press **F4** *while building a formula, Excel cycles through absolute and relative cell addressing.*

The dollar signs are inserted automatically when you press **F4**.

	Product Description	Product ID	Price	Quantity on hand	Quantity on backorder
2			Elvis Memorabilia Inventory		
5	Product Description	Product ID	Price	Quantity on hand	Quantity on backorder
6	Elvis hand towels	E3492	12.99	124	200
7	Elvis bath towels	E4344	16.99	155	150
8	Elvis pillow cases	E4533	15.99	34	205
9	Elvis sheet sets, twin	E4534	20.99	75	100
10	Elvis sheet sets, queen	E4535	40.99	25	100
11	Elvis sheet sets, king	E4536	60.99	150	100
12	Elvis desk lamp	E5696	52.99	23	75
13	Elvis floor lamp	E5697	125.99	14	50
14	Elvis pajama sets	E3221	19.99	78	500
15	Elvis pajama sets, knit	E3222	19.99	32	400
16	Elvis toothbrush holder	E3299	15.99	78	175
17	Elvis soap dish	E3230	14.99	212	500
18	Elvis soap dispenser	E3240	19.99	12	500
20		Tax rate	5%		
21		Total	=SUM(C6:C18)*$C$20		

4. To change to a mixed reference, keep pressing **F4** until you get the mixed reference you want to use. The **F4** key cycles through the choices.

5. Continue building your formula, pressing **F4** to set absolute or mixed references as you go; then press **Enter** to calculate the formula.

The **F4** key is the key to absolute and mixed references. For example, if you enter the reference C6, pressing **F4** will cycle through $C$6, C$6, $C6, and C6. Just stop on the reference you want. Is that a great trick or what?

Using Range Names in Formulas

Back in Chapter 7, "Working the Wide-Open Ranges," you learned how to name ranges in your worksheets. You can use assigned range names in your Excel formulas, which is pretty darned handy if you ask me. This greatly speeds up the time it takes to build a formula. It's a lot easier to remember a named range rather than a generic range (such as B4:E25).

You can type in the range name directly into the formula, or you can use the Paste Name dialog box. Follow these steps to paste a name into a formula:

1. Start your formula as usual. Then, enter an equal sign and any necessary cell references or operators.

2. When you come to the spot in the formula where you want to use a range name, open the **Insert** menu and select **Name**, and then select **Paste**. This opens the Paste Name dialog box, as shown in the following figure.

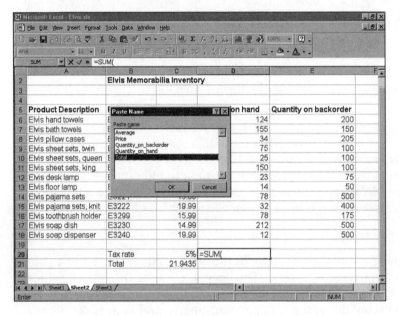

Use range names from the Paste Name dialog box to paste into formulas.

3. Select the range name you want to use from the **Paste Name** list box.

4. Click **OK** to exit the dialog box. The range name is immediately entered into the formula.

Now finish building the formula.

Of course, none of this will work if you haven't previously named ranges in the active worksheet. For more information about naming ranges, turn back to Chapter 7.

Referencing Cells from Other Worksheets

One more thing to cover regarding formula building—how to reference formulas from other sheets or workbooks. Yes, in addition to absolute and relative cell addressing in your formulas, you can also reference cells or ranges from other worksheets and workbook files.

To reference a cell on another sheet, you must enter the sheet name as part of the cell reference. For example, to refer to cell C10 on the third sheet, enter the address Sheet3!C10 in your formula. Remember that sheet names, when referenced, include the sheet and an exclamation mark. If you've given the sheet a specific name, such as SALES, use the specific name and an exclamation mark (SALES!C10). If the sheet name includes spaces, such as SALES TOTALS, you must surround the name with single quote marks ('SALES TOTALS'!C10).

Another way to enter a cell address from another sheet is to use the mouse. When you get to the point in the formula where you need to enter a cell reference from another sheet, click the sheet's tab and select the cell or range you want to use. Excel inserts the complete reference, including the sheet name, into the Formula bar.

Use 3D references to designate a cell range that includes two or more sheets in the workbook. For example, you may have a worksheet for each sales quarter that totals each salesperson's amounts. Each worksheet looks almost the same with slight differences in the number amounts. You can use a 3D reference to reference the same cells in each sheet. When entering 3D references, use a colon to indicate the range of worksheets. For example, if you're creating a formula that uses data from the same range in four different worksheets, the 3D reference might look something like this:

```
Sheet1:Sheet4!$D$5:$G$12
```

You can type 3D references or select them with the mouse. When you get to a point in the formula where you need to enter a 3D reference, click the first worksheet tab containing the cell or range you want to reference, hold down the **Shift** key, select the last worksheet tab containing the data you want to use, and then select the cell or range you want to reference.

Are You a Multiplan User?

If you're using Microsoft Multiplan, you may be used to entering the R1C1 style of referencing cells. This style identifies a cell by its row number and then its column. If you prefer this style of referencing, you can set up Excel to use the same style. Open the **Tools** menu, select **Options**; then click the **General** tab and select the **R1C1 Reference Style** check box. Click **OK** to exit the dialog box and apply the new setting.

The Least You Need to Know

➤ All formulas must begin with an equal sign.

➤ Use operators in formulas to define the calculations or arithmetic functions you want to perform.

➤ Excel always performs operations following the order of precedence: anything in parentheses first, followed by exponential equations, multiplication and division, and then addition and subtraction. When in doubt, use parentheses!

➤ You can enter a formula directly into a cell or you can use the Formula bar.

➤ Excel assumes you're using relative cell referencing unless you tell it otherwise, which means the references you use in a formula are relative to the formula's location.

➤ Use absolute referencing to assign fixed references in your formulas. Absolute references are preceded by dollar signs, as in $A$1.

➤ You can reference named ranges as well as cells found on other sheets.

➤ When you reference another sheet, use an exclamation mark along with the name—Sheet2!, for example.

Chapter 9

Functions: Fast Formulas for Fast Results

In This Chapter

➤ The dirt on Excel functions—what are they and how do you use them?

➤ Find out how to start your own arguments

➤ Learn how to enter functions painlessly

➤ Popular functions you can use almost every day

If you thought formulas were fun, wait until you get a load of functions. Excel functions make worksheet work fast, easy, and fun, which is quite a feat when it comes to dealing with the often humdrum nature of some spreadsheet data. Functions are the sports cars of the world of fast-paced formulas. They're sleek, glamorous, and exceedingly speedy, and every spreadsheet user wants to drive one. When you get tired of one, trade it in for another—there's a veritable stable to choose from.

In this chapter, you learn the ins and outs of Excel's many functions and how they make your work much easier. After all, isn't that why you use a computer anyway?

What's a Function?

If you're looking for a speedier way to enter formulas, Excel's functions are the way to go. Functions are built-in Excel formulas. For a lengthier definition, functions are complex ready-made formulas that perform a series of operations on a specified range of values. Got that?

Functions

Functions are prebuilt formulas you can use to quickly calculate data in your worksheet. Excel has over 300 functions.

As it turns out, you've already had a glimpse at what a function can do (if you read the previous chapter, that is). I mentioned the SUM function in Chapter 8, "Concocting Formulas," which automatically sums your data. Here's an example to refresh your memory. Suppose you want to determine the total of a series of numbers in cells A5 through G5. You could enter a formula that went something like this:

=A1+B1+C1+D1+E1+F1+G1

However, it would really simplify things if you could just enter this instead:

=SUM(A1:G1)

The SUM function tells Excel to add everything in the parentheses, without you having to insert all those operators and cell references. With functions, you can use range references (such as C4:F12), range names (such as EXPENSES), or numerical values (such as 585.86).

To qualify as a true function, each function must consist of these three elements:

➤ It must possess an equal sign (=), of course, because every Excel formula starts with an equal sign.

➤ It must have a name; every function has a specific name, such as SUM or AVG.

➤ It must have an argument. No, I don't mean it picks a fight with other data; rather, it has to act upon spreadsheet values. The argument you use with a function, such as (A3:F11), indicates the cell addresses of the values the function will act on. The argument is often a range of cells, but it can be much more complex.

Exceptions to the Rule

Actually, not all functions require an argument. For example, the NOW function, which inserts the current date and time, doesn't need one. Typically, the most commonly used functions do require arguments.

You can enter functions, like other data, by typing them in the cells. You can also enter them by using the mystical Paste Function feature. Sound interesting? Then let's get started.

The Awesome AutoSum Function

Argument

The values you plug into a function to calculate a result.

We might as well begin with a really whiz-bang function—Excel's AutoSum feature. One of the tasks you'll perform most often is summing up values you've entered in your worksheet cells. Because summing is so popular, Excel provides a super fast way to perform this function—you simply click the **AutoSum** button on the Standard toolbar. AutoSum guesses at what cells you want summed based on the currently selected cell. If AutoSum selects an incorrect range of cells, you just set it straight and tell it exactly which cells to sum.

The AutoSum tool is actually a deployment of the SUM function, which, as I already explained, sums your values. With the AutoSum feature, however, you don't even have to enter the function name—AutoSum takes care of that for you.

AutoSum makes its most accurate guess if you click a cell at the end of a row or column of data, that is to say, a cell next to the data you want to sum. If you click a cell that's not contiguous (next to) with the data you want to sum, AutoSum won't come up with the right total. If you do insist on using AutoSum in a noncontiguous cell, you have to tell AutoSum which range to use by dragging over the correct range.

To use the awesome AutoSum feature, follow these steps:

1. Select the cell in which you want to insert the sum. Try to choose a cell at the end of a row or column of data that you want to sum. The following figure shows an example.

2. Click the **AutoSum** button on the Standard toolbar.

I want to sum the col-
umn above the selected
cell.

AutoSum button

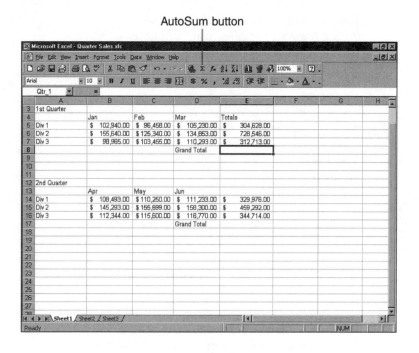

3. AutoSum inserts =SUM and the range of the cells to the left of or above the
   selected cell, as shown in the following figure. If this is the correct range, skip
   to step 5.

AutoSum guesses at
which range you want
to sum.

The SUM function is
added to the formula.

The selected range is out-
lined with a flashing border.

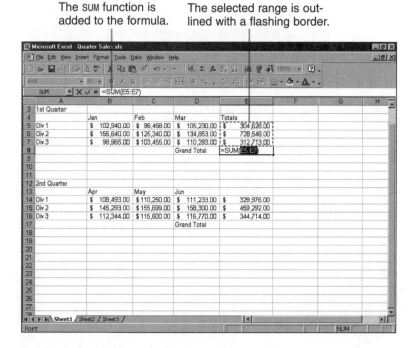

4. If AutoSum didn't guess the correct range, you can edit the selection. You can adjust the range of cells by clicking inside the selected cell or the Formula bar and editing the range. Type in the correct range or just drag the mouse pointer over the range of cells.

5. Press **Enter**. Lo and behold, Excel calculates the total for the range and enters it in the selected cell, as shown in the following figure.

Formula with function   Result

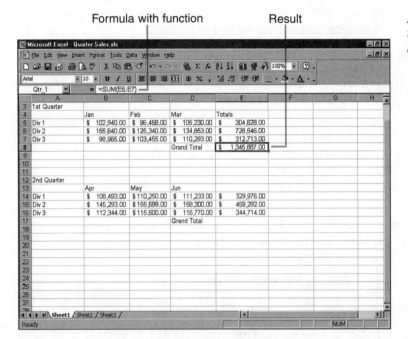

It's awesome—AutoSum totals the values in a blink of an eye.

See the Formula

As soon as you press Enter, you advance to the next cell in your worksheet. To back up and view the results as well as the formula that got you those results, just click the cell containing the results again and you'll see the formula in the Formula bar.

Functions in Action

Excel provides many calculation functions for you, and SUM is just one out of hundreds. You'll also find functions to help you calculate a loan payment, find the square root of a number, calculate an average, count items in a list, and much more. Let's see some more functions in action.

Keeping in mind that functions are simply a shorthand way for entering complex formulas, take a look at the AVERAGE function. It condenses a longer formula into a shorthand version. For example, rather than using the formula

    =(A+A2+A3+A4+A5)/5

you can use the following function instead:

    =AVERAGE(A1:A5)

Like a formula, a function starts with an equal sign. The next part is the function name, usually a short, abbreviated word that indicates what the function does. After the function name, you see a set of parentheses and the arguments enclosed within. If a function uses more than one argument, commas are used to separate the arguments.

As you work with more functions, you'll notice they can save considerable room in the Formula bar and cut down on the amount of typographical errors you might make when manually entering formulas.

Here's another function in action (guess what it does):

    =MAX(A1:F20)

It returns the largest number in a range—the maximum. Here's its opposite:

    =MIN(A1:F20)

This function returns the smallest number in a range, or the minimum. Are you starting to see how much fun this can be? It beats having to type in long formulas with lots of operators.

All About Arguments

Most functions have a particular syntax you must use. By that, I mean you have to write the formula so it includes the arguments you want the function to act on, presented in the manner the function expects. Syntax includes not only the order and format of the arguments, but punctuation and spacing as well. For example, the syntax =SUM(A1:G1) specifies a range of cells to add up (the range being the arguments used in the formula) enclosed in parentheses with no space between the word SUM and the opening parenthesis.

However, not all of us are expert typists, so occasionally, you may make a mistake in entering a function and leave out the proper spacing or mistype a key. When this happens, Excel warns you of the error with a prompt box. For example, if you type in =SUM (A1:G1) (see the space after the word SUM?) or =SUM(A1;G1) (a semicolon instead of a colon), Excel displays a prompt box telling you it has found an error in the function and proposes a correction. Click **Yes** and Excel fixes the punctuation or spacing error for you in the function.

Some of the simpler functions don't require any arguments. If you enter the function =NOW(), it returns the current date and time. No arguments are required (but notice that you still have to use the parentheses).

Some functions use just one argument. For example, to find the square root of a number, you can use the SQRT function, like this:

```
=SQRT(12)
```

However, most functions require several arguments. The SUM function can use as many as 30 arguments. Others, however, use a fixed number of arguments, such as the PMT function, which figures the periodic payment for a loan. Each argument is separated by a comma in the formula. Take a look at the syntax for the PMT function:

```
=PMT(rate,nper,pv,fv,type)
```

What's with all the funny abbreviations? It turns out that each one represents an argument. The following is a breakdown:

➤ **rate**   This is the first argument in the function and it represents the percentage rate per payment period.

➤ **nper**   This argument stands for the number of payment periods for the life of the loan.

➤ **pv**   This argument stands for the present value; it tells how much money was borrowed or loaned at the beginning of the loan.

➤ **fv**   This argument stands for the future value; it represents the amount of value remaining at the end of the loan. This argument is optional. You would define this argument if the loan has a balloon payment at the end, or if it's a lease and you have a purchase option amount to specify.

➤ **type**   This argument is optional, too. It defines how payments on the loan are entered for the payment period, either at the beginning or the end. The argument can be expressed as a blank or 0, which means payments are at the end of the payment period, or as a 1, which means the payments are at the beginning.

Now take a look at the mumbo jumbo at work with actual values plugged in. Let's say you take out a five-year loan for $10,000. There are 60 payment periods with an interest rate of 12 percent per year (12 percent appears as .12 in decimal form; divide it by 12 months and you get the monthly rate of 0.01). Because you're borrowing money, the amount is expressed as a negative value. There's no future value to worry about (it's just money), and let's assume the payments occur at the end of each period and not worry about entering a type argument. Therefore, your formula would look like this:

```
=PMT(0.01,60,-10000)
```

And what would be the result? If you guessed $222.44, you're absolutely right. Your monthly loan payment would amount to $222.44. The formula contains three out of five possible arguments.

What about those extra two arguments (future value and type)? Those were optional, remember. What if you wanted to skip one optional argument, but define the other? For example, what if you wanted the formula to figure in the payment occurring at the beginning of each period, which is expressed as 1, but not define a future value. Your formula would look like this:

```
=PMT(0.01,60,-1000,,1)
```

The extra comma near the end of the formula tells Excel that you're skipping an optional argument, but defining the argument to the right of the optional argument. You enter a comma just as if you were going to define the argument and then enter another separator comma to define the next argument. If you didn't do this, Excel assumes the argument for the type (1) is the future value argument. That's because the PMT function is based on fixed arguments. In other words, the PMT function is expecting each argument to be in the right order.

Now, what if you used cell references that pointed out these arguments instead? Your formula might look like this:

```
=PMT(C5,C6,C7)
```

or like this:

```
=PMT(C5,C6,C7,,1)
```

Getting confused? Don't be. Functions may appear extremely difficult at first, but Excel has a feature that helps you build them with minimal effort. You learn more about this feature later in the chapter. In the meantime, let's take a look at the kinds of results you can expect to see when using functions.

Examining the Result Types

Much of the time, the functions you plug into your spreadsheet will produce number results. But that's not always the case. Because functions use different types of arguments, you can get different types of results, as explained in this list:

➤ **Number**   This one's pretty obvious, and you've already seen such results when I explained how to use the PMT function in the previous section. Number results can include any integer or decimal number.

➤ **Time and Date**   When you're working with time and date functions and values, you can expect time and date answers.

➤ **Logical values**   These kinds of results include TRUE, FALSE, YES, NO, 1, 0, which follow logical arguments.

➤ **Text**   When a function displays a text result, it's surrounded by quote marks.

➤ **Arrays**   An array is a column or table of cells that are treated as a single value. Array formulas operate on multiple cells.

➤ **Cell references**   Believe it or not, some function results might display references to other cells instead of actual values.

➤ **Error values**   Some functions use error values as arguments, such as the ISERROR function; therefore, some results appear as error values as well. Error values aren't the same as error messages, which simply tell you you've entered something incorrectly in the function arguments.

The point of this list is to stress that you need to provide the correct types of arguments in order to see the correct results. If you enter a text function and then proceed to use number values as arguments, you're not going to get the right results. Of course, one way around possible mix-ups is to use Excel's Formula palette or Paste Function dialog box, both of which happen to be covered next.

Entering Functions into Formulas

Are you about ready to start entering functions for yourself? Okay then, here's what you need to do: You can choose to enter a function and its arguments by directly typing them into the cell or Formula bar. However, that's not necessarily the easiest way to go. For real speed, use the Formula palette or the Paste Function dialog box (actually, these two features work hand in hand).

Follow these steps:

1. Click inside the cell where you want to enter a function.

2. Click the **Edit Formula** button on the Formula bar. This immediately opens the Formula palette, as shown in the following figure.

141

Welcome to the Formula palette, the starting point for building formulas with functions.

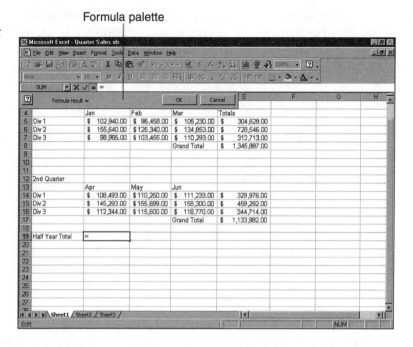

3. Click the function drop-down list (normally the Name box when you're navigating the worksheet) to display a list of recently used functions, as shown in the following figure. If the function you want to use is listed, select it and skip to step 6. If not, select **More Functions** from the list and proceed to step 4.

Use the drop-down list to select from recently used functions.

4. The Paste Function dialog box opens, as shown in the following figure. This dialog box lists all the available functions and their category headings. To find your function, select a category on the left. A list of functions appears on the right. Click the **All** category to see every Excel function, using the scrollbar to view them all.

5. When you locate the function you want to use, select it from the **Function Name** list box and click **OK**.

Another Route

Another way to open the Paste Function dialog box is to click the **Paste Function** button on the Standard toolbar.

Select a category.

Click here for help with the function.

Select a function.

A description of the function appears here.

The Paste Function dialog box is your source for Excel functions.

6. The Formula palette now displays the function and fields for each argument needed to build the formula (see the following figure). You can enter values directly into the fields or click the cells you want to reference.

Instructions   Fields   Collapse button   Formula palette   Click here to calculate the results.

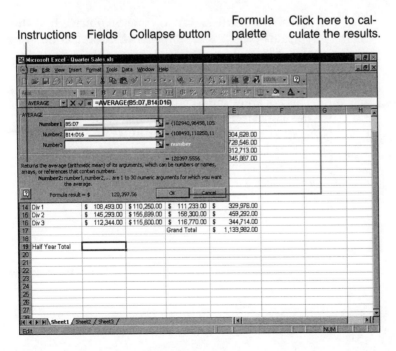

The Formula palette now has fields for each argument the function needs in order to produce results.

7. When you're finished entering arguments, click **OK**. The result now appears in the worksheet cell. Click the cell to see the complete formula in the Formula bar, as shown in the following figure.

The function calculates the result based on the function type and arguments, displaying it in the cell.

Formula

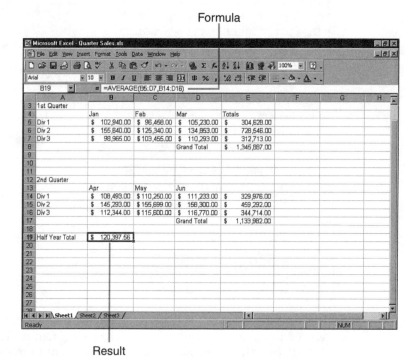

Result

Drag It!

You can also drag the Formula palette out of your way rather than collapsing it; just click on a blank area of the palette, hold, and drag it.

The most effortless way to enter arguments into the Formula palette is to simply click the cell containing the value you want to use (or select the range). If the palette is in the way, click the **Collapse** button to the far right of the field you're currently using. This collapses the palette to a bar, and you can see the worksheet without hindrance. Select the cell you want and then click the **Expand** button on the palette bar to expand the palette to full size again. The following figure shows the Formula palette collapsed.

144

Collapsed Formula palette   Click here to expand the palette again.   *Here's an example of a collapsed Formula palette.*

Useful Functions You Won't Want to Live Without

Excel has more than 300 functions you can use (of course, many of them appeal only to accountants, engineers, and other pocket-protector types). That's not to say you won't find at least a few functions incredibly useful for your own worksheet tasks. To help you sort through them all, they're grouped into categories based on type. Here's a brief overview of what you can expect to find in each category:

➤ **Database & List Management** If you're using Excel as a database program (for organizing lists of data), use the database functions to count, add, and filter database items.

➤ **Date & Time** You'll find all kinds of functions for calculating dates, times, minutes, and so forth. For example, you can calculate the number of days between billings or how many hours have passed since your birth and the current hour.

➤ **Financial** The financial category houses all the functions for calculating and tracking loans, principal, interest, yield, depreciation, future values, and so forth.

➤ **Information** The information functions help test your data—whether it's a number, a blank, or so on.

➤ **Logical** The logical functions will appeal to the philosopher or Mr. Spock (the Vulcan, not the baby doctor) in you; create if-then statements that apply logical conjectures to your data.

145

➤ **Lookup & Reference**   Use the lookup and reference functions to help you locate references or specific values in your spreadsheets. For example, you can use a lookup function to look up a particular value in a table of values. Use reference functions to determine cell contents or ranges.

Nesting Functions

You can nest a function inside a function. When building a formula with a function, you can include another function as part of the arguments. For example, when applying logical functions, it's quite common to use one or two additional functions as part of the argument syntax. Here's an example:

`=IF(RAND()>.5,"Heads","Tails").`

➤ **Mathematical & Trigonometric**   The mathematical and trig functions cover all the calculation tasks you might need to perform, and not just basic math. You'll find functions for rounding off, calculating logarithms, square roots, and much more.

➤ **Statistical**   You'll find functions to calculate averages, probabilities, rankings, trends, bell curves, and more.

➤ **Text**   In the midst of all these high-minded mathematical-based functions, Excel also has functions for working with text. Use them to search and replace data, as well as to perform other text-based tasks in your spreadsheet.

So, what kind of functions do you think you might be interested in? Can I suggest something from the Math & Trigonometry category, or perhaps something a little more Statistical? Our Financial functions are extremely popular, and we're having a special today on Date & Time functions.

To help the discerning function connoisseur, Table 9.1 is a handy list of functions you simply wouldn't want to live without.

Table 9.1   Popular Excel Functions

Function	Category	Description	Syntax
PMT	Financial	Finds the periodic payment for a fixed loan or annuity	`=PMT(interest_rate,number of_periods,present_value, future_value,type)`
DB	Financial	Returns the depreciation of an asset based on a declining balance	`=DB(cost,salvage,life, period,month)`
FV	Financial	Finds the future value of an investment based on periodic payments and a fixed rate	`=FV(rate,number_of_periods, payment,present_value,type)`

Function	Category	Description	Syntax
RATE	Financial	Returns an interest rate	`=RATE(number_of_periods, payment,present_value, future_value,type,guess)`
EFFECT	Financial	Returns the effective annual interest rate	`=EFFECT(nominal_rate,number_ of_payments_per_year)`
TODAY	Date	Returns the current date	`=TODAY()`
NETWORKDAYS	Date & Time	Returns the number of whole workdays between two specified dates	`=NETWORKDAYS(start_date,end_ date,holidays)`
DAYS360	Date & Time	Returns the number of days between two dates using a 360-day calendar	`=DAYS360()`
DCOUNT	Database	Counts the cells within a database field that match the criteria	`=DCOUNT(database,field, criteria)`
DGET	Database	Returns the record from a database that matches the criteria	`=DGET(database,field, criteria)`
DSUM	Database	Finds the sum of a field's values that match the criteria	`=DSUM(database,field, criteria)`
CELL	Information	Returns information on the formatting, location, or contents of a cell	`=CELL(info_type,reference)`
IF	Logical	Returns one of two results you specify based on whether the value is TRUE or FALSE	`=IF(logical_text,value_if_ true,value_if_false)`
AND	Logical	Returns TRUE if all the arguments are true, FALSE if any are false	`=AND(logical1,logical2,...)`
OR	Logical	Returns TRUE if any argument is true, or FALSE if all arguments are false	`=OR(logical1,logical2...)`

continues

Table 9.1   Popular Excel Functions CONTINUED

Function	Category	Description	Syntax
VLOOKUP	Lookup & Reference	Returns a value found in a cell by using a column-based lookup in a table	=VLOOKUP(lookup_value,table_arrow,col_index_numb, range_lookup)
HLOOKUP	Lookup & Reference	Returns a value found in a cell by using a row-based lookup in a table	=HLOOKUP(lookup_value,table_array,row_index_num, range_lookup)
REPLACE	Text	Replaces characters in text entries	=REPLACE(old_text,start_num, num_chars,new_text)
TRIM	Text	Removes space from text entries, except for single spaces between words	=TRIM(text)
INT	Math & Trig	Returns a number rounded down to the nearest integer	=INT(number)
ABS	Math & Trig	Returns an absolute (positive) value of a number	=ABS(number)
PI	Math & Trig	Finds the value of pi	=PI()
SUM	Math & Trig	Adds up values	=SUM(number1, number2,...)
ROUND	Math & Trig	Rounds a number specified by the number of digits	=ROUND(number,num_digits)
ROUNDDOWN	Math & Trig	Rounds a number down	=ROUNDDOWN(number,num_digits)
SQRT	Math & Trig	Returns the positive square root	=SQRT(number)
AVERAGE	Statistical	Returns the average of a series of arguments	=AVERAGE(number1,number2,...)
PERCENTILE	Statistical	Returns the *K*th percentile of an array of values	=PERCENTILE(array,k)
MEDIAN	Statistical	Returns the middle (median) value in a series of arguments	=MEDIAN(number1,number2,...)
MAX	Statistical	Returns the largest value in a series of arguments	=MAX(number1,number2,...)

Function	Category	Description	Syntax
MIN	Statistical	Returns the smallest value in a series	=MIN(number1,number2,...)
COUNT	Statistical	Returns a count of text or numbers in a range	=COUNT(value1,value2,...)

More Functions

For a complete listing of Excel's functions, let the Office Assistant help you out. Click the **Help** button in the Paste Function dialog box.

The Least You Need to Know

➤ Functions are formulas that are included in Excel. You can use more than 300 functions.

➤ Functions are grouped into categories, which you'll find listed in the Paste Function dialog box.

➤ When writing functions, start with an equal sign, followed by the function name, and then the arguments enclosed in parentheses.

➤ You can quickly enter functions by using the Formula palette.

Chapter 10

Fixing Formula Problems

In This Chapter

➤ Tips for how to deal calmly with a worksheet error

➤ Learn how to trace your errors with the auditing tools

➤ Find out what the most common formula errors are and how to fix them

Rest assured that Excel never makes a mistake—but that doesn't mean you won't. When you encounter an error in building formulas, it's a human one, never a computer one. However, knowing whose fault it is doesn't take away any of the frustration you experience when your formula won't work and you feel like throwing your keyboard against the wall or at least strangling your mouse.

Before you damage any equipment, an act you may later regret, peruse this chapter. I offer you some practical solutions to your formula problems. What's more, Excel has a few formula fixes up its proverbial sleeve, as well.

What's Wrong?

When something's wrong with your formula, Excel displays an error message, usually in the cell containing the formula results. The following figure shows an example of an error message. Unfortunately, the error message doesn't always make it clear what might be causing trouble in the formula or identify what you need to do to fix it.

When you do experience problems, you should first look at a few things before you begin yelling at your computer. Of course, the best advice I can give you is to tell you to look over your worksheet for obvious errors first. However, much of the time, the error isn't quite so obvious.

Here's an example of an error message in a cell. You see I tried to divide by zero (a no-no in mathematics).

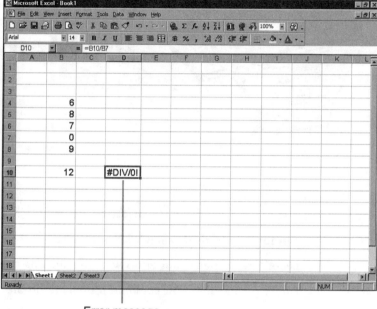

Error message

Here's a check list of items to go over when you see those (usually) cryptic error messages in your own worksheets:

➤ Check your cell references. If you used cell references in your formula, make sure they're correct. It's a bit embarrassing to find out you clicked cell B7 when you really meant to select B8.

➤ If you're referencing other worksheet cells or other workbooks, be sure to check those references for accuracy as well. Did you reference the correct worksheet or workbook name as well as the correct cell? Also, remember that range names with spaces must be enclosed in quotation marks.

➤ Check the data in the cell references you used; Excel can't calculate an answer if you try to divide by zero or use a nonnumeric value in mathematic formulas.

➤ Is your punctuation correct? Maybe you typed a semicolon instead of a colon or a comma.

➤ Have you got your parentheses in order? Make sure you've got a beginning and an ending parenthesis for each use and that they surround the formula arguments properly. When dealing with nesting arguments (using parentheses inside parentheses), you can easily let one single parenthesis drop out of sight without realizing it.

152

➤ Don't forget the rule of operator precedence. Make sure your cell references and parentheses follow the order of precedence you learned about in Chapter 8, "Concocting Formulas."

➤ Have you used the right data with the right function? Remember, some functions require a certain type of data in order to perform a calculation. For example, if you use text data and the function is expecting numeric data, you'll get an error.

➤ Check for missing arguments in the formula.

➤ Try removing any formatting from the cell references used in the formula. Some functions don't like to work with data that's formatted with different number formats (percent signs, for example).

Okay, those are some practical things you can do yourself. Now let me show you how Excel can help you trace your errors using the auditing tools.

Try an Audit

The larger the worksheet, the harder it is to figure out what's wrong when you've got a formula error. Also, what happens when you're checking over someone else's worksheet and can't readily see the problem because you don't know what the other person did to create the formula? Excel's auditing tools can help you out.

Lest you fear, the auditing tools have nothing to do with the IRS (but you should still save every receipt, just in case). You can use Excel's auditing tools to trace the path of your formula components and check each cell reference that contributes to the formula.

Basically, you use the tools to trace the relationships between cells. You can display tracer lines in your worksheet to find *precedents* (cells referred to in a formula), *dependents* (cells with formulas that refer to other cells), and errors.

Strange terminology, huh? Let me try to clarify things for you. Think of your worksheet as a family tree of data. When you perform an audit on a formula, you're tracing the formula's genealogy, the cells that feed into the formula. Like a real family tree, *dependents* are cells that descend from other cells in the worksheet, and *precedents* are the new family tree members, thrown into the mix, that aren't related to any other cells in the worksheet (new blood, so to speak). For example, you might reference a cell you used to display formula results based on a range of other cells. The cell containing the results is a dependent cell because its value is based on a calculation performed on other cells in the worksheet.

Precedent cells are those that contribute to a formula's result, and dependent cells rely on the results or contents of other cells. Clear as mud, right? Don't worry, the auditing tools will clear it all up.

Using the Auditing Toolbar

Before you start a trace, let me introduce you to the Auditing toolbar. Open the **Tools** menu and select **Auditing,** then select **Show Auditing Toolbar**. This opens the toolbar displayed in the following figure. The Auditing toolbar is a *floating toolbar,* which means you can drag it around the screen to move it out of your way or position it where you like.

The Auditing toolbar has buttons to help you trace formula errors.

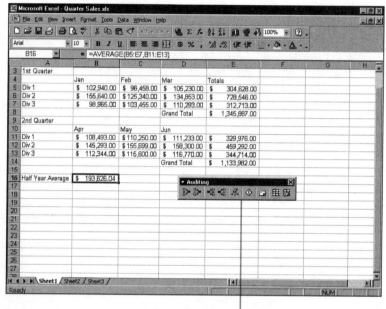

Auditing toolbar

Table 10.1 explains what each button on the Auditing toolbar does.

Table 10.1   The Auditing Toolbar Buttons

Button	Description
	Trace Precedents Shows the source of a cell's results by displaying tracing lines on the worksheet
	Remove Precedent Arrows Removes arrows created by the Trace Precedents command
	Trace Dependents Shows the source of a cell's results that are based on other cells by displaying tracing lines on the worksheet
	Remove Dependent Arrows Removes the tracing lines showing dependent cells
	Remove All Arrows Removes all dependent and precedent trace arrows

Button	Description
	Trace Error Locates the cells that contribute to a formula's error
	New Comment Lets you insert a comment into a cell so you can jot down a note
	Circle Invalid Data Draws a circle around invalid cell data defined using Excel's Validation feature
	Clear Validation Circles Removes circles drawn around invalid cell data

The Auditing Tools at Work

Ready to try an audit on your own worksheet? To trace your cell's precedents, follow these steps:

1. Select the cell containing the results or content you want to trace.

2. Click the **Trace Precedents** button on the Auditing toolbar.

3. The Excel worksheet displays a trace line tracing the path of the cells related to the selected cell, as shown in the following figure.

Close It

To close the Auditing toolbar, click the toolbar's close button located in the upper-right corner of the bar.

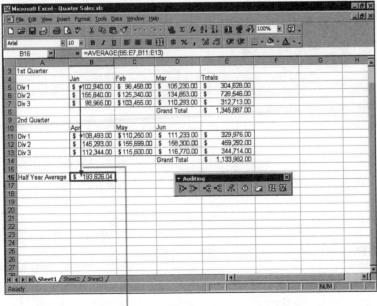

After clicking the Trace Precedents button, the trace line shows a clear relationship of the precedents.

Trace line

If the preceding figure were in color, you would see a blue line linking the related cells. The ranges are surrounded in a blue outline, as well. In this particular worksheet example, I suspected my average formula in cell B16 might have produced a wrong result; the number seemed too high. When I traced the precedents, Excel pointed out which ranges I used to get the formula results. As it turns out, I accidentally included the numbers in the Totals column as part of the range, which threw off my average. Thank goodness for the auditing tools; they pointed out the error of my ways...and means.

To trace your cell's dependents, select the cell containing the results or content you want to trace, then click the **Trace Dependents** button on the Auditing toolbar. Excel displays a trace line tracing the path of the cells related to the selected cell, as shown in the following figure.

In this example, I'm tracing several cells back to the cell where they're used in a formula.

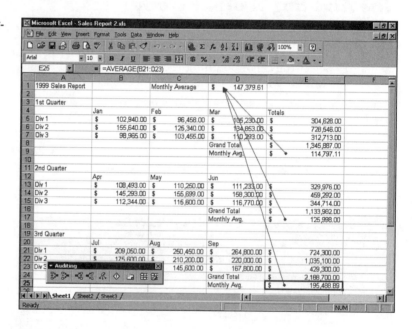

Take a look at the preceding figure. I wanted to find out where each cell containing an average formula result was linked, so I traced the dependents. I clicked cell E25 and performed a dependent trace to see if it linked to the results in cell D1. Notice that I did the same for cells E17 and E9; therefore, three different trace lines appear on my worksheet.

You can perform as many traces as you like. Just remember, the more you do, the more confusing your worksheet might appear. To remove a trace, select the cell and click the appropriate Auditing toolbar button; to remove them all, click the **Remove All Arrows** button.

If you've got a really big worksheet, it's not easy to see where the trace arrows go. If you double-click the arrow line, you'll immediately be taken to the cell at the other end of the arrow. Double-click again to return to the arrow's source.

Adding Comments

As you're straightening out your related worksheet cells, it might be helpful to add a comment from time to time. Comments are just notes you add to the cell that aren't visible unless you hover your mouse pointer over the cell. To add a comment to a selected cell, click the **New Comment** button on the Auditing toolbar. This inserts a comment box with your name on it. Enter your note text and press **Esc** to close the comment. To see the comment, hover your pointer over the cell.

Another way to attach comments is to open the **Insert** menu and select **Comment**.

Tracing an Error Message

When a cell displays an error message, you can trace the error. Select the cell and click the **Trace Error** button. In the following figure, I used the **Trace Error** button to help me realize I used the wrong range name in my formula. I meant to indicate Qtr_2 and instead I used Qtr_3, which isn't a valid range name in my worksheet.

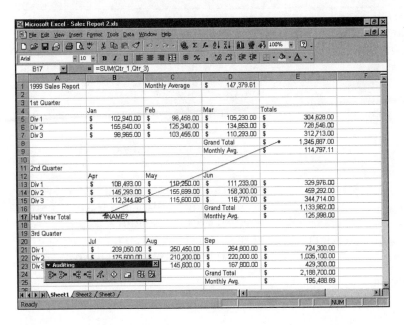

In this figure, I'm tracing an error message to find out what's wrong.

157

What About the Other Auditing Button?

The Auditing toolbar's Circle Invalid Data button lets you assign restrictions on the values in worksheet cells, but its use is beyond what most Excel users do with the auditing tools. To learn more about this button, be sure to check out the Help tools.

Common Error Messages and How to Get Rid of Them

What if I show you some of the most common Excel worksheet errors you can expect to encounter? Table 10.2 lists these errors and possible actions you can take. When you run into an error, you can just flip back to this chapter to find out what to do.

Table 10.2   Common Errors and Corrective Actions

Error	What It Means	What to Do
#NULL	Wrong range operator or cell reference.	You probably forgot to insert a comma to separate cell ranges that don't intersect.
#REF!	Invalid cell reference.	This happens if you overwrite or delete the range to which the formula was referring. Recheck your ranges referenced by the function.
#DIV/0!	You tried to divide by zero.	Make sure your cell references don't contain zeros or blanks.
#VALUE!	Incorrect data type.	The function you used expected a certain data type, and your cell references didn't contain the right type (the cell contains text instead of numbers, for instance). Recheck your cell data and the data type required by the function.
#N/A	The required value can't be found.	This is typical of lookup functions: The data can't be found, so you'll have to enter it.

Error	What It Means	What to Do
#NUM!	Either the argument needs a numeric value or a number exceeds Excel's maximum.	Excel supports numbers up to $1*10^{307}$ (and the same in negative numbers).
#NAME?	The range you referenced doesn't exist.	Recheck your range names, or the syntax (punctuation, spaces, parentheses) may be incorrect.

Call for Help!

Don't forget about Excel's Help features, which can always assist you when you're trying to figure out formula errors. To learn more about Excel Help, check out Chapter 5, "Help Me, Please!"

The Least You Need to Know

➤ Always stop and check over your worksheet data before panicking.

➤ Check and see if you used the correct cell references in the formula.

➤ Use Excel's auditing tools to visually trace the relationships between cells.

➤ When you see an error message in your worksheet, recheck your formula arguments, including the syntax, and data types.

Part 3

Worksheet Grooming

My mom always said, "Good grooming is important." This applies to your worksheets, too. Oh sure, you can slap on some data using all the default settings and call it a spreadsheet, but is that any way to present your work? No way. If you plan on handing over your data to anyone else to look at, whether it's a lowly colleague or your company's president, then you need to know how to tap into Excel's formatting options.

With Excel's formatting tools, you can change how your data appears, including fonts, styles and sizes, and how the worksheet is structured. In this section of the book, you learn how to add and delete rows and columns, move data around, insert graphics, and make your cells stand out with snazzy backgrounds and borders. You find out how to draw your own shapes, apply patterns, and fiddle with alignment controls. You also learn how to preview and print your data. If your worksheet needs a makeover, this is the place to be.

Formatting for Fun or Profit

Formatting. What is it? Why do it? And does it involve a lot of effort? Formatting is simply applying commands to your worksheet data and structure to change the way it all appears. It's a competitive world out there, and you need to make your worksheets stand out from all the rest. You know what they say—whoever *they* are— *presentation is everything.* Plus, you'll be happy to know, formatting doesn't take much effort (unless you think clicking a couple of buttons is a major workout).

Performing a Data Makeover

Does your data look dull and lifeless? Does your worksheet lack the bounce and body that other worksheets have? Then you need a data makeover. With Excel's fast and affordable formatting commands, your data can look its best. After all, if your data looks good, you look good.

I know it sounds like I'm trying to sell you something, and I am. I'm trying to sell you on the importance of formatting your worksheets. Don't settle for the default formatting that's applied every time you open a new workbook. Instead, give your data some dazzle.

Let's start with a makeover of your characters. These tips are good for number characters as well as text characters.

Ye Olde Bold, Italic, and Underline Commands

One Underline Style

The Underline button applies only one line style (a single line) to your data. To apply a different line style, you must open the Format Cells dialog box and use the **Underline** drop-down list on the **Font** tab.

One of the most popular methods of changing the way your characters look is to apply bold, italic, or underline formatting. Because these three character attributes are so popular, you'll see them available as buttons on just about every Formatting toolbar in every Microsoft program, and Excel is no exception.

B *I* **U** The following figure shows an example of each of these formatting attributes applied to worksheet data. To apply any of these formatting styles, select the cell or data you want to format and then click the appropriate toolbar button; click **Bold**, **Italic**, **Underline**, or any combination of the three. These buttons toggle the attribute on or off, so to remove the style, select the cell or data and click the appropriate button again.

A quick way to change the appearance of your data is to apply bold, italic, or underline formatting.

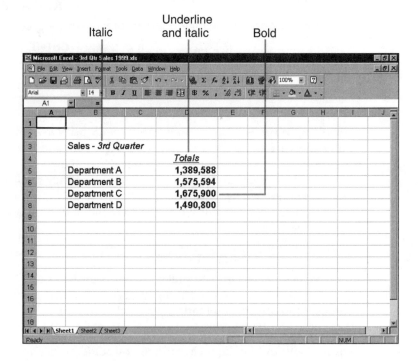

Oops!

If you make a mistake and decide you don't like the formatting you just applied, click the **Undo** button on the Standard toolbar immediately after applying the formatting. If you don't want to move your mouse, the keyboard shortcut is **Ctrl+Z**.

Changing the Font and Size

If you've ever worked with a word-processing program, such as Microsoft Word, then you already know how font and sizes can change the appearance of your data, whether it's text or numbers. By default, Excel automatically assigns 10-point Arial every time you start a new workbook, but you can easily change the font and size as needed. After using Excel for any amount of time, you start to notice how incredibly small 10-point type is; it's hard to read, particularly when it's surrounded by intersecting columns and rows.

You can change the font and size whenever you like. Select the cell or cells, or select the data within a cell (such as a single word you want to stand out or a single character within a word); then use the commands on the Formatting toolbar to select a new font and size.

To change the font, click the **Font** drop-down arrow on the Formatting toolbar and select another font from the list, as shown in the following figure.

Keyboard Shortcuts to Try

To quickly make data bold, press **Ctrl+B**. To italicize, press **Ctrl+I**, and to underline, press **Ctrl+U**.

Font

A set of characters that have the same typeface and size, such as Times New Roman or Arial.

Use the Font drop-down
list to change your font.

Click here.

To change the font size, click the Font Size drop-down arrow and choose another size, as shown in the following figure.

Use the Font Size drop-
down list to change your
font size.

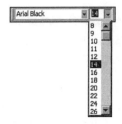

Font Size

The size measurement of a font. Font size is actually measured in points; 72 points equal one inch.

Using the Format Cells Dialog Box

If you're looking for one-stop shopping for all your formatting needs, then look no further than the Format Cells dialog box (see the next figure). You can access the dialog box through the Format menu (open the Format menu and select Cells), or you can right-click the worksheet and choose Format Cells. One of the best things about this dialog box—besides the fact that you find all the formatting commands you could possibly want here—is that you can also preview how your selections will look before actually applying the formatting to your data.

Click the Font tab to check out formatting options for controlling your data's fonts and sizes. The other tabs have plenty of formatting options, too, and you learn all about them later in this chapter, as well as in the rest of Part 3.

To apply formatting from the Format Cells dialog box, use these steps:

1. Select the data or cells you want to format.

2. Open the Format menu and select Cells (or right-click the selected cells and choose Format Cells from the shortcut menu).

166

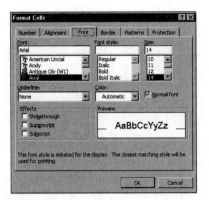

Use the Format Cells dialog box to access a cornucopia of formatting options.

3. Click the **Font** tab.

   ➤ Use the **Font** list to choose a new font.

   ➤ Use the **Font Style** list to apply bold or italic formatting.

   ➤ Use the **Size** list to select a font size.

   ➤ Need an underline? Click the **Underline** drop-down arrow and choose from the available styles.

   ➤ Want to change the font color? Click the **Color** drop-down arrow and select a color from the palette.

   ➤ Use the **Effects** options to assign formatting such as Strikethrough, Superscript, or Subscript. Click the appropriate check box to select the option.

   ➤ Look in the **Preview** area to see how your formatting changes will affect the data.

4. To apply the new settings to the worksheet data, click **OK**.

Got Color?

You can easily add color to the data you enter in Excel. Whether you're viewing a spreadsheet onscreen or looking at the output from a color printer, you can really add some pizzazz to your work with color formatting. Use the **Font Color** drop-down button on the Formatting toolbar to change colors, or you can use the **Color** drop-down list on the **Font** tab of the Format Cells dialog box.

Copying Formatting

Let's say you've spent some time formatting a range of data and it now looks just the way you want it. But then you find you have to add another range of data. Does this mean you have to spend precious time formatting it the same way? No, grab the Format Painter tool from the Standard toolbar and copy the formatting from one worksheet range to another.

Start by selecting the first range that has all the formatting you want to copy; then click the **Format Painter** button on the Standard toolbar. Now drag the Format Painter across the new range you want to format and release the mouse button. The formatting is copied to the new selection. You can keep copying as many times as you need to; double-click the button and the feature remains turned on. When you're finished, click the button again to turn it off.

How to Make Your Numbers Attractive

Numeric values are usually more than just numbers. They represent dollar values, dates, percentages, and other real values. So instead of just showing plain old digits on your worksheet, why not indicate what particular value they stand for? If you're working with dollars, let's see some dollar signs! If you're calculating percentages, let's see some percent signs! Number formatting can help you present your data in the way you intend your audience to view it.

Numbers have their own formatting controls, and you'll find them on the **Number** tab in the Format Cells dialog box (see the following figure). There are 12 different number categories, or styles, from which to choose. General is the default style, which merely formats your numbers plainly.

Depending on which category you select, the area on the right side of the Number tab will vary. For example, if you select **Currency** format (which formats your numbers with dollar signs and decimal points and is shown in the next figure), you see an option for specifying the number of decimal points, an option for selecting which currency symbol is used, and options for dealing with negative numbers. At the top of the Number tab, you see a **Sample** area that gives you a preview of what the formatting will look like when applied to your worksheet numbers. Table 11.1 explains each of the number format styles.

Use the Number tab in the Format Cells dialog box to change the numeric format.

Table 11.1   Number Format Styles

Style	Description
General	Default; no specific formatting applied
Number	General number display with two default decimal points
Currency	Use to display monetary values
Accounting	Lines up currency symbols and decimal points in a column
Date	Use to select the format of the date display
Time	Use to select the format of the time display
Percentage	Multiplies cell value by 100 and displays percent sign
Fraction	Displays value as a specified fraction
Scientific	Uses scientific or exponential notation
Text	Treats values as text
Special	Works with list and database values
Custom	Enables you to create your own custom format

Use these steps to format your numbers with the Format Cells dialog box:

1. Select the number data or cells you want to format (see the following figure).
2. Open the **Format** menu and select **Cells** (or right-click the cells and choose **Format Cells** from the shortcut menu).
3. Click the **Number** tab.
4. In the **Category** list, select the number style you want to use.
5. Excel displays the styles and options for the category you selected. If you select a format that requires you to specify additional options, such as decimal points, make your selections.
6. Preview the selected number style and options in the **Sample** area.

Here's what my work-sheet data looks like before I apply a number format.

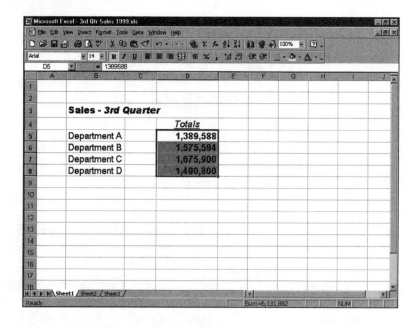

7. To apply the style to the worksheet data, click **OK**. The format is applied to the selected cell or range, as shown in the following figure.

In this example, I applied Currency style to my numbers.

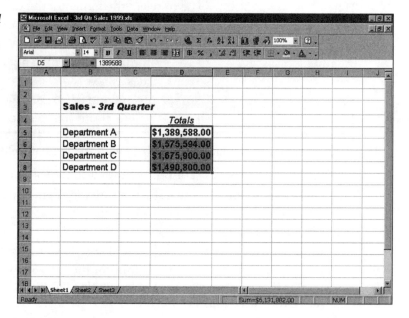

170

Using Euro Currency

To use currency symbols from other countries in your worksheet, including Euro currency, click the **Symbol** drop-down arrow in the **Number** tab and scroll through the available symbols. You'll find currency symbols for countries around the world. Select the one you want, and the **Preview** area displays a sample.

Changing Number Formats with the Toolbar Buttons

The three most common number styles people apply to worksheet data are dollar signs, commas, and percent signs. All three of these styles are available as toolbar buttons on the Formatting toolbar. Select the data to which you want to apply a style and do one of the following:

Keyboard Shortcuts

To quickly set the currency style, press **Shift+Ctrl+$**. To assign the percent style, press **Shift+Ctrl+%**. To assign the comma style, press **Shift+Ctrl+!**.

 ➤ To add dollar signs to your number data, click the **Currency Style** button.

 ➤ To add percent signs to your number data, click the **Percent Style** button.

 ➤ To use commas with your number data, click the **Comma Style** button.

Formatting with the Styles Dialog Box

To really speed up number formatting, try using Excel's Style dialog box. It contains a list of predefined number formats you can choose from, as explained in Table 11.2. Unlike the formats found in the Format Cells dialog box, with the Style dialog box, you can turn specific options on or off, essentially tailoring the style to suit your needs.

Table 11.2 Styles in the Style Dialog Box

Style	Description	Example
Comma	Adds commas to numbers with four or more digits and adds two decimal points	5000.00 becomes 5,000.00
Comma (0)	Same as Comma style but rounds decimals up	5000.75 becomes 5,001
Currency	Adds dollar signs to plain numbers, and inserts commas and two decimal points	5000 becomes $5,000.00
Currency (0)	Same as Currency style but rounds decimals up	5000.75 becomes $5,001
Hyperlink	Formats text to Arial, 10-point type, blue, and underlined	5000 becomes <u>5000</u>
Followed Hyperlink	Same as Hyperlink but formats text to another color	5000 becomes <u>5000</u>
Normal	Applies default formatting	5000 appears as 5000
Percent	Multiplies decimal number by 100 and adds a percent sign	.50 becomes 50%

To assign a style using the Style dialog box, follow these steps:

1. Select the cell or range you want to format.

2. Open the **Format** menu and select **Style**. This opens the Style dialog box, as shown in the following figure.

Use the Style dialog box to assign preset styles.

3. From the **Style Name** drop-down list, select the style you want to use.

4. Turn off any options you don't want included with the style or turn on any options that you do want to use. Mark the check boxes to turn options on or off.

5. Click **OK** to exit the dialog box and apply the style.

Do You Need an Alignment?

By default, Excel automatically aligns data in the worksheet cells based on data type. Text data is always aligned on the left. Number data is always aligned on the right. In addition, both text and numbers are initially aligned vertically and sit at the bottom of the cell. However, you can change all that. You can control your own alignment. Want to know how?

The easiest way to make any simple alignment changes is to use the alignment buttons on the Formatting toolbar. Select the data you want to align and then apply one of the following:

➤ To align the data entry (or entries) to the left, click the **Align Left** button.

➤ To align data to the right, click the **Align Right** button.

➤ To center data in the cell or cells, click the **Center** button.

You can also use the Format Cells dialog box to designate alignment. It has a tab dedicated to alignment options, as shown in the following figure. Take a look at this list to help you decipher your choices:

➤ **Horizontal options** Enable you to specify a left/right alignment in the cell(s). With the **Center Across Selection** option, you can center a title or other text across a range of cells.

➤ **Vertical options** Enable you to specify how you want the data aligned in relation to the top and bottom of the cell(s).

➤ **Orientation options** Let you flip the text sideways or print it from top to bottom (as opposed to from left to right).

➤ **Text Control check boxes** Enable you to wrap long lines of text within a cell (normally, Excel displays all text in a cell on one line), shrink text to fit inside a cell, and merge cells.

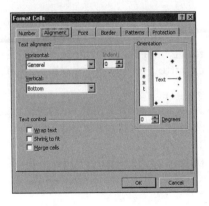

The Alignment tab has numerous alignment choices for controlling how data is positioned in your cells.

173

What About AutoFit?

The Shrink to Fit option on the Alignment tab is not the same as Excel's AutoFit. AutoFit simply widens or narrows the column to fit your data. The Shrink to Fit option reduces the size of your data.

Repeat Alignment Formatting

After aligning one range, you can repeat the same alignment formatting in another range. Select the new range and open the **Edit** menu and choose **Repeat Format Cells**.

To change alignment using the Format Cells dialog box, use these steps:

1. Select the cell or range you want to change; then open the **Format** menu and select **Cells**.

2. Click the **Alignment** tab (see the previous figure).

   ➤ To change the horizontal alignment, use the **Horizontal** drop-down list. Choices include **General** (default), **Left**, **Center**, **Right**, **Fill**, **Justify**, and **Center Across Selection**.

   ➤ To change vertical alignment, select an option from the **Vertical** drop-down list. Choices include **Top**, **Center**, **Bottom**, and **Justify**.

   ➤ To wrap text onto other lines inside the cell, select the **Wrap Text** check box. Use this option if you have a lengthy text entry and want the cell to contain multiple text lines.

   ➤ If you're having trouble fitting text in a cell, you may want to use the **Shrink to Fit** option. It automatically shrinks the size of the text to fit in the cell.

   ➤ Use the **Merge Cells** option to combine two or more cells into one.

3. Click **OK** to exit the dialog box and implement your alignment changes.

Centering a Title

One of the most common alignment tasks you'll want to perform in a worksheet is centering a title or heading across a range of cells. For that reason, the creators of Excel have placed a Merge and Center button on the Formatting toolbar. Use these steps to center a title or heading:

1. Select the cell that contains the heading or title text and the range you want to center across (see the following figure). If you just select the cell with the entry, this feature won't work properly.

2. Click the **Merge and Center** button on the Formatting toolbar.

174

Selected heading   Selected range

To center a heading in your worksheet, first select the range you want to center across.

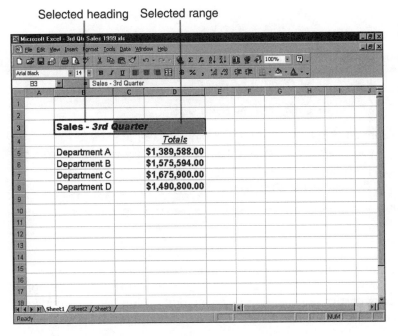

3. Excel centers the text across the selected range, as shown in the following figure. Now doesn't that look much better?

The heading is now centered across a range of cells.

With a click of the Merge and Center button, Excel centers the heading across the range.

175

Same Cell, Different Look

Even though a centered title looks as if it's in a different cell, it's still in the same cell in which you originally entered it. Sometimes it's easy to forget which cell holds the original title text. If you try to edit the cell and it looks blank, try selecting the first cell in the row.

Rotating Text

For most worksheets, the default horizontal text orientation is the norm. However, to help clarify drawings, tables, or charts you insert into your worksheets, you can apply vertical orientation to worksheet entries. Excel's orientation option lets you rotate text or numbers to create effects, such as those shown in the following figure.

Use rotated text to help label drawings and charts in your Excel worksheets.

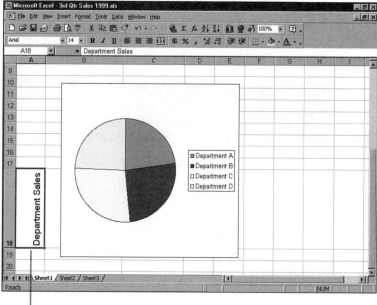

Rotated text

176

To apply rotation effects, use these steps:

1. Select the cell or range you want to change; then open the **Format** menu and select **Cells**.

2. Click the **Alignment** tab.

3. Under the **Orientation** options, drag or click the pointer in the **Orientation** gauge up or down to specify a rotation in degrees (see the following figure). Alternatively, you can type in a degree of rotation in the **Degrees** box or use the spin arrows to set a rotation.

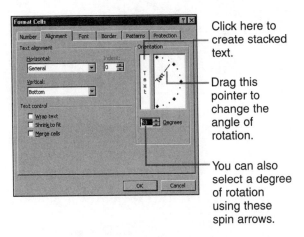

Click here to create stacked text.

Drag this pointer to change the angle of rotation.

You can also select a degree of rotation using these spin arrows.

Drag or click the pointer in the Orientation gauge to change the rotation setting.

4. To set a stacked orientation, where numbers or letters are stacked to be read from top to bottom, click the box to the left of the gauge.

5. Click **OK** to exit the dialog box and apply the rotation settings.

AutoFormat: Easy Formatting for the Formatting Impaired

If you're not too confident about your own formatting tastes and prefer a more tried-and-true approach, let Excel's AutoFormat tool do all the work for you. AutoFormat has 16 different autoformats (predefined sets of formatting styles) you can choose from and apply to your Excel worksheet cells. The following figure shows just two AutoFormat styles applied. Rather than worry over what formatting choices you should apply to your worksheet, use any of the professional-looking preformatted styles.

To use AutoFormat, follow these steps:

1. Select the data you want to format.

177

Here you can see how two different AutoFormat styles compare.

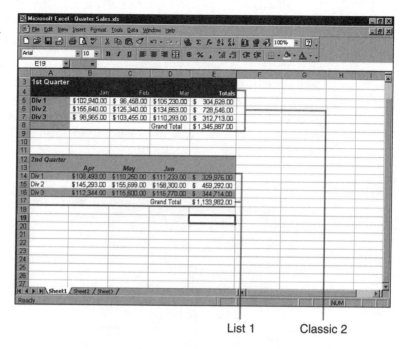

List 1   Classic 2

2. Open the **Format** menu and select **AutoFormat**. The AutoFormat dialog box appears, as shown in the following figure.

The AutoFormat dialog box has a lot of formats you can use, and many of them are quite stunning.

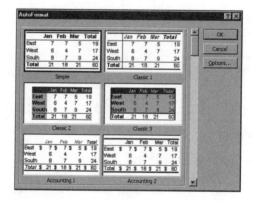

3. Look through the list to find a style you want to try. Use the scroll arrows to move up and down the list until you find something you like.

4. Select a style and click **OK** to exit the dialog box and apply the formatting.

If you don't like the format you've chosen, click the **Undo** button on the Standard toolbar or open the **Edit** menu and select **Undo** immediately. If you make any edits to the data in a formatted table, the new data will reflect the formatting you've chosen.

178

If you like certain parts of a preset AutoFormat, but not others, you can choose to apply the formatting only to certain portions of your data. Click the **Options** button in the AutoFormat dialog box to display a group of options (see the following figure). For example, if you want to apply only the font or pattern of a particular format, you can mark the check boxes for those particular options and deselect the rest. When you click **OK**, only the formatting options you selected are applied.

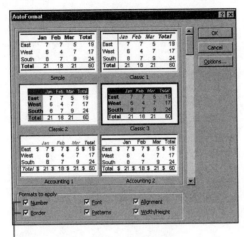

Choose only the formats you want.

When you want to apply only certain parts of an AutoFormat style, click the Options button and choose the options you want to apply.

The Least You Need to Know

➤ Excel data uses the same kind of formatting controls found in word processing programs, such as Word, for changing fonts and sizes.

➤ You can find quick formatting options on the Formatting toolbar.

➤ For one-stop format shopping, use the Format Cells dialog box (open the **Format** menu and choose **Cells**).

➤ Numbers have different meanings, so help your audience know what your numbers represent with Excel's number styles.

➤ Alignment options are available for every kind of data type you can imagine; check them out on the **Alignment** tab of the Format Cells dialog box.

➤ If formatting isn't your bag, use Excel's AutoFormats, which are preset formatting styles you can apply to spruce up worksheet data.

PUT ALL THOSE RECORDS IN BACK AND LEAVE THOSE HERE.

Chapter 12

Rearranging Your Worksheet Data

In This Chapter

➤ Learn how to resize columns and rows with one arm tied behind your back

➤ Find out how to insert and delete columns and rows at a moment's notice

➤ Discover top-secret ways to hide your data

➤ Learn how to move your data around on the worksheet and copy it to other places

➤ Find out how to locate data after you've moved or copied it

Before the advent of computers, the very act of making changes to a spreadsheet, document, or any other paper-based item was time-consuming, messy, and incredibly inconvenient. You had to get out your eraser to make simple changes, which most people could live with, but when it came to radical changes, such as deciding that the data on page 10 needed to be moved to page 2, well, you can imagine the frustration of having to write everything all over again.

With computers and programs like Excel, you can make all kinds of changes to the worksheet structure before ever committing the work to paper. What a relief, eh? In this chapter, you learn how to rearrange data, columns, and rows to make your worksheet look just right.

Changing the Worksheet Structure

The vast, sprawling worksheet grid you see before you in the Excel program window is not a permanent structure. In fact, it's far from permanent. The columns and rows are exceedingly flexible; you can easily remove or add columns and rows as needed, and you can resize them to suit your needs. In this first section, we explore all the techniques for adjusting the worksheet structure.

Making It All Fit Fast

Okay, you've just completed a wonderful, nicely formatted worksheet, and suddenly you notice that your data isn't fitting into the cells as you thought it would. What do you do? I'll make it easy for you; here's a list of multiple-choice answers:

a. Panic and reformat all the data into smaller point sizes.

b. Try using less data. Go through your worksheet and start cutting out data you think you might not need.

c. Adjust your column widths and row heights.

If you answered (c), you're on your way to true Excel success. If you're having trouble making your data fit completely into the default size columns and rows, you can just resize the columns and rows. No need to reformat your data to fit the worksheet structure; instead, make your worksheet structure fit your data. Think of your worksheet grid as being made of rubber; you can stretch it or squish it to your heart's content.

Automatic Resizing

When entering lengthy data into a cell, such as a really long number, you may have already noticed how Excel automatically resizes the entire column to fit the entry. However, if you want all your columns the same size, you can use the skills you learn in this chapter to resize them.

To resize your columns or rows really fast, just hover your mouse pointer over the appropriate row or column border and drag it to a new size. For example, perhaps your data isn't fitting completely in the default column width. Move your mouse pointer up to the top of the column (called the *header area*, where the column labels reside); then hover your mouse pointer over the left or right edge of the column. The pointer takes the shape of a double-sided arrow. Now hold down the left mouse button and start dragging the border. As you drag, the column gets wider or narrower, depending on which direction you're dragging. When the column is as wide or narrow as you want, release the mouse button. That's all there is to it. (I told you this was easy.)

Resizing Multiple Columns and Rows

Need to adjust the size of more than one column or row? Select as many columns or rows as you need (highlight them by dragging across them on the column or row header area); then resize one column or row border. The rest resize right along with it. To select nonadjacent columns or rows, hold down the **Ctrl** key while clicking the columns or rows.

As you drag the column to a new size, a ScreenTip appears, giving you the exact dimensions (see the following figure). This little tidbit is for those of you setting precise column widths so you can see where you're at, sizewise. A dotted line follows the pointer as you drag (as you can see in the figure), showing you the width of the entire column on the worksheet itself. Of course, wherever the dotted line is when you release the mouse button is where the resized column border will sit.

Measuring Up

The column width and row height are measured in points, just in case you were wondering. One inch equals 72 points.

You can resize your rows the same way you do columns: Move your mouse pointer over the row header area until it takes the shape of a double-sided arrow and then drag the border to a new depth. Again, the ScreenTip box appears, giving you exact dimensions.

Yet another way to fit your data is to use the **Format** menu. Click inside the cell you want to adjust, open the **Format** menu, select **Column, AutoFit Selection**. To do the same with a row, open the **Format** menu and choose **Row, AutoFit**.

183

Drag your columns and rows to new sizes by clicking and dragging the column or row header borders.

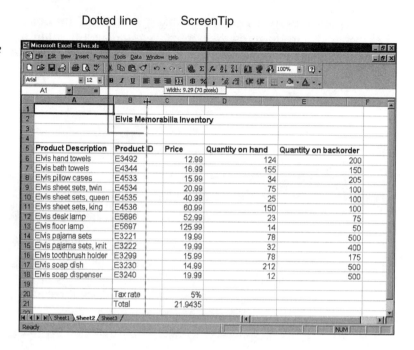

Dotted line   ScreenTip

Quick Fit

Data won't fit? No problem. Just double-click the column header edge (the border right next to the column header label). The column resizes itself to fit your widest entry.

Changing Column Width

If you'd rather specify an exact column width for a single column or multiple columns, use these steps:

1. Select the column or columns you want to change.

2. Open the **Format** menu and select **Column**, and then select **Width**. This opens the Column Width dialog box, as shown in the next figure.

3. Click inside the **Column Width** text box and enter a new width (in points).

4. Click **OK**. The measurement adjustment is then made to the column(s) you specified.

The Column Width box lets you type in an exact measurement.

184

Changing Row Height

To specify an exact measurement (in points) for a single row or multiple rows, use these steps:

1. Select the row(s) you want to change.

2. Open the **Format** menu, select **Row**, and then select **Height**. This opens the Row Height dialog box, as shown in the following figure.

3. Click inside the **Row Height** text box and enter a new depth (in points).

4. Click **OK**. The measurement adjustment is then made to the row(s) you specified.

Back to the Default

To return a column to its default size, open the **Format** menu, select **Column, Standard Width,** and click **OK**.

My, what a dainty little dialog box.

To let Excel automatically adjust the row height to fit the tallest cell's contents, use the AutoFit command (open the **Format** menu, choose **Row**, and then **AutoFit**).

Adding Columns and Rows

Here's another problem for you to solve. Let's say you've completed your worksheet only to find you left out a column of data. Now what are you going to do? The multiple-choice thing worked well last time; let's try it again:

a. Panic, open a new workbook, and start all over.

b. Pretend you didn't notice the problem and move on.

c. Add a new column in the middle of the existing data.

If you answered (c) again, you're getting pretty good at this Excel stuff. If you answered (a), you're a glutton for punishment. One of the easiest things to do with your worksheet structure is add or delete columns and rows.

When you add rows or columns, Excel moves the existing rows and columns over to make room for the new ones. To insert a row, follow these steps:

1. Select the row below where you want a new row inserted (see the following figure).

2. Open the **Insert** menu and select **Rows**.

185

I'm about to insert a new row above the one selected. Keep your eyes on row 6.

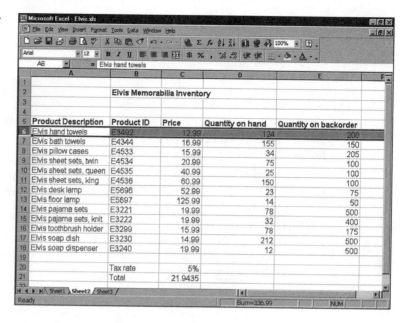

3. Excel inserts the new row and shifts the other rows down (including any data they might hold), as shown in the next figure.

Abracadabra! A new row is added, and all the rows beneath move down to make room.

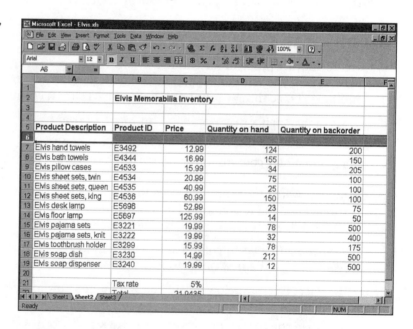

To insert a new column, follow these steps:

1. Select the column to the right of where you want a new column inserted.

2. Open the **Insert** menu and select **Columns**.

3. Excel inserts the column and shifts the other columns to the right (including any data they might hold).

Deleting Columns and Rows

The worksheet creator giveth, and the worksheet creator taketh away. It's just as easy to delete columns and rows as it is to add them. Follow these steps:

1. Select the column(s) or row(s) you want to delete.

2. Open the **Edit** menu and select **Delete**.

3. Excel deletes the column(s) or row(s) and shifts the remaining cells over to fill the gap.

I Only Want to Delete the Data!

No sweat. To leave the selected column or row intact but delete only the data found within, open the **Edit** menu and choose **Clear**. This leaves the column or row in place and clears the contents of the cells.

Hiding Columns and Rows

Do you plan on sharing your workbooks with other users? If you do, you might be interested in this handy little feature. You can hide confidential information from view by using a couple of different methods. You can even hide columns and rows before printing your workbook so that the confidential data doesn't appear on the printout. Sounds sneaky, right? Well, it's not exactly a top-secret security maneuver by any means, but it does keep your confidential data out of sight.

One way you can hide a column is to drag the right border of the column past the left border (see the next two figures). To quickly hide a row, drag the bottom row border up past the top border edge. To unhide the data, move the pointer so that it touches the column or row border; then drag the border to the right or down to display the column or row again.

I'm about to hide column E, so pay attention. Now you see it...

Click and drag to the left.

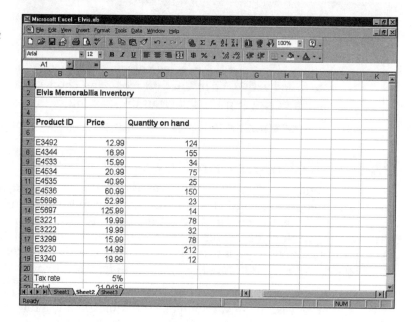

...now you don't. Column E is now hidden from view.

Another way to hide a column or row is to use the Hide command. Follow these steps:

1. Select the column(s) or row(s) you want to hide.

2. To hide a column, open the **Format** menu, choose **Column**, and then **Hide**. To hide a row, select **Format**, **Row**, **Hide**.

3. Excel hides the column or row you specified.

To unhide your data again, choose **Format**, **Column**, **Unhide** or **Format**, **Row**, **Unhide**.

Rearranging Data on the Worksheet

Just because you choose to enter data in certain cells doesn't mean it has to stay there forever. You can freely move your data around the worksheet as needed. For instance, you might want to move a range of cells from one sheet in your workbook to another, or maybe you want to copy a value from one cell to a completely different workbook. Perhaps you'd like to get rid of worksheet data you no longer need. Excel offers numerous ways to move, copy, and delete your data, as I'm about to explain in this section.

Move Your Data

What's the quickest way to move something from point A to point B? The Cut and Paste commands, of course. Yes, the good old Cut and Paste commands have been a staple of Windows programs since, well, since way back in Windows 1. (Were you around for Windows 1?)

When you cut data from your worksheet, you're sending it to the Windows Clipboard, a temporary storage area. It waits there until you paste it into a new location (or in the case of Windows 95, it waits until you cut something else to the Clipboard). To move your data with the Cut and Paste commands, follow these steps:

I Don't Want to Overwrite Existing Cells!

Use the **Insert,Cut Cells** command if you don't want to overwrite existing data in the cells you're pasting to. This command moves the existing cells aside to make room for the new data.

1. Select the data you want to move.

 2. Click the **Cut** button on the Standard toolbar, or open the **Edit** menu and select **Cut**, or right-click and select **Cut** (quite the smorgasbord of methods, eh?). Notice that the message at the bottom of the screen prompts you to select a destination.

3. Now click inside the cell where you want the data moved to (or open the sheet or

workbook where you want to move the data). If you're moving a range, click the upper-left corner where you want the cells pasted. Keep in mind that Excel will overwrite any cells in the destination area with the data you paste.

 4. Click the **Paste** button or open the **Edit** menu and select **Paste**.

This works great when moving data, but what about moving formulas? What happens when you move or copy a formula depends on the type of reference you used—Excel adjusts all relative references, but all absolute references stay the same.

The New Clipboard Toolbar

A new feature added to Excel 2000 is the Clipboard toolbar. It allows you to paste multiple items you cut or copy in your workbooks. For example, you might cut two or three different ranges, and then paste them back into your spreadsheet in a different order. The Clipboard toolbar lets you pick exactly which item to paste, and you can choose to cut or copy up to 12 items. The Clipboard toolbar appears as soon as you cut or copy two items. To paste an item, click in the cell where you want the data to go, and then from the Clipboard toolbar, choose the item you want to paste. If you're not too sure which item is which, hover your mouse pointer over an icon and a ScreenTip appears describing the cut or copied data. Click the icon representing the item you want to paste, and it is immediately pasted into your worksheet. To paste another Clipboard item, use the same steps. To close the Clipboard toolbar when you're finished pasting, click the **Close** button. Learn more about this feature in Chapter 23, "Integrating Excel with Other Office Applications."

Copying Data

To copy data from one cell or range to another, try these steps:

1. Select the cell or range you want to copy.

 2. Click the **Copy** button on the Standard toolbar, or open the **Edit** menu and select **Copy**, or right-click over the selected data and choose **Copy**, or stand on your head and spell **Copy**. (That last one won't work, by the way.)

3. The status bar prompts you to select a destination. Select the cell at the upper-left corner of where you want the cells pasted.

 4. Click the **Paste** button on the Standard toolbar or open the **Edit** menu and choose **Paste**.

Using the Drag-and-Drop Technique

Now let's try something a little different. If you're moving or copying data around a screen full of cells showing in the work area of the Excel window, use the drag-and-drop technique:

1. Select the cell or range you want to move.

2. Hover your mouse pointer over the selection's border until the pointer looks like an arrow, as shown in the next figure.

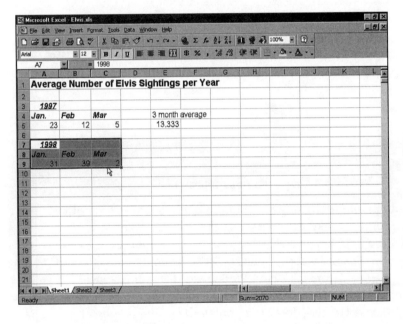

To start a drag-and-drop operation, select the cell or range and then start dragging the selected area's border.

3. Drag the selected data to a new location onscreen. As you drag, you see an outline of the data. When the data is in the spot you want, release the mouse button. The data is moved, as demonstrated in the following figure.

To copy the data instead of just moving it, hold down the **Ctrl** key while dragging.

191

Release the mouse button to drop the data in place.

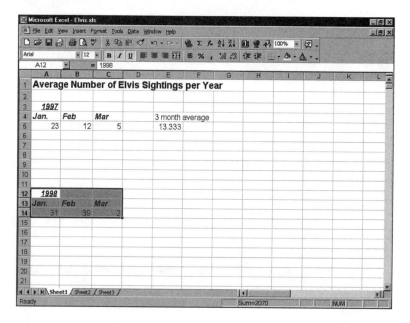

Want to Copy Across Sheets?

To copy the contents and formatting of cells from one worksheet to another, first click the tab for the worksheet containing the cells you want to copy. Next, hold down the **Ctrl** key and click the worksheet tab you want to copy to. Select the cells you want to copy, open the **Edit** menu, choose **Fill**, and then **Across Worksheets**. The Fill Across Worksheets dialog box appears. Select **All** (to copy cell contents and formatting), **Contents** (to copy contents only), or **Formats** (to copy formatting only). Click **OK**, and Excel copies the data.

Using the Paste Special Command

What's so special about the Paste Special command? Well, I was just about to tell you. The ordinary Paste command copies entire cell contents from one place to another. The Paste Special command lets you copy certain cell attributes, instead of everything. For example, you might want to copy only the formula, just the values, or only the formatting.

The Paste Special command combines the cell attributes of one cell or range with those of the cell or range you're copying to. To use the command, follow these steps:

1. Select the cell or range you want to copy.

2. Click the **Copy** button on the Standard toolbar or open the **Edit** menu and choose **Copy**.

3. Select the cell or range you want to copy to.

4. Open the **Edit** menu and choose **Paste Special** (don't even think about clicking the Paste button, or none of this will work). This opens the Paste Special dialog box, as shown in the next figure.

Use the Paste Special dialog box to copy cell contents, formulas, or formatting.

5. Under the **Paste** options, choose the attributes you want to copy to the new cell or range.

6. Under the **Operation** options, choose how you want the copied attributes combined with the cell or range you're copying to.

7. If you don't want to paste any blank cells on top of existing cells, select the **Skip Blanks** check box.

8. To change columns to rows or rows to columns, select the **Transpose** check box.

9. Click **OK**, and Excel transfers the attributes you selected.

Are You Linking?

If you're linking data from another application into an Excel cell or range, use the **Paste Link** button in the Paste Special dialog box. Learn more about linking and embedding in Chapter 23.

Deleting Data

One last thing about rearranging worksheet data: What do you do with data you no longer want? Obviously, you delete it, right? As usual, you have about a dozen different ways to delete your data. For instance, you can choose to clear out your cell's contents or completely delete the cells. If you do the latter, all the other cells move over to fill the void.

193

Select the data you want to remove and then use any of these deletion techniques:

➤ Press the **Delete** key on your keyboard.

➤ Click the **Cut** button or open the **Edit** menu and select **Cut**.

➤ Press **Ctrl+X**.

➤ To clear the contents but leave the cell(s) intact, including formatting, open the **Edit** menu, select **Clear**, and then **Contents**.

➤ To clear the formatting but not the data, open the **Edit** menu and choose **Clear**, **Formats**.

➤ To clear everything, open the **Edit** menu and choose **Clear**, **All**.

➤ Open the **Edit** menu and select **Delete**. This opens the Delete dialog box, as shown in the following figure. Designate how you want Excel to handle the void: **Shift Cells Left** or **Shift Cells Right**, or you can choose to delete the **Entire Row** or **Entire Column**. Click **OK** to exit the box.

Use the Delete dialog box to delete cells.

Seek and Ye Shall Find, and Then Ye Can Replace

I've explained how to change your worksheet structure and move things around. For balance, I guess I ought to fill you in on how to find data (especially after you've moved it). The bigger your worksheets, the harder it is to locate the data you want to view. Oh sure, you could waste your time scrolling around and squinting into the screen trying to read every cell, but why do that when Excel has a handy feature for looking for data? Not only that, but you can look up and replace data, too.

To find data in a worksheet, follow these steps:

1. Open the **Edit** menu and choose **Find**. This opens the Find dialog box, as shown in the following figure.

2. Click inside the **Find What** text box and enter the data you want to find.

3. Use the **Search** drop-down list to specify how to conduct the search (by rows or columns).

4. Use the **Look In** drop-down list to specify the type of data you're looking for: **Formulas**, **Values**, or **Notes**.

The Ever-Dependable Go To Command

If it's just a particular cell you're looking for, use the Go To command. Press **Ctrl+G** (or open the **Edit** menu and select **Go To**), enter the cell reference you want to locate, and then click **OK**.

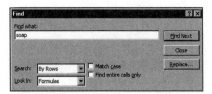

Enter the data you want to search for in the Find dialog box.

5. If you want Excel to match the case as you've typed it, click the **Match Case** check box. If you want to find only entire entries (not partial entries), click the **Find Entire Cells Only** check box.

6. To start looking, click the **Find Next** button, and Excel locates the first matching entry and highlights it, as shown in the next figure. If this isn't the occurrence you're looking for, click **Find Next** until you locate your data.

7. Click **Close** to exit the dialog box.

Move It!

If the Find dialog box is in the way, you can move it. Drag its title bar to a new location onscreen.

When Excel finds the entry, its cell is selected in the worksheet.

Found entry

What if you typed the wrong values for Department C's sales figures, and they're all over the worksheet? Don't sweat it; you can perform a find-and-replace operation all at the same time. Use these steps:

1. Open the **Edit** menu and choose **Replace**. This opens the Replace dialog box, as shown in the next figure.

Enter the data you're looking for, as well as the data you want to replace it with, in the Replace dialog box.

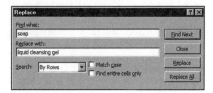

2. Click inside the **Find What** text box and enter the data you want to find.

3. Click inside the **Replace With** text box and enter the data you want to use as a replacement.

4. Use the **Search** drop-down list to specify how to conduct the search (by rows or columns).

5. If you want Excel to match the case as you've typed it, check the **Match Case** check box. If you want to find only entire entries (not partial entries), click the **Find Entire Cells Only** check box.

6. To start looking, click the **Find Next** button, and Excel locates the first matching entry. Do one of the following:

   ➤ If this isn't the occurrence you're looking for, click **Find Next** until you locate your data.

   ➤ Click **Replace** to replace the occurrence and move to the next.

   ➤ Click **Replace All** to replace all occurrences in the worksheet.

7. Click **Close** to exit the dialog box.

Use Undo

If you accidentally replace data you didn't want replaced, immediately click the **Undo** button on the Standard toolbar.

The Least You Need to Know

➤ You can resize columns and rows to fit your data, rather than the other way around. Just drag the column or row borders in the header area.

➤ To quickly insert a row, select the row you want to appear below the new row, right-click, and select **Insert**.

➤ To quickly insert a column, select the column to the right of where you want the new column, right-click, and select **Insert**.

➤ To delete a column or row, select it and then open the **Edit** menu and choose **Delete**.

➤ To delete cell contents, select the cell and press the **Delete** key on your keyboard.

➤ Use the old Cut, Copy, and Paste commands to move data around your worksheet.

➤ Use the Find and Replace commands to search your worksheet for specific data and replace it with new data.

Chapter 13

Getting Graphic

In This Chapter

➤ Spruce up your worksheet with clip art

➤ Learn how to insert image files

➤ Find out how to draw your own shapes

➤ Discover tips for turning words into art

You may not have thought about adding graphics to your worksheets. They say (it's "them" again) that a picture is worth a thousand words, right? So why not spruce up your worksheets with images, pictures, graphics, clip art, objects, or whatever else you want to call them. Not only can you insert graphic files from other programs, you can use Excel's drawing tools to create your own.

The World of Spreadsheet Art

Got graphics? You can insert them into your worksheet. For example, you may want to illustrate your data, add the company logo to the top of the sheet, or just insert a bold graphic to add pure visual interest to the worksheet.

The term *graphic* includes image files, clip art, photo images, WordArt images, and any other graphic image file that can be copied, pasted, or inserted into your worksheets. Once placed on a worksheet, the graphic object can be moved, sized, and formatted to suit your needs.

What About Chart Art?

An obvious graphic element that works hand-in-hand with Excel is charts. You can learn all about inserting charts in Chapter 16, "Charts That Say It All."

Inserting Clip Art

Excel comes with a collection of clip art files you can use to illustrate your data or convey an idea. Right up front, I need to advise you not to use too many clip art pieces in a worksheet, because they'll compete with your data. In most instances, one piece is sufficient.

Ready to give clip art a try? If so, then follow these steps:

1. Click the cell where you want to insert the clip art. Regardless of which piece you end up selecting, you'll need to resize it to fit properly on a spreadsheet; therefore, just indicate in the worksheet a general area in which to place the piece.

2. Open the **Insert** menu and select **Picture, Clip Art**. This opens the Insert ClipArt dialog box, as shown in the following figure.

Use the Insert ClipArt dialog box to search for and insert clip art.

Back button
Forward button
Categories

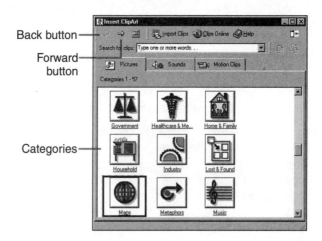

3. Click the category you want to view on the **Pictures** tab. (Use the scrollbar to view all the available categories.)

4. Scroll through the clip art list and locate the image you want to use. If you can't find a picture in that particular category, click the **Back** button and choose another category. The **Back** and **Forward** buttons let you navigate the Clip Art Gallery.

5. When you finally locate a picture you want to use, click it to select and then click the **Insert Clip** button, as shown in the next figure.

More Clips

Some categories may have links to additional clip files; click the link to see more clip art. To search for a clip, type a keyword (such as *desk*) in the **Search For Clips** text box and press **Enter**. If you still can't find a clip art piece, use the **Clips Online** button at the top of the box to log on to the Internet and look for more clip art on the Microsoft Web site.

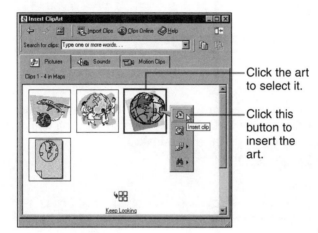

Select the clip art you want to use to display a menu of buttons.

Click the art to select it.

Click this button to insert the art.

6. To close the dialog box, click the **Close** (x) button in the upper-right corner of the box.

You can now resize and move the image as needed on your worksheet. It remains selected after you close the dialog box; selection handles appear around the object. The floating Picture toolbar also appears onscreen, as shown in the next figure. (If it doesn't, open the **View** menu and choose **Toolbars, Picture**.)

To resize the clip art, drag a selection handle. Depending on which selection handle you drag, the resizing options vary. Drag a corner handle to resize the entire object. Drag a top or bottom handle to resize the object's height; drag a side handle to resize the object's width.

To move an object, hover your mouse pointer over the selected object until the pointer takes the shape of a four-sided arrow; then drag to move the object anywhere on the worksheet.

201

I had to resize this clip art to fit; you'll probably have to resize the image you choose, too.

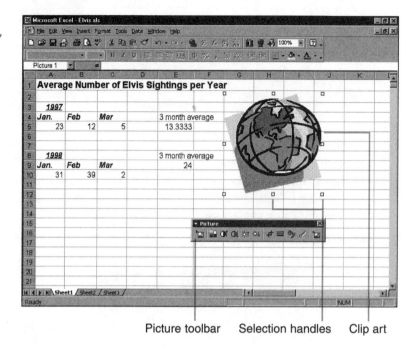

Picture toolbar   Selection handles   Clip art

Table 13.1 explains how to use the Picture toolbar buttons to make changes to the clip art object. Try experimenting with the buttons to change the clip art's appearance. If you don't like any of the changes you make, click the **Reset Picture** button to return the clip art to its original state.

Table 13.1   Picture Toolbar Buttons

Button	Function
	Opens the Insert Picture dialog box for inserting image files.
	Lets you specify how the image appears—in color, grayscale, black and white, or as a watermark background (a transparent background).
	Lets you increase the image contrast.
	Lets you decrease the image contrast.
	Lets you adjust the image brightness to a higher degree.
	Lets you lessen image brightness.
	Use to crop the image.

Button	Function
	Use to set a line border around the clip art.
	Opens the Format dialog box.
	Lets you set a transparent color.
	Resets the clip art to its original size and formatting.

Inserting Image Files

Perhaps you have a graphic file you want to use from another program. You can easily insert it into your worksheet and resize or move it as needed. Use these steps:

1. Click the cell where you want to insert the image file.

2. Open the **Insert** menu and select **Picture**, **From File**. This opens the Insert Picture dialog box, as shown in the following figure.

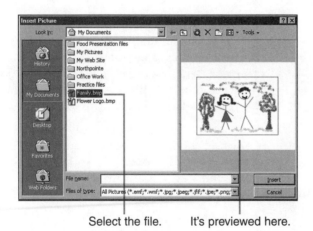

Use the Insert Picture dialog box to insert image files from other programs and folders.

Select the file.   It's previewed here.

3. Locate the file you want to insert. If necessary, use the Places bar or the Look In drop-down list to find the folder where the file is stored.

4. Select the file, and the preview area displays the image. To insert the file, click the **Insert** button.

5. Excel inserts the image file into your worksheet and opens the Picture toolbar, as shown in the next figure.

After inserting the image, you can resize and move it around. Notice that the Picture toolbar appears along with the image. You can use the toolbar buttons to change the image. Revisit the previous table to learn what each button does.

Like clip art, the image file is treated as a graphic object.

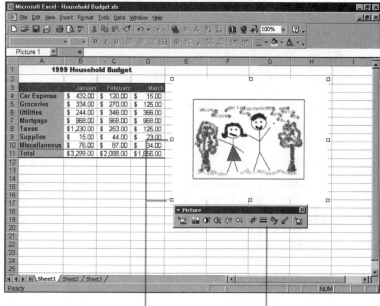

Selection handles   Picture toolbar

Now You See It, Now You Don't

You see the Picture toolbar only when the object—whether it's clip art or an image file—is selected. When you click anywhere outside the object's selection handles, the Picture toolbar disappears.

Draw Your Own Art

If you can't find an image file or clip art to use in your worksheet, consider drawing your own art. Excel comes with a set of excellent drawing tools. Of particular interest are the AutoShapes, which I'll show you how to use later in this section.

First up, open the Drawing toolbar—that's where all the drawing goodies are located. Open the **View** menu and select **Toolbars**, **Drawing** or right-click over an empty area of any displayed toolbar and choose **Drawing**.

The following figure shows the Drawing toolbar. The figure also illustrates several different kinds of objects you can draw on a worksheet. Each item you create with the Drawing toolbar tools is an object and can be resized and moved just like the clip art or image files you insert into your worksheets. When you select the object, such as the text box in the following figure, it's surrounded by selection handles.

As you can see, you can draw all kinds of objects on a worksheet. You're only limited by your imagination. Be sure to check out all the tools on the Drawing toolbar to see what you can come up with. Table 13.2 explains each button found on the Drawing toolbar and how it's used.

204

Rectangle object   AutoShape   Oval object

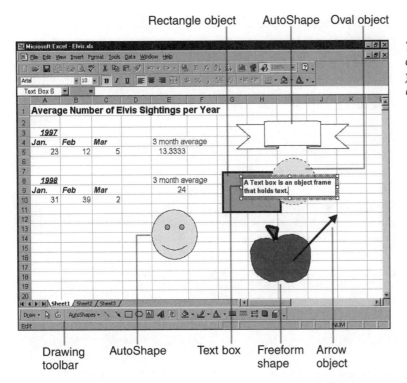

The Drawing toolbar is chock full of tools to help you create shapes, forms, and freehand drawings.

Drawing   AutoShape   Text box   Freeform   Arrow
toolbar   shape   object

Table 13.2   Drawing Toolbar Buttons

Button	Function
Draw ▾	Displays a menu of drawing control commands
�	Selects the pointer tool for manipulating drawn objects
↻	Lets you rotate an object by dragging the rotation handles
 AutoShapes ▾	Opens a list of predrawn shapes you can insert
\	Draws a straight line
↘	Draws a straight line with an arrow on the end
▢	Draws a rectangle or square object
○	Draws an oval or circle
▤	Draws a text box into which you can type data

continues

Table 13.2   Drawing Toolbar Buttons Continued

Button	Function
	Opens the WordArt tool
	Opens the ClipArt Gallery
	Fills the object with a color you designate
	Changes the line color
	Changes the font color
	Displays a list of line styles you can choose from
	Displays a list of line dash styles
	Displays a list of arrow styles
	Displays a palette of shadow effects you can apply to an object
	Displays a palette of 3D effects you can apply to an object

After drawing an object, you can select it to display selection handles; then you can resize or move it as needed.

Drawing AutoShapes

If you're not too keen on drawing your own shapes, you can tap into the available predrawn shapes. AutoShapes is a fairly large collection of predrawn shapes. Click the **AutoShapes** button on the Drawing toolbar to see what I mean. The figure below shows the **AutoShapes** menu with the **Stars and Banners** category displayed.

To draw an AutoShape object on your worksheet, follow these steps:

1. Click the **AutoShapes** button on the Drawing toolbar, select a category, and then click the exact AutoShape you want to draw.

Open the AutoShapes menu to display a list of categories.

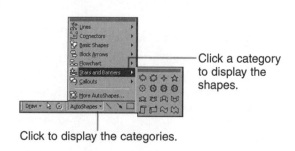

Click a category to display the shapes.

Click to display the categories.

206

2. Move your mouse pointer to the worksheet area; then click and drag to draw the shape, as shown in the following figure. The mouse pointer looks like a cross hair as you're drawing.

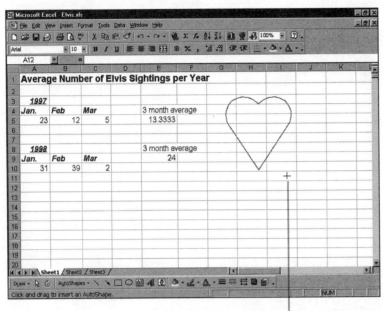

Click where you want the shape drawn, then drag to begin drawing.

Click and drag to draw and size the shape.

3. Release the mouse button. The shape is drawn, as shown in the following figure. Notice that it's surrounded by selection handles.

Now use the Drawing toolbar buttons to change your shape's appearance. You can resize or move it as you please.

Object Tips

Once you've got an object, such as an AutoShape, drawn on your worksheet, you can do quite a few things with it. Here are just a few examples:

➤ If you want to draw a perfectly proportioned shape, hold down the **Shift** key while dragging.

➤ To delete a selected shape, press the **Delete** key.

➤ Double-click an object to open the Format dialog box, where you can change the object's formatting settings. For example, you can change the object's color or line styles.

➤ Use the layering tools to place objects on top of other objects. Click the **Draw** button on the Drawing toolbar, select **Order**, and then choose how you want the object placed.

The finished shape appears surrounded by selection handles.

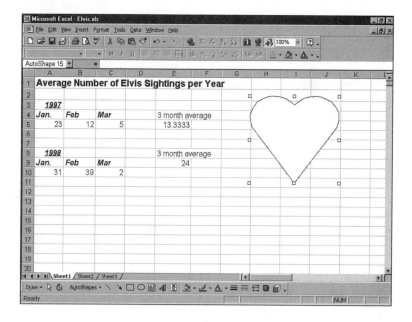

➤ If you group objects, you can move or resize them together. To turn two or more selected objects into a group, select the objects (use the **Shift** or **Ctrl** key as you click each one) and then click the **Draw** button and choose **Group**. (To ungroup, click the **Draw** button and choose **Ungroup**.)

➤ To rotate an object, select it, click the **Rotate** button, and then drag a rotation handle on the object.

➤ If you're trying to draw fine details, try zooming in at 200%. (Use the **Zoom** button on the Standard toolbar; click the drop-down arrow and select **200%**.) You'll be able to see things better.

That should be enough to whet your appetite. Take time to explore the many tools and options available on the Drawing toolbar to find out what else you can do with the art you insert.

Turning Words into Art

There's one more graphics technique I want to tell you about—WordArt. The WordArt tool lets you turn ordinary text into works of art. Mind you, we're not talking Monet or anything, but rather special effects. Try it yourself:

1. Click the **Insert WordArt** button on the Drawing toolbar. This opens the WordArt Gallery dialog box, as shown in the following figure.

2. Click the style you want to use and click **OK**.

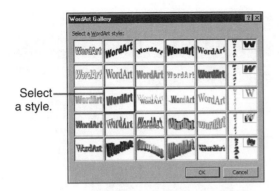

Select a style. ←

First, select a WordArt style to use.

3. In the Edit WordArt Text dialog box, shown in the following figure, enter the text you want to turn into WordArt. It can be a word or a phrase. Use the **Font** and **Size** lists as well as style buttons to change the character attributes of the text.

Click here to display the font list.   Click here to display font sizes.

Enter your text and choose a font style or size.

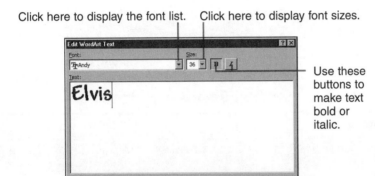

Use these buttons to make text bold or italic.

4. When the text looks the way you want it to, click **OK**.

5. The WordArt object is inserted into your worksheet, as shown in the following figure. You can move or resize the object as needed, just like any other graphic object.

As soon as Excel places the WordArt object onto your worksheet, the WordArt toolbar appears. Table 13.3 explains how to use the toolbar buttons. You can resize and move your WordArt object as needed.

I resized my WordArt and placed it over an Auto-Shape. Pretty cool, eh?

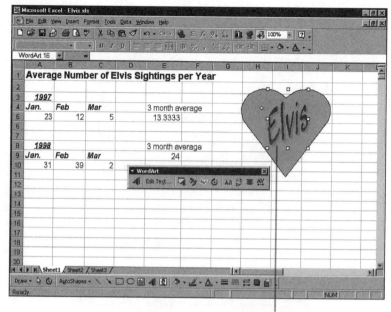

WordArt object

Table 13.3   WordArt Toolbar Buttons

Button	Function
	Click to add new WordArt (same as Insert WordArt button on Drawing toolbar).
Edit Te**x**t...	Opens the Edit WordArt Text dialog box, where you can change the text or font.
	Opens the WordArt Gallery so you can choose another WordArt effect.
	Opens the formatting dialog box for changing the object's appearance.
Abc	Displays a palette of WordArt shapes you can choose from.
	Lets you rotate the WordArt object.
Aa	Makes all the letters the same height.
Ab	Redraws the WordArt object with vertical text.
	Changes the text alignment.
AV	Changes how tightly the letters are spaced.

The Least You Need to Know

➤ It's easy to insert clip art into your workbooks using the clip art collection that comes with Excel.

➤ You can also insert image files from other programs.

➤ Use Excel's Drawing toolbar buttons to add your own shapes and objects.

➤ AutoShapes has a large collection of predrawn shapes you can insert.

➤ All graphic elements you add to a worksheet are treated as objects. When selected, an element is surrounded with selection handles for moving, shaping, and resizing.

➤ To move an object, hover your mouse pointer over the selected object until the pointer becomes a four-sided arrow pointer; then drag the object to a new location.

➤ Drag a selection handle to resize an object.

Chapter 14

Adding Borders and Backgrounds

In This Chapter

➤ Discover tips for setting up borders to keep out unwanted data

➤ Learn how to set a custom border using the Format Cells dialog box

➤ Find out the various ways you can use color formatting in your Excel worksheets

➤ Learn how to apply patterns to your cell backgrounds

You may be thinking, "Hey, haven't we just about covered every possible formatting tool in Excel yet?" Yes, just about. There's still a few more you might be interested in—that is, if you've got the stamina to see this through. You wouldn't wimp out on me now, would you?

A lot of people never take the time to learn about Excel's lesser-known formatting tools, such as those for controlling cell borders and backgrounds. True, these features aren't as glamorous or as popular as changing fonts and number styles—but, darn it, they're just as important. If only people would take the time to learn how to add a border or apply a background color or pattern, worksheet cells would never have to look ordinary again. Won't you give these formatting options a try? (Yes, I'm on a campaign to raise support for underused formatting tools. Please give generously.)

Bordering on Borders

Borders, schmorders. When you're working with an endless worksheet grid, the need for borders isn't exactly at the forefront of your mind. Heck, every cell seemingly already has a border on the worksheet. But when it comes time to print out your worksheet data, ah-ha...then you'll see. You'll see a need for distinguishing your columns and rows of data.

Printing Gridlines

If you do want your worksheet's gridlines to print, open the **File** menu and choose **Page Setup**. Click the **Sheet** tab and then click the **Gridlines** check box. Click **OK**.

As it turns out, your worksheet gridlines don't print (unless you've turned them on to print), so your data appears in tabular form on the printout. Not that there's anything wrong with that! But sometimes you need something more: something defining, strong, and linear. You need a border.

You can add a complete border to any cell or range, or you can add partial borders to one or more sides of a cell. You can also select from several line styles when using borders. For example, you can add a double-underline to a cell holding your totals, or you can draw a thick outline around your headings to make them stand out. The following figure shows some examples of borders used effectively in a worksheet. I turned off the worksheet gridlines so you can see how everything looks.

Borders can make a spreadsheet easier to read and make for a professional presentation.

A top and bottom border   A top-only border

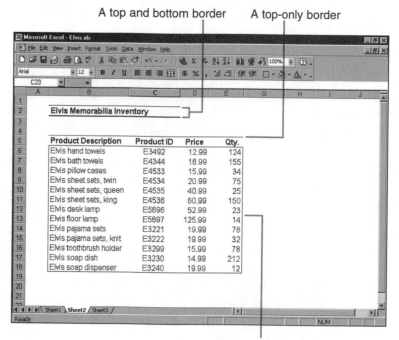

An all-sides border

Turn the Gridlines Off?

Yes, you can do this, didn't you know? Open the **Tools** menu and select **Options**. Click the **View** tab and deselect the **Gridlines** check box. Click **OK**. To turn them on again, repeat this action, this time clicking the check box to turn the gridlines on again.

To quickly add a border using the toolbar buttons, follow these steps:

1. Select the cell or range to which you want to add a border.
2. Click the **Border** drop-down arrow on the Formatting toolbar.
3. This opens a palette of border styles, as shown in the following figure.

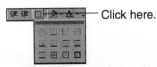 ──── Click here.

Click the Border button's drop-down arrow to see a palette of border styles.

4. Click the style that represents the side(s) you want to border and the line style you want to use.

5. As soon as you make a selection from the palette, it's applied to your cell or range, as shown in the following figure.

If you change your mind about the border after adding it to your worksheet, click the **Undo** button on the Standard toolbar. You can also display the Border palette again and choose the **No Border** option button. If you're trying to delete a border you assigned quite a while back and you can't seem to delete it, try selecting the cell next to, above, or below the cell you think has the border. Remember, a cell can have a border on the left, right, top, or bottom.

Use the Same Border Again

When you use the **Border** toolbar button to apply a border, it always reflects the last border you assigned. To reassign the same border style elsewhere, you don't have to display the palette again; just click the **Border** button itself.

215

I chose a thick border to add to this range. How do you like it?

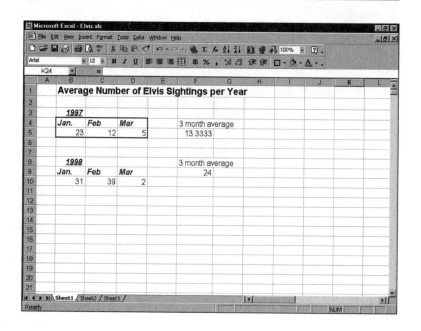

Tear-off Palettes

The Border palette is one of Excel's many tear-off palettes, which means you can drag it off the toolbar and turn it into a floating palette that you can move around freely on the screen. To tear off the Border palette, drag its blue bar at the top of the palette. When you're done with it, click its **Close** button.

Although the Border palette has plenty of border styles to keep you happy, if you're looking for greater control and additional border options, you need to open the Format Cells dialog box and click the **Border** tab, as shown in the following figure.

As you can see from the figure, you can specify exactly what you want your border to look like, including choosing from a variety of line styles. Use these steps to create your own custom border:

1. Select the cell or range to which you want to add a border.

2. Open the **Format** menu and select **Cells**. This opens the Format Cells dialog box.

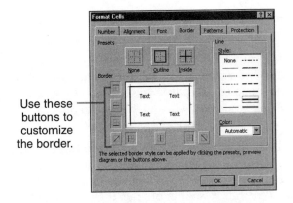

Use these buttons to customize the border.

The Border tab in the Format Cells dialog box lets you customize your border exactly how you want.

3. Click the **Border** tab to bring its options to the front.

4. In the **Presets** area, select the border style you want: **None**, **Outline** (all-sides), **Inside** (inside lines only). The third option works only if you select more than one cell.

5. In the **Line** area, choose a line style for the border. Scroll through the list to see what's available. When you find something you like, click it.

6. Want to add color? Click the **Color** drop-down list and choose a color from the palette.

7. To customize which sides of the border are included, click the individual buttons representing the sides you want in the **Border** area. You can then preview how the border will look in the middle area.

8. To exit the dialog box and apply the new border settings, click **OK**.

Print 'Em or Preview 'Em

To really check out how your borders look, print them out. Click the **Print** button on the Standard toolbar. If you're conserving paper, you can use Print Preview mode to preview the borders instead; click the **Print Preview** button. To learn more about printing and previewing worksheets, turn to Chapter 15, "Printing and Previewing."

Here's a Little Background Information

Borders aren't the only thing you can add to your cells. You can also add background patterns and colors. Why? Because it not only looks nice, it can make a large spreadsheet a lot easier to read, that's why. In some instances, adding background elements to a range of cells can really make your data pop off the page. However, in other instances, the background can compete with the data, making it equally difficult to discern. Use good judgment, of course, but don't be afraid to explore all the possibilities.

If you've got a color printer, you're all set to jump in and see what you can create. If you have a black-and-white printer, you may not feel as inclined to learn about the pattern, color, and shading options. Let me assure you that you can still fully utilize the background options—they'll just come out in shades of gray, that's all. The figures in this book aren't in color (in case you haven't noticed); however, take a look at the next figure. The examples of backgrounds added to the cells look pretty good in grayscale, if you ask me.

Just because you don't have a color printer doesn't mean you can't take advantage of the colors and backgrounds Excel offers.

Background color and pattern   Background color   Background pattern   Colored text

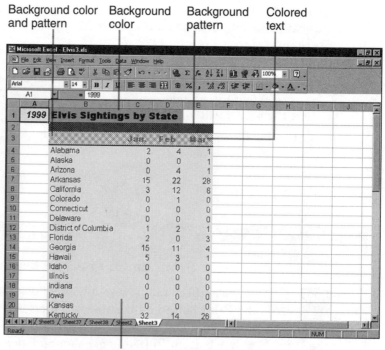

Background color

Regardless of what kind of printer you have, colors and backgrounds can greatly enhance the presentation of your worksheet data. If you played with any of Excel's AutoFormat styles (see Chapter 11, "Formatting for Fun or Profit"), you've already seen what a difference such formatting can make. Backgrounds and colors, even printed in grayscale, can make your worksheet look polished and professional.

Don't Get Carried Away

Just a word of warning: Don't get too carried away assigning lots of backgrounds and borders to a single worksheet. Too many formatting effects can really work against the appearance of your data. If you ever have any doubts about what's acceptable, check out Excel's AutoFormats. To learn more about this feature, turn to the section "AutoFormat: Easy Formatting for the Formatting Impaired" in Chapter 11.

Strictly Color

You can use color in several ways with Excel. You can assign a color to your cell contents, or you can assign a color to the cell background. If it's colored text you want, look no further than the **Font Color** button on the Formatting toolbar. A click on the **Font Color** drop-down arrow will reveal a palette of colors you can assign (see the following figure). As soon as you select a color, it's applied to the data in the selected cell or range.

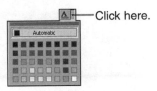
Click here.

Use the Font Color palette to color your cell contents.

You might use color to distinguish different data types or make your totals stand out. You might also use color to differentiate headings from data.

Like the **Border** button you learned about earlier, the **Font Color** button always reflects your last selection. Therefore, if you want to assign the same color again to other cells, just click the button instead of displaying the entire palette.

You can also apply color to your data via the Format Cells dialog box (open the **Format** menu and choose **Cells**). Use the **Color** drop-down list on the **Font** tab to change the font color.

219

Tear One Off

The Font Color palette is another of Excel's tear-off palettes, which means you can drag it off the toolbar and turn it into a floating palette that you can move around freely on the screen.

If it's background color you want, try the **Fill Color** button on the Formatting toolbar. A click on its drop-down arrow reveals yet another color palette, as shown in the next figure. Any selection you make from this palette is applied to the background of the selected cell or range.

The **Fill Color** button remembers the color you last selected; the color appears on the button itself. To assign the same color again, click just the **Fill Color** button, not the drop-down arrow.

Another way to assign a background color is to use the Format Cells dialog box. (We just can't get enough of this dialog box!)

Use the Fill Color palette to apply a background color to your cell or range.

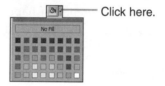

Click here.

Follow these steps:

1. Select the cell or range to which you want to add background color.
2. Open the **Format** menu and select **Cells**.
3. Click the **Patterns** tab, as shown in the following figure.

Here's the Format Cells dialog box again. This time, check out the Patterns tab.

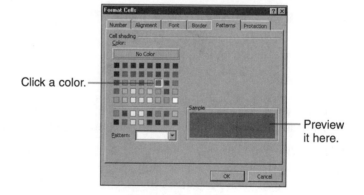

Click a color.

Preview it here.

4. From the **Color** palette, click the color you want to use.
5. The **Sample** area gives you a preview of the color.
6. Click **OK** to exit the dialog box and apply the color to your cell(s).

No More Color

If you don't like the color you assigned to the background, click the **Undo** button. If you want to lose the color you assigned a long time ago, select the cell or range and click the **Fill Color** drop-down arrow and choose **No Fill**.

Following a Pattern

Finally, one piece of background information—patterns. You can use patterns to create shading in your worksheet background. First, though, just a heads-up: You've got to be careful about applying patterns to your backgrounds. Some patterns are pretty busy and will definitely detract from your data or make it difficult to read. However, who says your cells always have to hold data? You can choose to apply a pattern to a range of cells without data. Check out the next figure to see what this scenario might look like.

This range has no data, just a pattern.

Background patterns can really spruce up a worksheet, but use them wisely.

221

If you do pick a particularly busy pattern, compensate for it by using bold text or numbers, or you can use a font that's really bold and blocky looking so that it stands out against the pattern. You can also try using other font colors. White text against a darkly patterned background can be quite appealing.

To assign a pattern to your cells, use these steps:

1. First, select the cell or range you want to add background color to. (I have an overwhelming sense of déjà vu here. Do you?)
2. Open the **Format** menu and select **Cells**.
3. Click the **Patterns** tab.
4. This time, click the **Pattern** drop-down arrow. This displays another palette— a palette of patterns (see the following figure).

Use the Pattern palette to experiment with various background patterns.

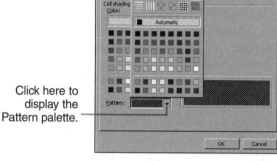

Click here to
display the
Pattern palette.

5. When you see a pattern you like, click it. The **Sample** area gives you a preview of the color.
6. Click **OK** to exit the dialog box and apply the pattern to your cell(s).

I Don't Like It

If you don't like the background pattern you assigned, click the **Undo** button immediately.

The Least You Need to Know

➤ For a quick border, use the **Border** button on the Formatting toolbar.

➤ For a custom border, open the Format Cells dialog box and check out the Border tab's options.

➤ Background colors and patterns can add to your worksheet, but don't get too carried away.

➤ For a quick background color, use the **Fill Color** button on the Formatting toolbar.

Chapter 15

Printing and Previewing

In This Chapter

➤ Find out how to preview your work before printing

➤ Learn how to print your data, whether it's a single range or an entire workbook

➤ Discover tips for using Excel's Page Setup options for controlling page layout

➤ Learn how to set a header or footer

➤ Find out how to control page breaks

All Excel roads inevitably lead to printing, even if you take some really wrong turns. Why printing? It's the easiest way to share your data. A printed worksheet is tangible and solid. It's printed right there in black and white (or color), so the data must be correct. Right?

A funny thing happens to people when they see facts and figures organized in nicely aligned columns and rows with totals, subtotals, and such. They start taking the data very seriously, even if you made it all up. That's because there's a real beauty in the presentation of data on a printed spreadsheet. It's elegant and refined, and by golly, it looks really good.

Although printing an Excel worksheet takes only a simple click, there are quite a few additional printing options available as well as formatting features you can use to improve the appearance of your worksheet on the printed page even more. In this last formatting chapter, you learn how to preview your worksheet pages before committing them to paper. Find out if your data is legible and whether you've used the appropriate fonts and sizes. Learn to change the page margins, paper size, and printer setup options. Best of all, learn how to add headers and footers to your worksheets to identify page contents, and use Excel's page-break features to control how your data prints out.

Preview It All

Here's another Excel feature that most people don't take nearly enough advantage of—previewing. When you're working in a worksheet, you see only a small part of the sheet in the Excel window. You can't tell how the whole page looks or how the fonts and sizes will appear on the printed page. Using Excel's Preview mode, you can see a full-page view of the file. You can examine how each worksheet page looks before ever committing a single piece of data to paper.

To open Excel's Preview window, click the **Print Preview** button on the Standard toolbar or open the **File** menu and select **Print Preview**. The Preview window appears, as shown in the following figure. You can click any of the toolbar buttons on the Preview toolbar to adjust your view of the worksheet. Table 15.1 explains each of the Preview buttons and their functions.

Excel's Print Preview window lets you see what your entire worksheet will look like once it's printed.

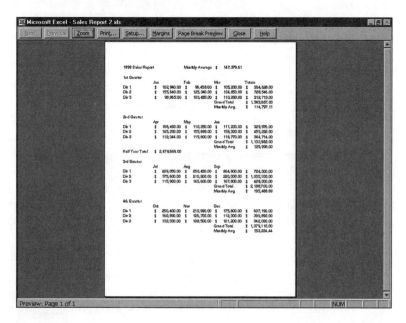

Table 15.1   Print Preview Buttons

Button	Function
Next	Displays the next page if your worksheet takes up more than one page.
Previous	Displays the previous page if you used the Next button to view multiple pages.
Zoom	Controls the zoom for viewing your workbook. Click to zoom in for greater magnification of your workbook. Click the button again to return to the original size. You can do the same thing using the mouse (which looks like a magnifying glass when zooming in and out).
Print...	Prints the workbook.
Setup...	Opens the Page Setup dialog box, where you can make changes to the layout of the page.
Margins	Displays onscreen margin indicators (see the following figure). You can drag these to change the page margins. The margin markers look like black squares. Column markers look like black Ts.
Page Break Preview	Lets you designate page breaks within your worksheet.
Close	Closes the Preview window.
Help	Opens Excel's Help feature.

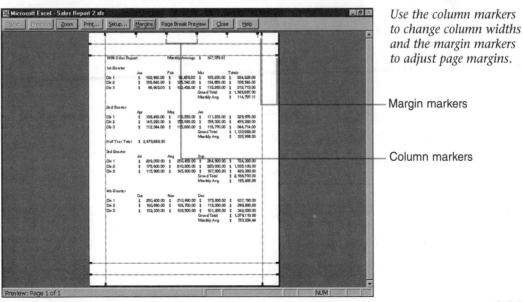

Use the column markers to change column widths and the margin markers to adjust page margins.

Margin markers

Column markers

You'll notice two sets of margin markers for the top and bottom of the workbook page. The extra set is for defining the area for headers and footers you might add to the page (headers and footers are text you enter that will appear on every printed page in the workbook).

Using the Zoom Command

If you're looking for more control of the zoom, use the Zoom command in the Excel window. You can quickly zoom a worksheet using the **Zoom** button on the Formatting toolbar; or if you want to customize your zoom percentage, use the **View** menu and select the **Zoom** command. When you select the **View** menu command, the Zoom dialog box opens, and you can specify the zoom percentage you want to use. Click **OK** to apply the new setting. To return to regular view, click the drop-down arrow on the **Zoom** button and choose **100%**.

Everything You Ever Wanted to Know About Printing, and More

All your hard work pays off when you can print your final worksheet. You may want to print a copy to review and mark up, or you may want to print a copy to distribute to others.

To print an entire file, no questions asked, simply click the **Print** button on the Standard toolbar. This little maneuver tells Excel to print one copy of the file using all the default printer settings. It's no-frills printing.

If you want to print only certain pages or selected ranges, print multiple copies, or otherwise control exactly how the file is printed, you need to open the Print dialog box.

Run a Spell Check

Did you know you can run a spell check on your worksheet data? You can, and you might want to do so before you print. Click the **Spelling** button on the Standard toolbar or press **F7**.

Follow these steps to print from the Print dialog box (if you want to print only the contents of a single cell or range, first select the cell or range before proceeding to step 1):

228

1. Open the **File** menu and select **Print**. This opens the Print dialog box, as shown in the following figure.

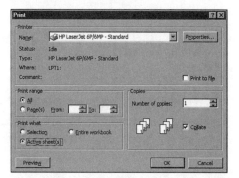

Use the Print dialog box to set your print options.

2. For the **Print Range** options, select which pages to print:

   To print the entire file, select **All**.

   To print a particular page or range of pages, select **Pages** and use the **From** and **To** boxes to identify the pages to print. You can type in the page numbers or use the spin arrows to set the page numbers.

3. To print certain portions of your worksheet data, use the **Print What** options:

   Choose **Selection** to print the selected cell or range (remember, you have to select the data before opening the Print dialog box in order to use this option).

   Choose **Active Sheet**(s) to print only the active worksheet.

   Choose **Entire Workbook** to print each worksheet in the file.

4. If you're printing just one copy of the file, make sure the **Number of Copies** box under the **Copies** options reads **1**. If you want more than one copy, type the number of copies you want or use the spin arrows to set a number.

5. Click the **OK** button when you're finally ready to print.

Got Lots of Pages?

If you're printing several copies of your workbook and the workbook has several pages, consider selecting the **Collate** check box to print out complete sets rather than three of page 1, three of page 2, and so on.

Changing the Default Printer

Most programs you use on your computer print to the default printer you have set up. In some situations, you may have more than one printer available, and you can select which printer is the default. For example, if you work in an office and are hooked up to a network, you may be able to select which network printer you want to use.

You can control which printer you use in the Print dialog box. To change the printer, click the **Name** drop-down list and choose another printer (see the following figure). Click **OK** to print to the printer you selected. Just remember, the next time you go to print a worksheet, it will use the printer you selected previously.

Use the Name drop-down list to choose which printer to use.

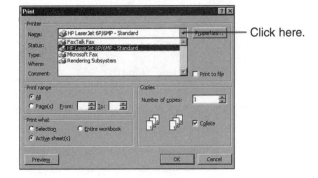

Click here.

Changing the Default Settings

If you need to change paper size, orientation, or paper source, click the **Properties** button in the Print dialog box. This opens the properties Setup dialog box, as shown in the following figure. When you make changes to any of the options in this dialog box, the changes are good for every file you print from Excel using the printer you selected in the Print dialog box, as well as from any other program you've installed (just thought I'd warn you). For example, if you change the paper size, the new size becomes the default for every program, not just Excel.

Use the properties Setup dialog box to change the default paper size and the orientation settings for printing from all the programs you use.

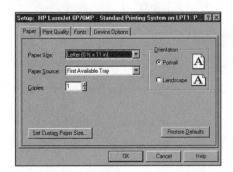

If you want to change only the paper size or orientation for the file you're working with, use the Page Setup dialog box instead. You learn all about this in the following section.

230

Setting Up with Page Setup

Before you run off and start printing everything in sight, you have a few more for-matting options to explore before printing your workbook file. For starters, you have a bevy of options available to you in the Page Setup dialog box (open the **File** menu and choose **Page Setup** to display the dialog box). This dialog box has options for controlling your page layout. You can use these options to fine-tune your worksheet before printing. For example, you may want to change the page margins or paper size and orientation, or you may want to add titles that repeat on every page.

You'll find four tabs in the Page Setup dialog box with options for changing your page layout:

➤ The **Page** tab has options for controlling paper size, print quality, and page orientation for the current worksheet.

➤ The **Margins** tab lets you specify top, bottom, left, and right margins.

➤ The **Header/Footer** tab lets you create headers and footers to print on each worksheet page. (You learn more about this topic later in the chapter.)

➤ The **Sheet** tab has options for printing titles, changing print order, and other sheet-related options.

Let me show you how to apply some of these options.

Changing Margins

Let's start with margins. If you want to change your worksheet's page margins, click the **Margins** tab in the Page Setup dialog box (see the next figure). Notice that the middle of the tab shows a sample page surrounded by spin boxes for setting margins for each side of the page. In addition, there are spin boxes for controlling header and footer margins.

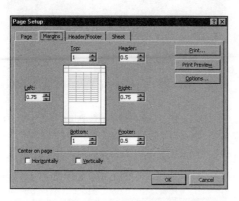

Use the Margins tab to set up page margins.

Mind you, for most users, the default margins are fine, but if you do need to adjust the margins, you can do so here or in the Print Preview window. To change a margin, click inside the appropriate margin text box on the Margins tab and type in a new setting, or you can use the spin arrows to increase or decrease the setting.

What About Those Other Buttons?

If you click the **Print Preview** button, the Print Preview window opens. If you click the **Options** button, the Setup dialog box opens (see the earlier section "Changing the Default Settings").

The bottom options in the Margins tab let you control how the printed worksheet is positioned on the page: **Horizontally** or **Vertically**.

When you're done, click **OK**. If you want to print right away, click **Print** instead of **OK**.

Changing Page Options

Click the **Page** tab of the Page Setup dialog box to find options for changing paper size or orientation, among other things. The following figure shows the Page tab. Under **Orientation** options, you'll find two choices: **Portrait** and **Landscape**. Choose **Portrait** to print your page across the 8½" width of the paper and down along the 11" length. Choose **Landscape** to print your page across the length of the paper (the 11" edge).

Change paper size and orientation for the current file by selecting from the options on the Page tab.

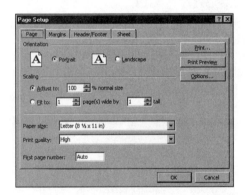

To change the paper size entirely, click the **Paper Size** drop-down list and choose a size. Depending on your printer type, the choices displayed in this list may vary.

If you're having trouble fitting all your data onto one page, try fudging a few things using the **Scaling** options. For example, if you've got one line of data that falls off the first page and onto a second page, and it's the only data on the second page, consider adjusting margins. If that doesn't work, use the **Adjust To** or **Fit To** option. To scale the worksheet to a percentage of its full size, enter a size in the **Adjust To** text box or use the spin arrows to enter a new setting. Any number you enter that is less than 100 will reduce the page to that percentage. For example, if you enter **50**, the page is reduced by 50 percent.

To tell Excel to fit the worksheet onto a specified number of pages, use the **Fit To** option. In the first text box, choose how many pages to fit to. This number will represent the number of page widths. In the second text box, enter the number of pages tall to fit the document to. For example, to fit a two-page worksheet onto one page, each text box should specify the value **1**. To fit a four-page worksheet onto two pages, the values in each **Fit To** box will be **2**.

Caution

If your printer doesn't support scalable fonts or TrueType fonts, you won't be able to use Page Setup's scaling options. Check your printer documentation if you have any doubts.

Dealing with Sheet Options

Click the **Sheet** tab on the Page Setup dialog box to reveal a tab of options that control which worksheet elements print. The following figure shows the Sheet tab in all its glory.

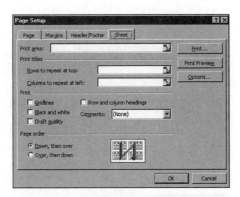

The Sheet tab has options for controlling which sheet elements print.

To help keep your printouts organized, consider adding titles to print on very page. You can repeat row or column titles on each page. To repeat rows, click inside the **Rows to Repeat at Top** text box; to repeat column titles, click inside the **Columns to Repeat at Left** text box. Click the **Collapse** button to reduce the Page Setup dialog box to a bar on the screen. Now select the row or column titles you want to use (they must be adjacent). Click the **Expand** button to return to the full-size dialog box. Now when you print the worksheet, the titles will print out on each page.

Here are a few more sheet options you might find useful:

➤ To print the worksheet gridlines, click the **Gridlines** check box.

➤ To print draft quality (which doesn't use as much printer ink as regular printing—or take as long to print), click the **Draft Quality** check box.

233

➤ Use the **Page Order** options to control which pages print first.

➤ If you've designed your worksheet to utilize color, but change your mind about printing it in full color for the time being, click the **Black and white** check box.

➤ If you've added comments to your worksheets, you can choose to print them out at the end of the sheet or as displayed on the worksheet. Use the **Comments** drop-down list to make your selection.

How About a Header or a Footer?

You can assign headers and footers to print on every worksheet page. A header appears at the top of the page, a footer at the foot of the page (like you didn't see that coming from a mile away). Headers and footers can be report titles, dates, the department name, the person creating the sheet—basically any text you want to include at the top or bottom (or both) of every page. Excel comes with several predefined headers and footers you can use, or you can enter your own.

Using Predefined Headers and Footers

To assign a predefined header or footer, follow these steps:

1. Open the Page Setup dialog box by selecting **File**, **Page Setup**.

2. Click the **Header/Footer** tab, as shown in the following figure.

Choose a predefined header or footer to use.

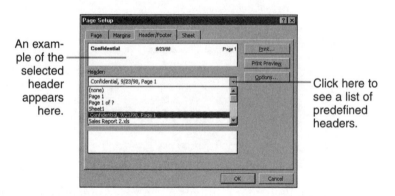

An example of the selected header appears here.

Click here to see a list of predefined headers.

3. To use a predefined header, click the **Header** drop-down list and make your selection. Excel displays a preview of the header in the Header text box.

4. To use a predefined footer, click the **Footer** drop-down list and choose one. Excel displays a preview of the selection in the Footer text box.

5. Click **OK** to exit the dialog box.

You won't see your headers or footers displayed in the worksheet window. Instead, you have to switch to Print Preview mode to see them (click the **Print Preview** button on the Standard toolbar).

To remove a header or footer you've assigned, reopen the Page Setup dialog box to the **Header/Footer** tab and select **(none)** from the **Header** or **Footer** drop-down list. Click **OK**.

Header/Footer Margins

By default, headers are printed a half inch from the top of the page and footers are printed a half inch from the bottom of the page. To change these margins, click the **Margins** tab in the Page Setup dialog box and enter new settings in the Header or Footer text box.

Setting Custom Headers and Footers

Now, if it's custom headers or footers you want to create, well, that's a whole other can of worms, so to speak. When you open the appropriate box to do this, you're presented with some odd-looking buttons for inserting codes for typical header or footer elements, such as page numbers, current date or time, and so on. Table 15.2 explains the special buttons.

Table 15.2 Header and Footer Toolbar Buttons

Button	Function
A	Changes the font (opens the Font dialog box)
#	Inserts a page number
#	Inserts number of pages (for instance, you can print page 1 of 12 using this button and the preceding button)
date	Inserts the date
clock	Inserts the time
file	Inserts the filename
sheet	Inserts the worksheet name

Use these steps to set a custom header or footer:

1. From the **Header/Footer** tab in the Page Setup dialog box, click the **Custom Header** or **Custom Footer** button. This opens a dialog box similar to the one shown in the following figure.

If the predefined headers or footers aren't what you want, you can create your own custom headers and footers.

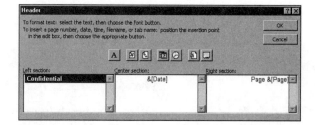

2. The dialog box is divided into three sections: **Left**, **Center**, **Right**. These represent the segments of the page where the header or footer will appear. Click inside the section you want to insert text into; then enter your text or use the buttons to insert codes. (You don't have to enter text for each section.)

3. When you're done, click **OK**. You're returned to the **Header/Footer** tab, where you can check your work.

4. Click **OK** again to exit the Page Setup dialog box.

Pondering Page Breaks

One more thing before you finish your worksheet-grooming crash course—page breaks. There are just a few things you should know about page breaks. When you print a worksheet, Excel breaks up the pages based on the margins you've selected, the column width, and any other page setup options you may have set. Page breaks appear as dashed lines on the worksheet. They're not always easy to see unless you switch over to Print Preview mode or turn off your gridlines.

Setting a Manual Page Break

If you don't like Excel's page breaks, you can insert your own. You can insert two types of page breaks: vertical and horizontal. A *vertical page break* breaks the print range at the current column. To insert a vertical page break, click the column heading to the right of where you want the vertical page break to appear and then open the **Insert** menu and choose **Page Break**.

A *horizontal page break* breaks the print range at the current row. To insert a horizontal page break, click the row just below where you want the horizontal page break to appear and then open the **Insert** menu and choose **Page Break**.

The following figure shows an example of both kinds of page breaks (I turned the gridlines off so you can see the breaks clearly).

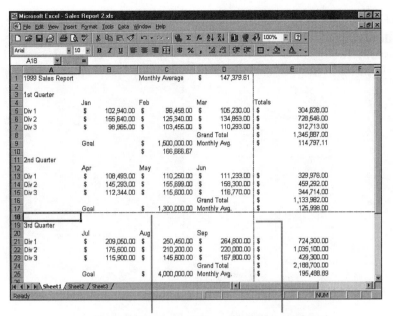

Here you see an example of both vertical and horizontal page breaks.

Horizontal page break   Vertical page break

Manual page breaks (those you insert yourself) appear with longer dashed lines than those indicating automatic page breaks (which are set by Excel).

Using Page Break Preview Mode

If you're working with a big worksheet that has lots of page breaks, use the Page Break Preview mode to check where your page breaks fall and make adjustments. To use this feature, open the **View** menu and choose **Page Break Preview**. A Welcome to Page Break Preview dialog box appears. Click **OK** to continue.

In Page Break Preview mode, page breaks appear as thick blue lines. The next figure shows the lines as thick black lines, but try to imagine them as blue, okay? Page numbers appear as shaded background numerals. To change the position of any page break, hover your mouse pointer over the line until it changes to a double-sided arrow; then drag the break to a new location on the worksheet. You can change the positions of both hard page breaks (those you insert) and automatic page breaks (those Excel inserts) from this view mode.

Here are a few more things you can do with this feature:

➤ To remove a manual page break, select a cell directly below or to the right of the break and open the **Insert** menu and choose **Remove Page Break**. The remaining pages readjust themselves accordingly.

➤ To remove all the manual page breaks, select the entire worksheet and open the **Insert** menu and choose **Reset All Page Breaks**.

➤ To exit Page Break Preview mode, open the **View** menu and choose **Normal**.

237

Use the Page Break Preview mode to adjust page breaks throughout your worksheet.

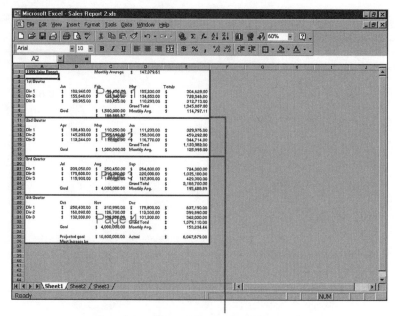

Page breaks

The Least You Need to Know

➤ Previewing your worksheets can save you from wasting paper.

➤ To print using all the default settings, just click the **Print** button.

➤ To make any changes to the printer settings, open the Print dialog box.

➤ Use the Page Setup dialog box to change page layout settings such as page size, orientation, and so on.

➤ Use headers and footers to help you organize your printed pages and define their contents.

➤ You can control how and where pages break on your worksheets and view them in Page Break Preview mode.

Part 4

Charting New Territory

The culmination of entering all that worksheet data, whipping up all those formulas, and calculating all the results is putting everything into a nice, professional chart. A chart shows everyone what a spreadsheet wizard you are and sets off your data like nothing else can. In this part of the book, you learn how to utilize Excel's chart features to create your own magnificent charts to share with the world. Just remember that a chart makes you look smart.

Charts That Say It All

If you ask an experienced Excel user what his or her favorite Excel feature is, you'll probably hear charts mentioned more often than not. You can't find a better way to present your data to an audience than a chart. A *chart* is simply a visual picture of your data that's easy to relate to, and certainly easy on the eyes. You'll find plenty of tips and tricks in this chapter to help you on your way to charting new chart territory of your own.

A Cornucopia of Charts

Before we jump in and start making charts, I need to tell you about the various chart types. You can create literally dozens of different charts in Excel. For example, the simple pie chart can be expressed in two ways—you can create regular pie charts or exploded pie charts. Each pie chart can spin off variations in design, such as 3D effects. Sometimes it's not easy figuring out which chart type works best with your data.

To give you an example, take a look at the following figure. In this spreadsheet, I'm tracking monthly Elvis sightings over the course of two years. The pie chart (the chart on the left) shows the sightings for 1997. The entire pie shows the entire year's sightings, and each piece of the pie represents a month's sightings. The column chart (on the right) shows the data for 1998's sightings. This time, each month is depicted as a column, and you can see the rise and fall of the frequency of sightings across a year's worth of time.

Here's an example of two charts depicting similar data.

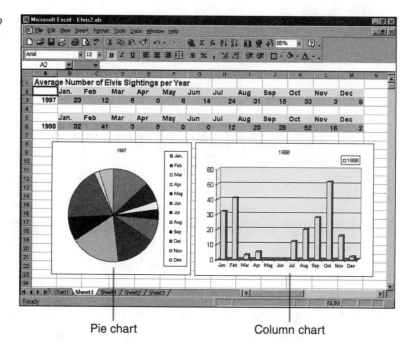

Pie chart   Column chart

Now, what if I had entered my data differently on the worksheet, and what if I compared the two years of sightings side by side (compared the data series)? The next figure shows a line chart doing just that. See how the presentation of data differs from the examples shown in the previous figure? As you can see, different chart types work better for different data series.

To help you make heads or tails of chart types, let's go over each major type and find out which kind works best for each type of data:

➤ **Column charts** When you're comparing data in two or more categories, or when you need to show changes over time, column charts work well.

➤ **Bar charts** A bar chart is similar to a column chart, but bars display the data horizontally instead of vertically.

➤ **Line charts** Again, a line chart is similar to a column chart, but instead of bars, the data is depicted in a series that looks like a connect-the-dots drawing (take a look at the following figure to see an example of a line chart). This chart type is great for showing changes across time.

242

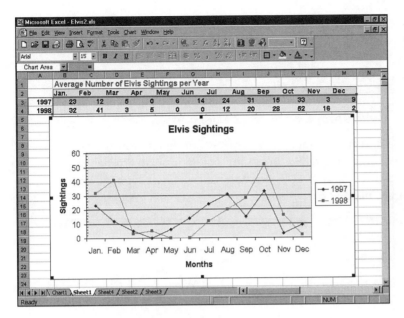

Here's an example of a line chart comparing two data series.

➤ **Pie charts** If you need to show percentages of a whole, you can't go wrong with a pie chart. You can use several styles, including 3-D, which shows the pieces of the pie in 3D.

➤ **Scatter charts** Use a scatter chart to show correlations between two value sets—one on the y-axis and the other on the x-axis.

➤ **Area charts** If you need to show changes over time, an area chart will help emphasize the individual contribution of each data part.

➤ **Doughnut** Use a doughnut chart to compare multiple series, much like a pie chart, but for several series instead of one.

➤ **Radar** A radar type lets you depict separate axes for each data category, radiating out from the center. It looks like a spider's web, in essence.

➤ **Surface** Use a surface chart to show how three sets of data interact. It's good for showing patterns.

➤ **Bubble** A bubble chart is a lot like a scatter chart, but bubble charts use three columns of data, and each data point indicates a third dimension.

➤ **Stock** As the name implies, you can use a stock chart to track stock market activity.

Cylinders, Cones, and Pyramids

Another way to make regular column and bar charts more interesting is to use 3D cylinders, cones, and pyramids instead of columns or bars to depict your data. You find these options at the bottom of the Chart Type list box in the first Chart Wizard dialog box.

Jumping In with the Chart Wizard

The easiest way to make a chart is to use Excel's Chart Wizard. The Chart Wizard walks you through the steps necessary for creating a chart. Want to try it? Then follow these steps:

1. Start by selecting the data you want to turn into a chart. Be sure to include any labels along with the data (such as column and row headings for the data). Excel recognizes the labels and turn them into labels on the chart.

2. Next, click the **Chart Wizard** button on the Standard toolbar or open the **Insert** menu and select **Chart**. This starts the Chart Wizard.

3. The first thing you need to do is select a chart type, as shown in the figure below. Scroll through the Chart Type list box to view the various types. When you select a chart type, the sub-type's list on the right displays a variety of chart styles for that particular category.

The Standard Types tab in the Chart Wizard dialog box invites you to select a chart type.

Choose a chart type here.

Choose a sub-type here.

Click here to preview how your data will look using the chart type you selected.

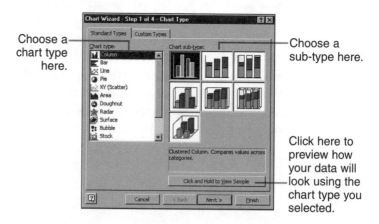

4. When you see a chart type you want to make, click it and then click **Next** to continue.

5. The next wizard box, shown in the following figure, lets you verify the data range. If you selected your data before starting the Chart Wizard, the range you specified is indicated. If you haven't selected your chart data, do so now. Click the **Collapse** button in the Data Range field and select the data on your worksheet (click the **Expand** button to expand the dialog box again).

Preview It!

To see how your selected chart type will look using the data you specified, click and hold the **Click and Hold to View Sample** button in the first Chart Wizard dialog box (see the previous figure).

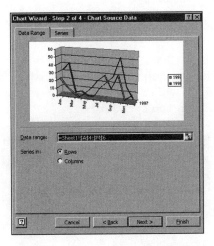

The Data Range tab in the Chart Wizard dialog box lets you verify the data change and check the series orientation.

6. Depending on your chart data, you may need to change the orientation for the series. If you choose **Rows**, each row of data in your selected range is treated as a data series. If you choose **Columns**, each column becomes a data series. The sample view at the top of this wizard dialog box lets you know immediately which series orientation is correct for the chart type you're creating.

Finished Now?

You can click the **Finish** button at any point during the Chart Wizard walkthrough, and the chart is immediately placed on your worksheet as is. To exit the Chart Wizard without inserting a chart, click the **Cancel** button.

7. After you've got the data range and series orientation cared for, click **Next** to continue.

8. Use the next sets of tabs in the Chart Wizard dialog box to set chart options (see the next figure). For example, you can enter titles, add gridlines, add a legend, and more. Check out the options on each tab, making any changes as needed. Click **Next** to continue.

The third wizard box to appear has a series of tabs with options for adding titles, a legend, and more.

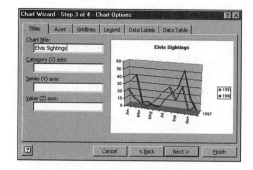

9. The final Chart Wizard dialog box, Chart Location, shown in the following figure, lets you choose to insert the chart onto the active worksheet or onto its own sheet in the workbook (which will be labeled **Chart1**, unless you enter another name). Make your selection and click **Finish**.

The fourth and final Chart Wizard dialog box, Chart Location, lets you choose a location for the chart.

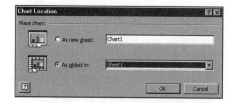

What About the Series Tab?

For more controls pertaining to your data series, click the **Series** tab in the second Chart Wizard dialog box. The options here let you add or remove a series, change a series, or name a series.

Excel inserts the chart as directed. In the next figure, I created a 3D line chart showing the two years' worth of Elvis sightings side by side for comparison. The selected chart, like any other object you add to a worksheet, is surrounded by selection handles (see Chapter 13, "Getting Graphic," for more information). To resize the chart, drag a handle. To move the chart, hover your mouse pointer over the chart until the pointer takes the shape of a four-sided arrow pointer; then drag the chart to a new location on the worksheet.

246

Title

Here's an example of a 3-D line chart.

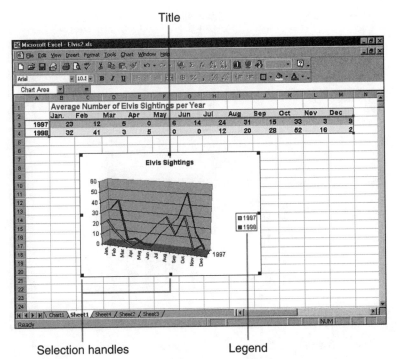

Selection handles   Legend

If, after creating your chart, you decide you don't like the chart type you specified, you can try another. If you right-click the selected chart, a shortcut menu appears with chart commands. Select **Chart Type** to reopen the first Chart Wizard dialog box, where you can choose another chart type.

You can also open the **Chart** menu and select **Chart Type**. The Chart menu appears only when a chart is selected on the worksheet.

The Lowdown on Chart Parts

So, you've created a chart. Now is a good time to familiarize yourself with your chart's parts, especially if you want to learn how to format your chart in Chapter 17, "Formatting Charts." As you can see from the following figure, a typical chart has many parts. When you're editing the chart, you can select each individual element and make changes.

➤ **Legend**   A guide to the data series on your chart. The legend tells what each series represents.

➤ **Chart title**   A headline for your chart.

➤ **Plot area**   The background of your chart, where the actual chart is drawn.

Learn the chart parts now so you can format them later.

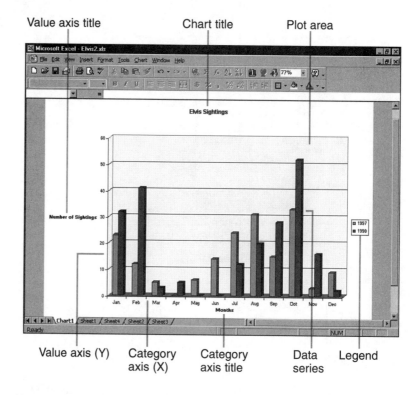

Value axis title   Chart title   Plot area

Value axis (Y)   Category axis (X)   Category axis title   Data series   Legend

➤ **Value axis**   The axis listing values for the data series; in the previous figure, this is the y-axis.

ScreenTips Galore

You can hover your mouse pointer over various chart elements to find out what they are; a ScreenTip appears, identifying the chart part.

➤ **Value axis title**   A headline identifying the value axis.

➤ **Category axis**   The axis listing categories for the data series; in the previous figure, this is the x-axis.

➤ **Category axis title**   A headline identifying the category axis.

➤ **Data series**   The data you're plotting on the chart. In the previous figure, this is the two years' worth of Elvis sightings data.

Naturally, you can make changes to any part of your chart, which you learn how to do in the next chapter. Now, at least you know what each part is.

248

The Least You Need to Know

➤ You can create a variety of chart types as well as dozens of sub-types in Excel, so you're bound to find something you like.

➤ Be sure to select a chart type that makes the best use of your data.

➤ The easiest way to create a chart is to use Excel's Chart Wizard tool.

➤ After you create a chart, you can go back and change the chart type whenever you like.

Chapter 17

Formatting Charts

In This Chapter

➤ Find out how to put the Chart toolbar to use

➤ Learn how to format chart elements by using the Format dialog box

➤ Discover tips for adding new chart elements

To really expand your chart smarts, you need to learn how to format your charts. You can change the way your chart's parts appear just as you can change the way data (text and numbers) and graphic objects appear in your worksheet. Most users feel the need to fine-tune their charts before printing them or passing them on to others. For example, you might want to set a new chart title or change the background color used to plot the chart. In this chapter, I show you how to change your charts by using the Chart toolbar and the Format dialog box.

Using the Chart Toolbar

Immediately after you insert a chart into a worksheet, the chart appears selected (surrounded by selection handles) and the floating Chart toolbar is displayed. This toolbar has shortcut buttons for making changes to the chart and the various chart elements.

As a floating toolbar, the Chart toolbar can be dragged around the screen or summarily closed whenever you don't need it anymore. When you click anywhere outside the chart, the toolbar disappears as well. If the toolbar doesn't appear on your screen, open the **View** menu and select **Toolbars**, and then **Chart** (or you can right-click a blank area of any toolbar and choose **Chart**).

Table 17.1 explains each of the Chart toolbar buttons and how you can use them.

Table 17.1   Chart Toolbar Buttons

Button	Function
Chart Title ▼	Use this drop-down list to select which chart element you want to edit.
🖺	Opens the Format dialog box for making changes to the selected chart element.
▣	Opens a palette of chart types to choose from.
▤	Turns the legend information on or off.
▦	Inserts a data table containing the worksheet data you based the chart on.
▤	Displays the data series by row.
▥	Displays the data series by column.
⤫	Angles text downward.
⤪	Angles text upward.

Because a typical chart is made up of several elements, you can select each one individually to make changes to that particular element. One way to select a chart element is to simply click it. For example, to change the chart title, click it. The chart title is now surrounded by selection handles, as shown in the following figure.

You can select individual chart elements by clicking them.

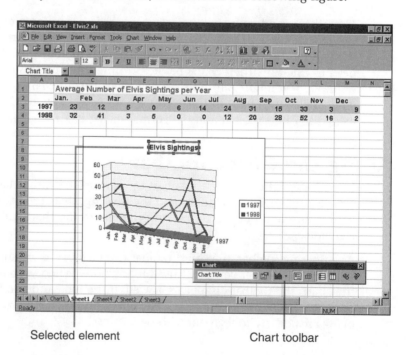

Selected element   Chart toolbar

To edit the chart title text, click again to place the cursor in the text box. Now you can make changes to the existing text or enter new text. Click outside the text box to deselect the chart element.

Objects Are Objects

Chart elements are objects just like graphic objects on a worksheet. They can be selected, resized, moved, and formatted. You can use the same skills you learned in Chapter 13, "Getting Graphic," to handle chart elements.

Another way to select chart elements is to use the **Chart Objects** drop-down list on the Chart toolbar. The next figure shows the list displayed. As it turns out, some chart elements aren't so easy to select on the chart because they're too small or layered with other chart elements. Thankfully, the **Chart Objects** list can help you out.

Click here to display the list.

Use the Chart Objects drop-down list to help you select individual chart parts.

Depending on the chart type you're working with, the elements displayed in the **Chart Objects** list vary. Rest assured, however, that it shows you every element that makes up your particular chart.

After you select an item from the **Chart Objects** list, it appears selected on your chart. You can now make changes to the element.

Changing the Chart Type

One of the most radical changes you can make to a chart is to change the chart type. Perhaps you don't like the way your column chart turned out and want to try some 3D effects, or maybe you want try another chart type altogether. For a quick change, click the **Chart Type** button on the Chart toolbar, as shown in the following figure. A palette of chart types appears. Click another type to apply it to your chart data.

The Chart Type button displays a palette of chart types.

Click here.

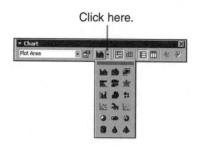

If you're looking for greater variety of chart types to choose from, use the **Chart** menu instead. Open the **Chart** menu and select **Chart Type**. This opens the Chart Type dialog box, as shown in the following figure. This box should look vaguely familiar—it resembles the first Chart Wizard dialog box. From the **Chart Type** list box, select a new chart type to use; from the **Chart Sub-type** box, choose another sub-type to use. A description of the selected type appears below the sub-type area.

Use the Chart Type dialog box if you want a greater variety of selection.

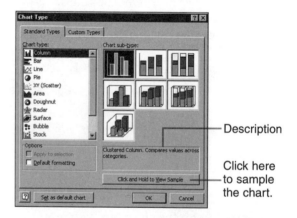

Description

Click here to sample the chart.

To see how the type and sub-type selections will look, click and hold the **Click and Hold to View Sample** button. You'll see a preview of how your data looks using the new chart type and sub-type. If you like what you see, click **OK**, and the new chart type is applied.

Formatting with the Format Dialog Box

If you want to fine-tune your chart elements, the Format dialog box is the way to go. Like the Format Cells dialog box you learned about in Part 3, "Worksheet Grooming," the Format dialog box offers one-stop shopping for all your chart part-formatting needs. The name of the dialog box will vary slightly depending on the particular chart item you're formatting. For example, if you select the category axis to format and display the Format dialog box, its name is Format Axis, as shown in the next figure. If you select the data series to format, the dialog box is called Format Data Series.

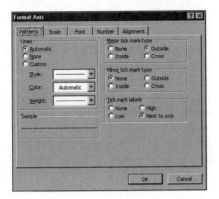

The Format dialog box changes its name based on the chart element you select.

Depending on the item you select, the Format dialog box will present different chart options. The next figure shows the Format Data Series dialog box. Notice it has different tabs than the Format Axis dialog box shown in the previous figure.

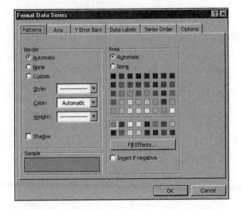

The Format dialog box offers different formatting options based on the chart element you select.

To display the Format dialog box for the element you want to format, first select the chart element and then use any of these methods:

➤ Click the **Format Object** button on the Chart toolbar.

➤ Right-click the selected element and choose **Format** *object* (*object* being the name of the element you've selected).

➤ Open the **Format** menu and choose **Selected** *object* (again, *object* being the name of the element you've selected).

Explore the various tabs and options available for the chart objects you select.

Data Series

If you're charting data from more than one row or column, each row or column is distinguished by a different color or pattern on the chart, called data points. Each color or pattern is a data series.

Formatting Colors, Lines, and Patterns

An easy modification you can make to any chart element is to change its color, line style, or pattern. With the Format dialog box open for the object you want to edit, click the **Patterns** tab. For example, in the following figure, I want to change the background color used for the plot area. To select a new color, just click a color in the color palette. The **Patterns** tab for this chart part also has options for changing the border; you can make it thicker or give it a new color. After making changes in the Format dialog box, click **OK** to apply them to your chart.

In this figure, the plot area is selected, and I'm changing the background color using the Patterns tab.

Click a new color.

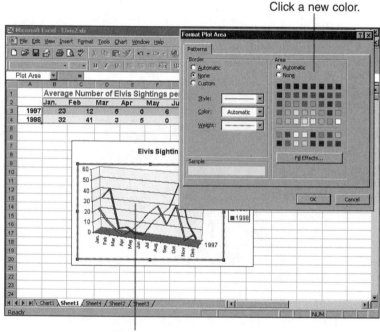

Plot area

To find a pattern to apply, open the Fill Effects dialog box, as shown in the next figure (click the **Fill Effects** button on the Patterns tab in the Format dialog box). The Fill Effects dialog box has numerous options for setting background patterns, textures, and gradient effects. You can even turn a picture file into a chart background. The following figure shows the **Gradient** tab options. These options let you create a one- or two-color gradient effect, which shades the background from one color or grayscale to another color.

256

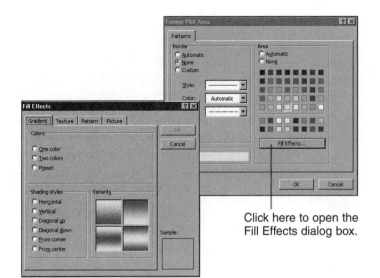

Use the Fill Effects dialog box to assign special background effects to your chart.

Click here to open the Fill Effects dialog box.

One of my favorite background effects is to assign a professional-looking texture. Click the **Texture** tab in the Fill Effects dialog box to discover what's available (see the following figure). Click the texture you want and then click **OK** to apply it.

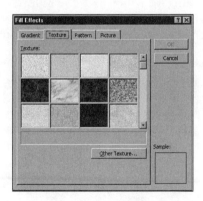

The Texture tab has lots of great background textures you can try.

Be careful, though! The background effects you apply to your chart may compete with your chart data. It doesn't do you any good to use a whiz-bang texture background if you can't see the chart data anymore. Just use good judgment when assigning fill effects to charts.

When changing line styles used in your chart, you have the choice of changing the style (such as dashed, dotted, or solid), color, or line weight (how thick or thin the line is). The next figure shows the Format Gridlines dialog box. To change any line option, click the appropriate drop-down arrow and select a new option from the list box. Click **OK** to exit and apply your changes to the selected chart item.

257

When changing lines, you can change style, color, and line weight.

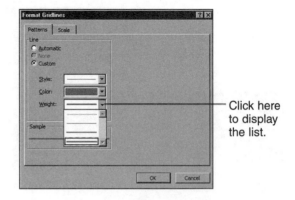

Click here to display the list.

Formatting Axes

Axes are an important part of your chart. To make them more meaningful to your audience, consider doing a little fine-tuning. For example, you can change how tick marks are displayed or how they are labeled. You can even get rid of them altogether. You'll find options for controlling the tick marks on the **Patterns** tab in the Format dialog box.

To control the range of values or how the category axis lists those values, click the **Scale** tab (see the next figure). Depending on which axis you're formatting, you'll see options for controlling the gridline units, reversing the order of categories or values, and other settings. Be sure to check them all out. Click **OK** to apply any changes to your chart.

Use the Scale tab when formatting an axis to change settings such as gridline units.

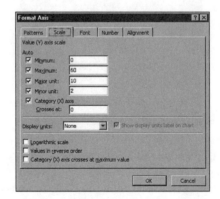

Formatting the Data Series

To control how your data series displays on the chart, open the Format Data Series dialog box (see the following figure). Here you'll find options for controlling colors, lines, the gaps between the series, and more. The options will vary in this dialog box based on the chart type you're using.

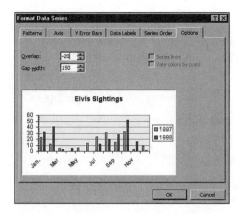

Change your data series using the Format Data Series dialog box.

For example, click the **Options** tab to find options for controlling how the data series displays. Use the **Overlap** control to change the amount that each series overlaps the one next to it. A positive number means the series overlaps; a negative number means there's space between the series. In the previous figure, I've set the overlap to –20. Use the **Gap Width** box to control the amount of space between categories.

If you're working with a line chart, the options on this tab will allow you to control colors for the line points, set drop lines (which show the minimum value for each marker), and set high/low lines (which show the spread between high and low values).

Adding New Chart Elements

What if you want to add more parts to your chart? Well, what's stopping you? You can add text labels, callouts (arrows and text that identify parts or portions of your chart), legends, and so on. Of course, you don't want to clutter your chart with too many elements; just remember that the data still has to be easily read and understood at a glance.

For example, if you chose not to create a legend for your chart while creating the chart with Chart Wizard, you can always add one now. Click the **Legend** button on the Chart toolbar. If you don't like where it's placed, drag it to a new position.

When creating a chart, the Chart Wizard creates labels for your title and axes, but you can change them. Select the label text box and edit the text. If you didn't set labels during the creation process, you can always add them later. With the chart selected, open the **Chart** menu and select **Chart Options**. This opens the Chart Options dialog box, as shown in the next figure. Click the **Titles** tab and enter any labels you want to create.

259

Use the Chart Options dialog box to change labels, titles, and more.

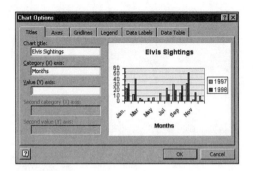

Adding a Free-Floating Label

Another way to add a text box to your chart is to click the chart and start typing. The text is entered into the Formula bar. As soon as you press **Enter**, the text becomes a free-floating text box on the chart. You can now move, resize, or format the text as needed.

Adding callouts to a chart can help point out important trends or notable peaks and lows. To add a callout to your chart, follow these steps:

1. Display the Drawing toolbar (right-click a toolbar and select **Drawing** or open the **View** menu and select **Toolbars**, **Drawing**).

2. Click the **Line** button or the **Arrow** button, depending on exactly what kind of callout you want to create (a plain line or one with an arrow).

3. Draw a line on the chart where you want the callout placed.

4. To add a text box to the callout, click the chart and enter the callout text. Press **Enter** when you're finished. Now you can resize and move the text box next to the callout and format the text as needed. You can select, resize, and move the arrow also.

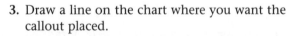

Drawing Recap

For a recap on how to use the Drawing toolbar tools, check out Chapter 13, "Getting Graphic."

The following figure shows an example of a callout used on a chart.

I drew an arrow...   ...then I typed in callout text.   *Here's an example of a callout on a chart.*

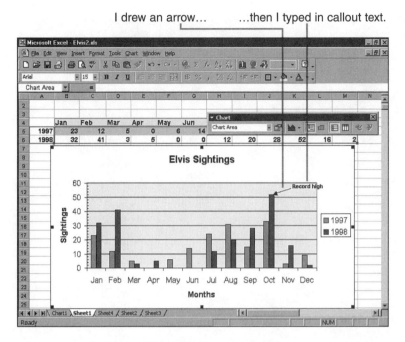

That about wraps up chart formatting. There are obviously a lot of different things you can do to your chart elements—too many to cover in this book. Take time to explore the available tools on your own and see what kind of effects you can create.

The Least You Need to Know

➤ The Chart toolbar has some useful tools for fiddling with your chart elements.

➤ For greater formatting options, use the Format dialog box.

➤ Chart elements are treated as objects, just like graphics. You can move and resize them as needed.

➤ If you don't like your chart, try another chart type.

➤ You can add new elements to your chart to help explain the chart data.

261

Chapter 18

Map It Out

In This Chapter

➤ Learn what a map chart is and how it's used

➤ Find out how to create your own map charts

➤ Create your own pin maps

Just when you thought we had covered everything chart-related, here's another topic. I must tell you, though, this one's pretty nifty. Did you know you can make map charts using Excel? Well, you can. I show you how in this chapter. Prepare to have some fun.

All About Map Charts

Another type of chart you can create with Excel is a map chart. Microsoft Map is a program that comes with Excel that you can install and use to chart geographical data. For example, you can turn regional data, such as regional sales numbers, into a map chart that clearly shows what's happening in each region.

With map charts, you can see at a glance how data compares between states, regions, or countries. You can take any kind of region-based data (such as state statistics or state-based sales figures, for example), population statistics, or anything else you can chart geographically and turn the data into a map chart.

The Microsoft Map feature is actually an add-in program; it's a module that contains a database of maps and demographic data. Microsoft Map includes maps of the

United States, Canada, Europe, Asia, Mexico, Australia, South America, North America, the UK, and more.

If you haven't installed the Microsoft Map add-in, take a moment and do so now. Insert your Excel CD-ROM into the CD-ROM drive. If AutoInsert notification is turned on, you'll see the Maintenance Mode dialog box. Select the **Add or Remove Features** button; then locate the **Microsoft Map** feature (you'll find it listed in the Excel folder) and select it for installing. Click the **Update Now** button, and the feature will be installed.

Creating a Map Chart

To use the map module, the data you chart needs to be geographical in nature. For example, if you're tracking division sales across the United States, the first column of data you want to chart should include the geographical data (that is, the names of the states or regions). Geographical data can include cities, states, or countries.

In the map example I'm going to show you, I'm tracking Elvis sightings recorded for each state during a three-month period, so my worksheet data lists each state, as shown in the next figure.

In this worksheet, I'm tracking statistics for each state.

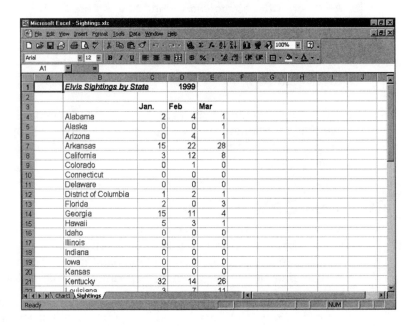

Ready to try this map thing? Then follow these steps:

1. Start by selecting the worksheet data you want to chart.

2. Click the **Map** button on the Standard toolbar.

3. Your mouse pointer changes to a crosshair symbol. Drag a chart shape on the worksheet where you want the chart to appear (see the following figure).

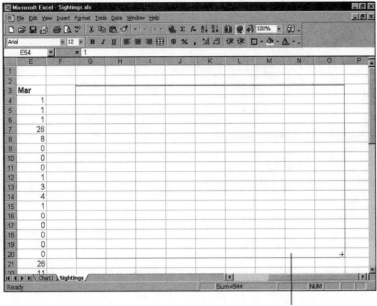

Draw where you want the map chart inserted.

Map chart shape

4. Release the mouse button after drawing the chart shape, and the Microsoft Map program stirs into action. It checks its database of maps to see which map would be most appropriate. If more than one map is applicable, you see a dialog box similar to the one shown in the next figure.

Select the map you want to use. In this case, you're asked whether you want to include Alaska and Hawaii or just show the continental United States.

5. Choose the map you want to use and click **OK**.

6. The map appears on the worksheet. The first column of data values is displayed on the map, along with the Microsoft Map Control dialog box (see the next figure).

The map chart appears along with the Microsoft Map Control dialog box.

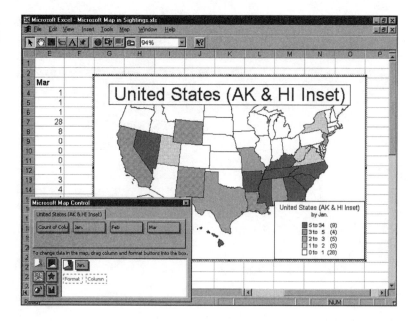

Notice that the Map toolbar replaces the other Excel toolbars at the top of the program window.

No Data? No Problem!

You don't have to have geographical data on your worksheet to use Microsoft Map. You can make maps without data—just click the **Map** button and choose a map from the Unable to Create Map dialog box. Click **OK**, and it's inserted onto your worksheet.

The Microsoft Map Control dialog box can be used to view different data columns on the map or to change the map format. For example, by default, the map shows the first column of data using the **Value Shading** format, which simply means the shading on the various map areas represents data values. To view another column of data, drag the column from the top of the box to the control box (the white box in the middle), as shown in the following figure. Each column of data appears as a button at the top of the Microsoft Map Control dialog box. Drag the column you want to view to the empty white box, and the map changes to show that column's data values.

You can easily change which column of data is displayed on the map by dragging that column heading into the control box.

Format buttons   Control box   Now I'm displaying the data values for February on the map.   Columns

You can drag various columns on or off the control box, or you can assign different formats using the format buttons. The format buttons determine how data is plotted on the map. Table 18.1 explains each of the format styles you can use on the map.

Table 18.1   Microsoft Map Control Buttons

Button	Format
	Applies light shading to the map to represent data values
	Applies colorful shading based on data categories
	Displays dot density formatting for data values
	Displays graduated symbol formatting for data values
	Displays values as pie charts
	Displays values as column charts

The next figure shows the data for the month of March displayed as dot density on the map.

267

I changed the formatting to show dot density on the map.

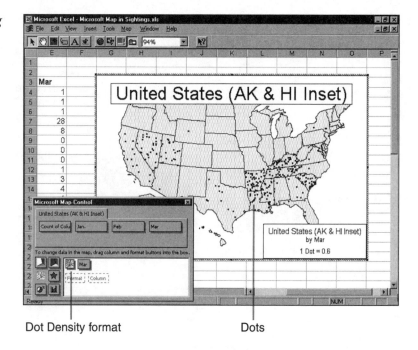

Dot Density format   Dots

In addition to the Microsoft Map Control dialog box, you'll also find a toolbar of map controls at the top of your program window. Table 18.2 explains what each control does.

Table 18.2   Map Toolbar Buttons

Button	Function
	Use the Select Objects button to point to and select objects on the map.
	The Grabber tool lets you adjust the map onscreen by dragging it.
	Use the Center Map button to designate a center point on the map.
	The Map Labels button lets you create text labels on the map.
	Click the Add Text button to enter text directly on the map.
	Use the Custom Pin Map button to spotlight areas of your map.
	Click the Display Entire button to display the entire map in the chart space you designated.

Button	Function
	After you make changes to the map, click the Redraw Map button to redraw the map.
	After you make changes to the spreadsheet data used in the map chart, click the Map Refresh button to update the map.
	Turns the Microsoft Map Control dialog box on or off.
94%	Use the Zoom button to set a zoom percentage to view your map.
	Opens the Help feature for the map chart.

When you click outside the selected map chart, you're returned to your worksheet, and the familiar toolbars appear onscreen again. To reselect the map chart, double-click it. This reopens the map tools, and you can once again make changes to the map display.

 When you change the data on the spreadsheet, be sure to update the display on the map chart. Click the **Map Refresh** button on the Map toolbar to update the map.

Moving Around Your Map

Once you've got your map chart created, you're probably wondering how you can move around or view different portions of the map. To move around the map chart, use any of these methods:

 ➤ Click the **Grabber** tool and drag to reposition the map.

 ➤ To center the map inside the parameters, click the **Center Map** button.

 ➤ To select a map item (such as a title or legend), click the **Pointer** button and then click the map item.

➤ To zoom your view, click the **Zoom** drop-down list and either choose a percentage or type one in.

Deleting the Map Chart

To rid your worksheet of a map chart, select it (don't double-click it or else you open the map tools) and then press **Delete**.

Changing the Map Features

You can enhance your map by choosing to view cities, roads, and airports. To do so, right-click the map and choose **Features** from the shortcut menu, or you can open the **Map** menu and select **Features**. This opens the Map Features dialog box, as shown in the next figure.

Use the Map Features dialog box to turn on highways, cities, and other map display features.

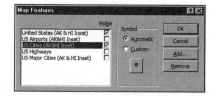

The Map Features dialog box shows a list of features already attached to your selected map, such as highways, surrounding countries, cities, and so on. Scroll through the list box to see what's available. To turn a feature on, click it to add a check mark in its box. To turn a feature off, deselect it. Click **OK** to exit the dialog box.

To add other features, such as additional cities, airports, and so on, click the **Add** button within the Map Features dialog box, or you can open the **Map** menu and select **Add Feature**. Select the type of feature you want to include and click **OK**. To remove a feature from the Map Features dialog box, select it in the list box and click the **Remove** button.

Adding Labels to Your Map Chart

To add your own labels, click the **Map Labels** button on the Map toolbar. This opens the Map Labels dialog box, as shown in the following figure. Choose which map feature you want to label. Click the **Map Feature to Label** drop-down arrow to choose an included feature (such as roads or cities) from the list. You can also select one of the **Create Labels From** options to create labels from your data. Make your selection and click **OK**.

Use the Map Labels dialog box to help make your data easily interpreted at a glance.

As soon as you exit the dialog box, your mouse pointer becomes a crosshair. You can now drag over the map to create your labels. Use the crosshair pointer icon to drag a text box, and then enter your label text.

The next figure shows data value labels added to each state with an Elvis sighting for January. Each data label is an object on the map chart, just like any other chart element. You can select and move labels around the chart.

For example, in the following figure, I dragged a tiny text box over each shaded state to create a label with that state's number of Elvis sightings.

270

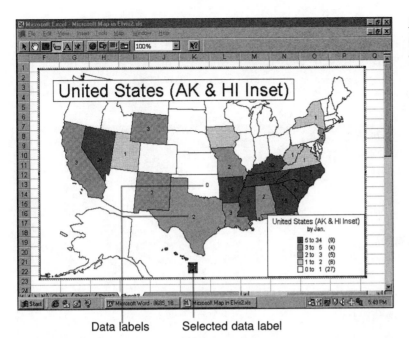

In this figure, data labels have been added to the shaded states.

Data labels   Selected data label

Create a Pin Map

Here's something handy. You know those bulletin board maps some people hang in their offices and fill with little pushpins marking important places? Well, you can create your own electronic version using Microsoft Map. You can use it to mark sales offices or places you've been; you can even print it out and pass it around.

To create your own pin map, follow these steps:

1. Open a worksheet but don't select any data.

2. Click the **Map** button on the Standard toolbar.

3. Draw an area on the worksheet where you want to insert a pin map.

4. From the Unable to Create Map dialog box, choose a map and click **OK**.

5. After your map is created, click the **Custom Pin Map** button on the Map toolbar. This opens the Custom Pin Map dialog box, as shown in the following figure.

Use the Custom Pin Map dialog box to create a pin map name.

6. Enter a name for the map and click **OK**.

7. The mouse pointer becomes a pushpin. Everywhere you click the map, a tiny pushpin icon is left behind, as shown in the next figure.

8. To turn off the pushpin pointer, click the **Custom Pin Map** button again on the Map toolbar.

Teeny-tiny pushpins appear everywhere you click the map.

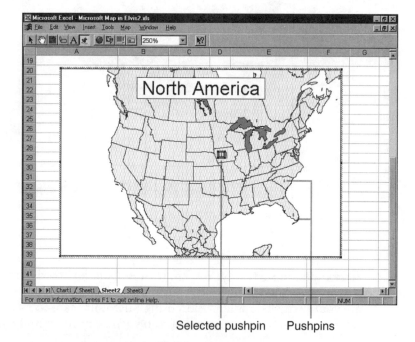

Selected pushpin   Pushpins

The Least You Need to Know

➤ Map charts can help you display your data geographically.

➤ Use the Microsoft Map add-in to turn your geographically based data into instant map charts.

➤ Use the Microsoft Map Control dialog box to change your map data and formats.

➤ Create your own pin map and fill it with pushpins marking your favorite locations.

Part 5

Building and Analyzing Databases

Pssst, over here. Want to learn how to turn Excel into a database tool? Yes, I said database. *Sure, most people think of Excel only as a spreadsheet program, but you can use it to create databases, too. If you want, I'll tell you how. Mind you, this kind of information isn't for everyone. But you seem trustworthy, and I think you'll use Excel's database powers for good, not evil. Right? Raise your right hand and repeat after me: "I will use Excel's database powers only for good and will manipulate my data for truth, justice, and strict organizational purposes only." Okay then, I have many things to teach you about this subject. Let's get started.*

OOOOH...

Chapter 19

Build Your Own Excel Databases

In This Chapter

➤ Find out just what's involved with building a database

➤ Learn database lingo to impress your friends

➤ Create your own database with minimal fuss

➤ Learn two different ways to enter database data

Many people buy database programs, such as Access, that are made especially to organize and manipulate lists of data. But you don't need a whiz-bang database program if you're using Excel. Excel can act like a database program, too, when you want it to. This chapter will explain database basics and how to use Excel to create your own databases.

The Dirt on Databases

Ever work with a database before? Believe it or not, you encounter databases every day. Do you look at a TV guide to plan out the evening's prime-time viewing (such as finding out whether *ER* is a repeat or a new episode)? A TV guide is a database of program listings. Do you ever need to look up a number using the phone book? A phone book is a database of telephone numbers. Or how about using the Rolodex on your desk? Same thing. Do you fill out your checkbook register when you write a check? It's a database, too. Do you check the paper to see how your stocks are performing? You guessed it; that's a database as well. Are you using a recipe for dinner tonight? Is it from a cookbook? Database again.

Databases are everywhere. Essentially, a *database* is a collection of related information, typically in list form. For example, do you keep a record of the addresses of your friends and family? That would be considered an address database. The key to using a database is the way in which the information is organized. In the example of an address database, you might organize your list of names and addresses in the following manner:

```
Last name    First name    Address    City    State    Zip code
```

So, when you make out your list of addresses, the best organizational approach is to write each person's address in the same format. There's a column for last name, first name, address, city, state, and zip code. Your list of addresses might look something like this:

```
Sechrest, Shawn, 1900 Cloud Drive, Bloomington, IL 61701
Willard, Dave, 1325 Ritchey Drive, Marion, IL 62959
Farmer, Scott, 8080 Hillcrest Rd., Denver, CO 80094
```

When you buy an address book at the store, it's typically arranged in the same fashion. It has preset columns for each part of the address, with rows to enter the individual addresses.

But what about an electronic database? As it turns out, it's arranged in the same manner as a paper database. Take a look at the next figure.

Here's an example of an address database created by using an Excel worksheet.

Last Name	First Name	Address	City	State	Zip
Cannon	Melissa	1325 Ritchey Dr.	Kewanee	IL	63939
Cannon	Joshua	394 E. Elm	Fishers	IN	46599
Cannon	Jacob	2001 Lionway	Fishers	IN	46599
Cannon	Doug	304 W. Chestnut	Vincennes	IN	47589
Willard	Pat	808 Hill Ct.	Marion	IL	62959
Willard	Dave	714 S. Chestnut	Marion	IL	62959
Willard	Mima	2004 North View	Marion	IL	62959
Sechrest	Shawn	1901 Cloud St.	Bloomington	IL	61701
Farmer	Scott	416 Hoover	Bloomington	IL	61701
Loving	Greg	807 Vale Drive	Bloomington	IL	61701
Loving	Kelly	30090 Jeremiah Dr.	Champaign	IL	63293
Howell	Teresa	715 Armadillo Ct.	Dallas	TX	79803
Toliver	Steve	9490 Main, Apt. B	Pinedale	WY	80934
Crosson	Tim	4080 Music Blvd.	Kansas City	KS	32920
Sechrest	Stacey	1032 Pine Drive	Raleigh	NC	20394
Janese	Jay	90 East Main	Mt. Vernon	IL	65940
Farmer	Bob	808 Toad Hill	Marion	IL	62959
Farmer	Rita	808 Toad Hill	Marion	IL	62950
Sechrest	Mildred	987 Aspen Way	Breckenridge	CO	79043

Excel's worksheet structure makes it perfect for organizing database data. The columns define the different parts of the address entries, and the rows are used to actually enter each person's address information.

Database Lingo

Time to learn the database lingo. (You knew this was coming, didn't you? You'd better memorize these terms, because I've heard rumors that there's a test at the end of the book.) Here are the basic components of a database:

➤ **Fields** The columns you use to break down your database list into manageable pieces. Fields categorize each part of the database record.

➤ **Records** The rows you use to enter each database entry; each row represents one record in the database.

➤ **Tables** The entire database collection of information is considered a table.

In the example of an address database, the categories for last name, first name, address, city, state, and zip code are all *fields*. Each is represented as a column in the database table. Individual entries are *records*, a complete row of data with each field filled in. The next figure shows each of these elements labeled on a database table.

Here's a breakdown of each database element.

After you have a database, you can perform several kinds of actions on it. For starters, you can keep adding more records to it, or you can delete old records. You can also sort the existing data. For example, in the address database, you might sort the records alphabetically based on the last name field. You can also filter the database to show only the records for a particular zip code, for example.

Relational Versus Flat Databases

If you've worked with database programs in the past, you're probably familiar with relational databases and flat databases. If you haven't, I'll explain the two. A *flat database* is a two-dimensional database, which simply means you see rows and columns on your screen that organize the data. This is the kind of database you can create in Excel. A *relational database*, on the other hand, lets you store lots of different tables or files that are in some way related (hence the name *relational*). This setup allows for a third dimension of data—the relationship. You can create relational databases only in database programs, such as Access or Paradox.

Planning Is Everything

Before you build a database, you should spend a bit of time planning it out. Good planning can alleviate having to reorganize your database later when you find out you left off important fields and such. Decide what kind of data you want to store and how it should be organized. Each table should have a topic (such as addresses or product inventory). Determine what actions you want to perform on the data and think about what information you want to extract from the database.

The following are a few things to consider:

➤ Most databases are comprised of several columns, so plan on at least two or more columns or fields.

➤ Don't combine fields. Instead, try to break data out into separate fields. For example, in an address database, it's not very helpful to combine the city and state fields into one. For sorting purposes, the database would be more useful if these two related items were two separate fields.

➤ It's not a good idea to have more than one database table on a single worksheet. Things can get a bit confusing performing filters when there's more than one database on a sheet.

➤ Decide in what order you want to enter data, which fields come first, and so on.

➤ When building your database, use a different font or size for your field labels as opposed to the font and size used for the record data. That way, you can easily see what your fields are because they're easier to read.

➤ No blank rows allowed. It's a database rule.

Techno Talk

Filters

You can choose to display only certain records in your database by filtering out records that don't contain the data you want to view. For example, in an address database you can choose to view only the records with the zip code 90210 by filtering out the records that don't have this data in the Zip Code field. Learn more about filters in Chapter 20, "Manipulating Your Data."

When planning your database, keep in mind that for all the data you enter, you can extract bits and pieces of it later.

Let's Build One Already!

Okay, okay. Hold your horses. Have you planned out your database first? If so, then follow these steps to start building your own Excel database:

1. Open a worksheet and click where you want the first column. (You can choose to build your database anywhere in the worksheet.)
2. Enter a field label, as shown in the following figure.

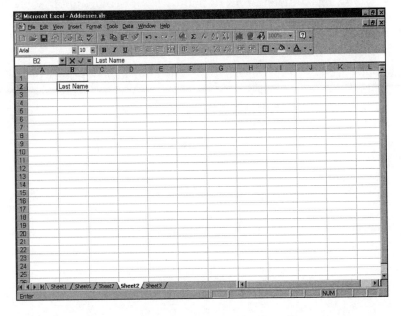

Choose a column for the first field and enter the field label.

3. Press **Tab** and enter the next field label.

4. Continue entering as many fields as you need. After typing the last field label, press **Enter**. Your worksheet will resemble the one shown in the following figure.

Here's an address database ready for entries.

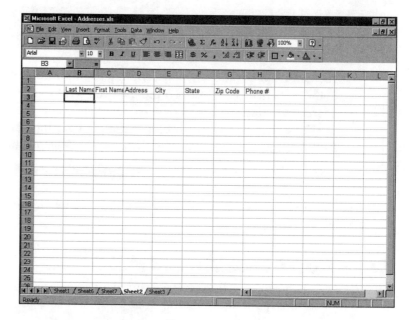

Now you can start entering records or make any adjustments to the column widths. Don't forget those worksheet structure formatting skills you learned in Chapter 12, "Rearranging Your Worksheet Data." For example, you ought to make your field labels stand out in some way. Try using a different font or point size, or perhaps apply some bold formatting. You should also resize your columns so your field labels are easily read. Take a look at my address database after I applied a little bit of formatting (see the next figure).

There are two ways to enter records into your database. The following sections will explain each.

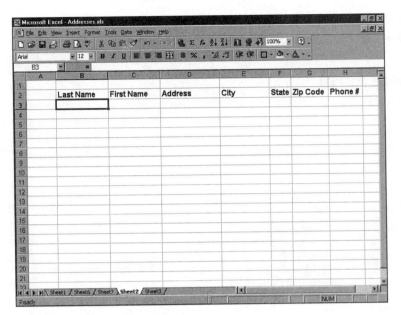

With a little formatting, my database already looks good.

Entering Records Directly

One way to enter records is to type them directly into the database table. Click inside the first row below the column fields and enter your first record. Use the **Tab** key to move from field to field. When you reach the last field in the table, press **Enter** to start a new record. The following figure shows several records recorded this way.

Records

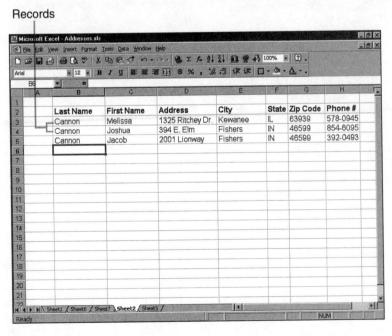

You can enter records directly into the database table just like any other Excel data.

You can't have any blank rows between the column fields and the first record. If you do, Excel won't know that the records and the fields go together.

Using a Database Form

Another way to enter database records is to use a form. Forms provide a handy way to enter records. This is particularly helpful if someone else is doing the data entry tasks for your database table. By using a form, you're less likely to enter the wrong information into a field. This is particularly true as the table grows and you can no longer see the column labels.

Freeze Your Field Labels

Way back in Chapter 4, "The Wonderful World of Worksheets," you learned how to freeze panes or sections of your worksheet. If you're working with a large database, you can freeze your field labels so they always appear at the top of the work area. To do so, click in the row directly below the labels, open the **Window** menu and choose **Freeze Panes**. (To undo a freeze, open the **Window** menu again and choose **Unfreeze Panes**.)

To create a database form, use these steps:

1. Click any cell in the row beneath your field labels; then open the Data menu and choose **Form** (see the next figure).

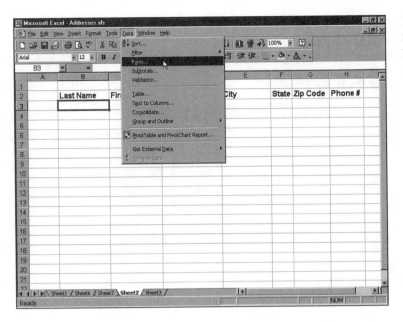

The Data menu has commands you can use when working with an Excel database.

2. If your database has no records yet, a prompt box appears alerting you to yada, yada, yada (it's just not that important). Click **OK** to continue (see the following figure).

Just click OK to move on.

3. The next box that appears is the data entry dialog box (see the next figure).

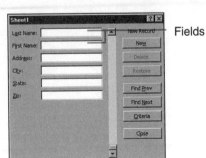

Fields

The data entry dialog box is customized to your database. A text box appears for each field you labeled.

4. Start entering data for each field. You can click inside each text box, but it's easier to just press **Tab**.

5. To start a new record, press **Enter** or click the **New** button (see the following figure).

*When one record is complete, click **New** to start another.*

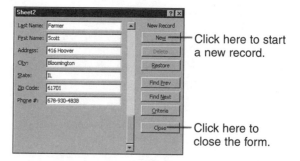

Click here to start a new record.

Click here to close the form.

6. Notice that the spreadsheet behind the dialog box shows the records you enter (see the next figure). When you're finished, click the **Close** button.

The database table behind the form shows the records you've entered.

Records already entered

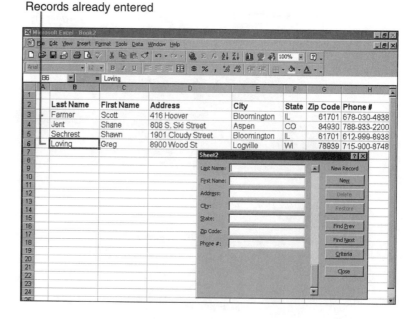

Navigating Records

To move back a record in the form, click the **Find Prev** button. To move forward again, click **Find Next**. To remove everything in the current record, click the **Delete** button. To undo changes in the current record displayed, click the **Restore** button.

You don't have to fill up your database table in one session. You can open it up at a later time (provided you've saved it) and use the form all over again to enter new records.

You can edit your records directly in the database table just like you edit any other Excel data, or you can reopen the entry form dialog box and navigate to find the records you want to edit. Make your changes and close the form.

Don't Forget to Save

Just a reminder: You ought to save your database after you create it, even if you haven't finished entering records. Use the **Save** button or open the **File** menu and choose **Save** command to save the file.

The Least You Need to Know

➤ A database is just an organized collection of data.

➤ Some common databases include those you create for organizing names and addresses or those you create for keeping track of inventory.

➤ In the big picture, a database is a table comprised of columns and rows.

➤ All database items are organized into fields (columns).

➤ Every entry in a database is a record (row).

➤ Use database forms to enter records into your table or simply type each record in directly.

Chapter 20

Manipulating Your Data

In This Chapter

➤ Find out how to manipulate database data

➤ Learn how to perform a sort without breaking a sweat

➤ Discover tips for filtering your data and finding the information you need

After you've compiled a database, you can start manipulating the data. You can sort, filter, and extract just the portions of data you want to see. Trust me, this is going to be fun…at least as fun as things can get with a database. Don't expect amusement park fun or anything—just fun with data.

I've Got a Database—Now What?

In all sincerity, a table of data really isn't that useful, even if it does look neat and tidy. What can you possibly do with it, aside from print it out and look at it? It's a static thing, in and of itself. Thankfully, Excel has some super tools for putting a bit of life into your database tables. These tools involve searching your database and extracting data.

Take a moment and think about what types of data you want to extract from your database. For example, if you have an inventory database that lists each item's price, you might want to extract all the items that are $24.99. By *extract*, I don't mean you destroy your hard-built table of data, but rather choose to view certain portions of it.

Perhaps your inventory database lists the on-hand quantity of each item. You can apply a filter to your table so it shows only products that have extremely low quantities on hand. That way, you can focus on items you know you need to restock.

Here's another example: Let's say you have an address database and want to send out a sales announcement to all your customers in a particular state. Rather than tediously look through your database to find the addresses you need, you can filter your table to show only the addresses for that particular state.

Not only can you filter your database table, but you can easily rearrange its data, too. For example, back to that address database. Perhaps you entered the records randomly in no particular order, but you want to reorganize the table alphabetically. No problem. You can sort the entire table and show the records in alphabetical order. Cool, huh?

Excel's data tools can really breathe some life into your plain old database tables. Want to see how for yourself? Then keep on reading.

Subtotal Your Data

To quickly create a subtotal for a column of sorted data in your database and enter the number into your database, click the column where you want to create subtotals and then open the **Data** menu and choose **Subtotals**. This opens the Subtotal dialog box. Use the **At Each Change In** drop-down list to specify the field by which you want to subtotal (only one field allowed). In the **Use Function** drop-down list, choose the SUM function. Use the **Add Subtotal To** list to choose the fields to subtotal (choose as many as you want). Finally, click the **Summary Below Data** check box and then click **OK**. To remove the subtotals, reopen the **Data** menu and choose **Subtotals**; then click the **Remove All** button.

A Sorting We Will Go

One of the easiest things you can do to a database table is to sort it. You can choose to sort your data by any field in the database. In the address database, for instance, you can sort the table by the State field. Or how about sorting by city, or even by zip code? Want to give it a try?

To sort a field in ascending order (top to bottom), follow these steps:

1. Click in any cell in the column you want to sort. For example, to sort by state in an address database, click inside the **State** field, as shown in the following figure.

Click in the field you want to sort.

Start by choosing a field to sort.

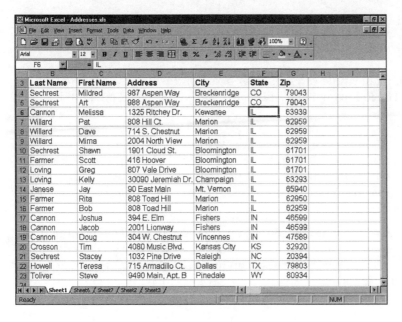

2. To sort the field alphabetically from A to Z or numerically from 1 to whatever, click the **Sort Ascending** button on the Standard toolbar.

3. Excel sorts your table alphabetically or numerically, based on the data type in the field you selected. The next figure shows the results of the sort by state.

	B	C	D	E	F	G	H	I
3	**Last Name**	**First Name**	**Address**	**City**	**State**	**Zip**		
4	Sechrest	Mildred	987 Aspen Way	Breckenridge	CO	79043		
5	Sechrest	Art	988 Aspen Way	Breckenridge	CO	79043		
6	Cannon	Melissa	1325 Ritchey Dr.	Kewanee	IL	63939		
7	Willard	Pat	808 Hill Ct.	Marion	IL	62959		
8	Willard	Dave	714 S. Chestnut	Marion	IL	62959		
9	Willard	Mima	2004 North View	Marion	IL	62959		
10	Sechrest	Shawn	1901 Cloud St.	Bloomington	IL	61701		
11	Farmer	Scott	416 Hoover	Bloomington	IL	61701		
12	Loving	Greg	807 Vale Drive	Bloomington	IL	61701		
13	Loving	Kelly	30090 Jeremiah Dr.	Champaign	IL	63293		
14	Janese	Jay	90 East Main	Mt. Vernon	IL	65940		
15	Farmer	Rita	808 Toad Hill	Marion	IL	62950		
16	Farmer	Bob	808 Toad Hill	Marion	IL	62959		
17	Cannon	Joshua	394 E. Elm	Fishers	IN	46599		
18	Cannon	Jacob	2001 Lionway	Fishers	IN	46599		
19	Cannon	Doug	304 W. Chestnut	Vincennes	IN	47589		
20	Crosson	Tim	4080 Music Blvd.	Kansas City	KS	32920		
21	Sechrest	Stacey	1032 Pine Drive	Raleigh	NC	20394		
22	Howell	Teresa	715 Armadillo Ct.	Dallas	TX	79803		
23	Toliver	Steve	9490 Main, Apt. B	Pinedale	WY	80934		

In this example, I've sorted my table alphabetically based on the State field. Can you tell the difference between this figure and the previous one?

289

Now try a descending sort:

1. Click in any cell in the column you want to sort. For example, to sort by product ID in an inventory database, click inside the **Product ID** field, as shown in the following figure.

Click in the field you want to sort.   Choose a field.

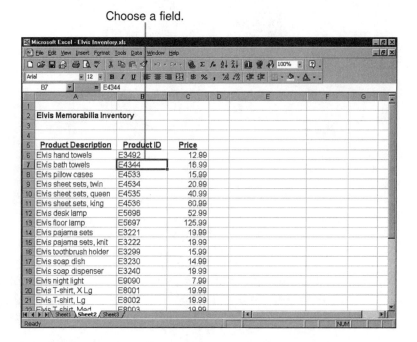

2. To sort the field alphabetically from Z to A or numerically from the highest number to the lowest, click the **Sort Descending** button on the Standard toolbar.

3. Excel sorts your table in descending order based on the data type in the field you selected. The following figure shows the sort results based on a product ID sort.

 Here's something important to remember: When you perform a sort, the original order of records is replaced with the sort order. If you don't want this order to remain permanent, click the **Undo** button after you're done using the **Sort** command. If you want to retain the sort and the original data order, consider saving the sorted table as a new file.

Are you looking for a more sophisticated sort, one that sorts your data by more than one field? Then you need the super-duper **Data**, **Sort** command. This command opens the Sort dialog box where you can sort up to three fields at a time. To employ this method of sorting, follow these steps:

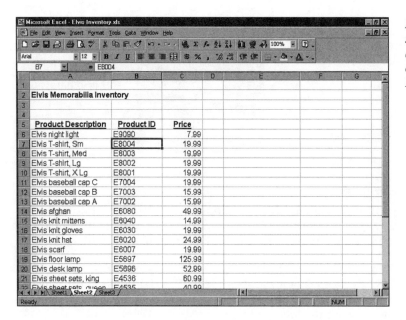

In this example, I've sorted my table in descending order numerically, based on the Product ID field.

1. Open the **Data** menu and choose **Sort**. This opens the Sort dialog box, as shown in the figure below.

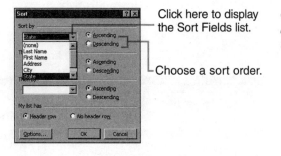

Click here to display the Sort Fields list.

Choose a sort order.

*Click the **Sort By** drop-down arrow and choose the first sort field.*

2. Click inside the first **Sort By** text box and choose the primary field to sort by. Click the drop-down arrow to select from a list of all your database fields.

3. Indicate whether you want to sort the field in ascending or descending order.

4. Select the second field you want to sort by using the **Then By** drop-down arrow (see the following figure).

5. Again, choose to sort the field in ascending or descending order.

6. If you want to designate a third sort field, click the second **Then By** drop-down arrow and choose a third field. Then choose which order to sort by: ascending or descending.

7. Make sure the **Header Row** option is selected at the bottom of the dialog box so that your column labels aren't included in the sort.

8. Click **OK**. Excel sorts your table in the order you requested.

291

To specify a second field to sort by, use the Then By text box.

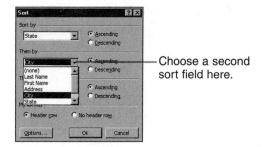

Choose a second sort field here.

Pass Me That Filter

A filter is a little different than a sort. When you apply a filter to your database, you're choosing to view only portions of your data, not the entire table. In effect, you're pulling out the important parts to look at and leaving the rest hidden.

The first step in filtering is deciding what data you want to extract. For example, you might want to filter your inventory database to show only certain prices or product names. You might want to filter an address database to show only the addresses from a particular state or city. You get the idea, right?

To perform a filter, use these steps:

1. Open the **Data** menu, choose **Filter**, and then **AutoFilter**. As soon as you do, your field labels suddenly have drop-down arrow buttons, as shown in the next figure.

When you perform a filter, use the field labels to select which fields to filter.

Filter arrows

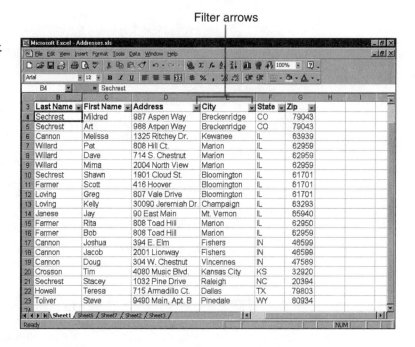

2. Click the drop-down arrow of the field you want to filter (see the following figure). A list of filter options appears.

Click here.　　　　　　　　　　　　　　　*Select the type of filter.*

	B	C	D	E	F	G	H	I
3	Last Name	First Name	Address	City	State	Zip		
4	Sechrest	Mildred	987 Aspen Way	(All)	CO	79043		
5	Sechrest	Art	988 Aspen Way	(Top 10...)	CO	79043		
6	Cannon	Melissa	1325 Ritchey Dr.	(Custom...)	IL	63939		
7	Willard	Pat	808 Hill Ct.	Bloomington	IL	62959		
8	Willard	Dave	714 S. Chestnut	Breckenridge	IL	62959		
9	Willard	Mima	2004 North View	Champaign	IL	62959		
10	Sechrest	Shawn	1901 Cloud St.	Dallas	IL	61701		
11	Farmer	Scott	416 Hoover	Fishers	IL	61701		
12	Loving	Greg	807 Vale Drive	Kansas City	IL	61701		
13	Loving	Kelly	30090 Jeremiah Dr.	Kewanee	IL	63293		
				Marion				
				Mt. Vernon				
				Pinedale				
				Raleigh				
				Vincennes				
14	Janese	Jay	90 East Main	Mt. Vernon	IL	65940		
15	Farmer	Rita	808 Toad Hill	Marion	IL	62950		
16	Farmer	Bob	808 Toad Hill	Marion	IL	62959		
17	Cannon	Joshua	394 E. Elm	Fishers	IN	46599		
18	Cannon	Jacob	2001 Lionway	Fishers	IN	46599		
19	Cannon	Doug	304 W. Chestnut	Vincennes	IN	47589		
20	Crosson	Tim	4080 Music Blvd.	Kansas City	KS	32920		
21	Sechrest	Stacey	1032 Pine Drive	Raleigh	NC	20394		
22	Howell	Teresa	715 Armadillo Ct.	Dallas	TX	79803		
23	Toliver	Steve	9490 Main, Apt. B	Pinedale	WY	80934		

3. Choose the filter type you want to apply:

   To filter your database based on certain data in a field, select the data from the list.

   Choose **Top 10** to display the 10 most-repeated items for this field.

   Choose **Custom** if you want to customize your filter (more about this later).

4. After you make your selection, the database is filtered. For example, in the following figure, I filtered my address database to show only records with the Bloomington entry in the City field.

Print It!

While your data is filtered, take this opportunity to print it out as a report. You can also save the filtered data as another workbook file.

You can filter again, if you want. The filter arrows on the fields you've already filtered appear in color so you know which fields you've worked with so far.

To redisplay all the records again, click the filter drop-down arrow on the field you filtered and select **All**. You can also open the **Data** menu, choose **Filter**, and then **Show All**.

Here are the results of a filter to show the entries containing a particular city in my database.

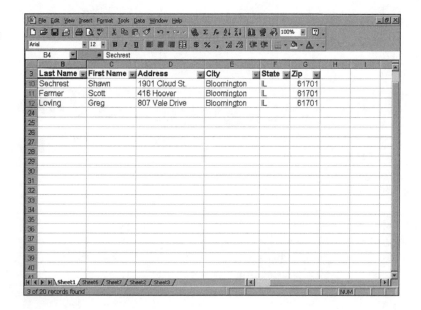

Custom Filters

Excel's Custom AutoFilter feature lets you define filter criteria, such as whether the field data is equal to or greater than another field or other specified data. To open the Custom AutoFilter dialog box for specifying filter criteria, click the filter drop-down arrow of the column you want to filter and then choose **Custom** from the list.

The Least You Need to Know

➤ A sort lets you reorganize your database table.

➤ A filter lets you bring out pertinent data and hide the rest.

294

Chapter 21

All About PivotTables

In This Chapter

➤ A full explanation of the use of PivotTables

➤ Learn useful PivotTable lingo

➤ Create your own PivotTables with the PivotTable Wizard

➤ Find out how to analyze your PivotTable data

Here's a topic unduly avoided by most Excel users—PivotTables. Sounding like some sort of obscure European sport, PivotTables can be intimidating and mind-numbing to many users. I caution you now; they're not for the faint of heart. So, who are they for? For people who want to analyze more complex data. Lest I frighten you off before I even get started, let me assure you that PivotTables are excellent tools for gauging different viewpoints of your data and looking beyond the surface. If you dare to master them, PivotTables can put you leaps and bounds ahead in data analysis. Therefore, don't let their seemingly complex name and function put you off. There's a lot you can do with PivotTables, as you're about to learn.

What's a PivotTable?

You won't find a better tool for analysis than Excel's PivotTables. PivotTables allow you to ask certain questions of your data to help you see beyond the obvious. Although PivotTables present your data in a tabular display, you can summarize different fields in different dimensions. If you have a pair of 3D glasses on hand, now is the time to put them on.

For example, the following figure shows an example of a sales order table describing products, quantities ordered, dates, amounts, buyers, and salespersons (which you can't quite see in the far-right column).

The bigger your spreadsheet, the harder it is to analyze.

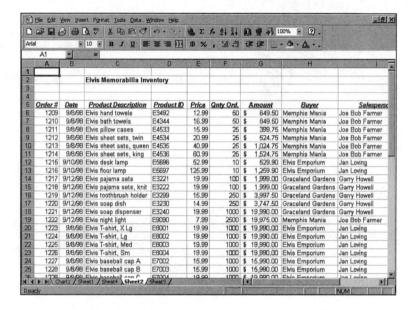

Here are some possible questions I might have regarding this data:

➤ What are the total sales for each product, and what items are the top sellers?

➤ Which salesperson has the most sales?

➤ Which buyer buys the most product?

➤ What product mix does each salesperson sell the most of?

➤ Who are the top 10 buyers?

➤ Who are the top 10 salespeople?

➤ What are the top 10 products?

➤ Who sold the most of what product on a given day?

Those are just a few of the analysis points I might want to glean from my database. Of course, I could spend hours examining my data, scrolling through the list, printing it out, reading it over, and trying to pull out the information I'm looking for to find answers for my questions. But why do all that when Excel's PivotTables can do it all in a second or two?

Suppose I want to find out which product the buyers are buying and the quantities of each. It's not going to be easy looking through my big old database and picking out which buyer is buying what product and in what quantity.

296

Now take a look at the next figure. This figure shows a PivotTable summarizing buyers and which products they're purchasing and in what quantities. From this table, I can see how many Elvis afghans the Memphis Mania buyer ordered. Can you see how this gets to the heart of my question?

Here's a PivotTable at work. It shows how much of each product has been ordered by the various buyers and at what cost.

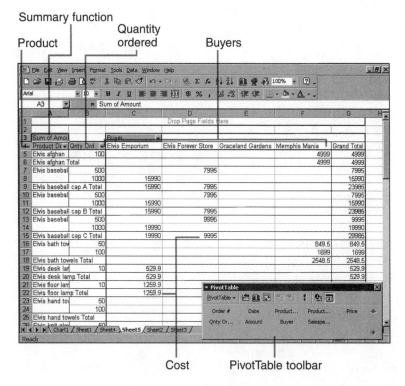

Summary function

Product

Quantity ordered

Buyers

Cost   PivotTable toolbar

Here's an example of an even simpler table, this time summarizing how much each salesperson has sold (see the next figure). As you can see from the figure, Jan's making a killing for us. Go, Jan, go.

Hopefully, you can begin to understand how PivotTables help you analyze data from your database tables in lots of different ways. Both of the PivotTable examples I showed you were derived from the giant database of sales orders back in the first figure.

Like every other wild and wacky computer feature, PivotTables have their own lingo (here we go again). Before you venture much farther into PivotTable territory, stop and review these terms:

➤ **Row field**   A PivotTable field that summarizes data across rows. (In the previous figure, **Product Description** and **Qnty Ord** are the row fields.)

➤ **Column field**   A PivotTable field that summarizes data across columns. (In the previous figure, **Buyer** is the column field.)

A simple PivotTable showing two fields— salespeople and amount sold.

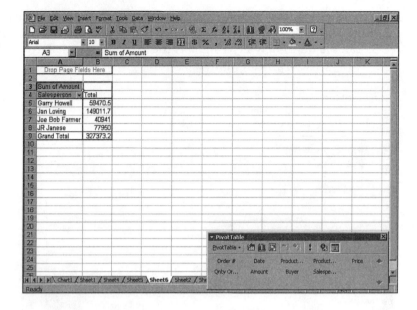

➤ **Page field**   You can break out individual fields into separate pages, called *page fields*, and view the data one field or record at a time.

➤ **Data area**   The middle area of a PivotTable where the actual data appears. (In the preceding figure, the data area shows sales totals.)

➤ **List**   The database table that's the basis for all your PivotTables. (The first figure shows the list on which the PivotTables in the second and third figures are based.)

➤ **Summary functions**   The calculations Excel performs on the values in the data area of the PivotTable.

➤ **PivotTable control**   When you designate fields to use in your PivotTable, the row and column labels become buttons, called *controls*, on the PivotTable.

Have another look at yet another PivotTable example—this time with the terms you just read about pointed out for you in the figure (except for *list*; you saw the actual database list back in the first figure). In the following figure, I'm analyzing how much each salesperson sold to each buyer on the date indicated in the page field area (9/8/98).

Granted, these terms still don't mean much to you now, but by the end of this chapter, you'll know what they refer to.

Row
field   Summary function   Page field

Column field   PivotTable control buttons

This figure identifies parts of the PivotTable.

Data area

Creating Your Own PivotTable

If your head's spinning right now, don't worry. PivotTables only seem complicated—wait until you see how they really work. For starters, the PivotTable Wizard will walk you through the procedure for creating a PivotTable. Shall I tell you how to use it? Follow these steps:

1. Click inside the database list from which you want to create a PivotTable. To show you how things work, I'm going to use the example of the inventory database list you saw in the first figure in this chapter.

2. Open the **Data** menu and choose **PivotTable and PivotChart Report**.

3. The first of three wizard dialog boxes appears onscreen, as shown in the next figure.

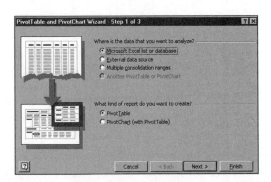

Use the first PivotTable wizard dialog box to designate your data source and PivotTable report.

299

4. At the top of the wizard box, indicate the location of the data you want to analyze. Because we're focusing on your Excel database list, which happens to be selected by default, you don't have to choose anything. However, if you're using another database, this is where you tell Excel.

5. At the bottom of the wizard box, indicate the type of report you're creating. Again, we're focusing on PivotTables here, so make sure the **PivotTable** option is selected (which it is, by default).

6. Click **Next** to continue.

7. Use the second PivotTable wizard dialog box, shown in the following figure, to verify your data list range. If you clicked inside the database before opening the wizard, the range appears in this dialog box. If the range is incorrect, you can enter the correct range. Be sure to include column labels in the range.

Use the second PivotTable wizard dialog box to designate your data range.

8. Click **Next** to continue.

9. In the final PivotTable wizard box, shown in the next figure, you can choose to insert the PivotTable as a new worksheet in your workbook or on the current worksheet. It's a good idea to place it in a new worksheet, which Excel will create for you, to avoid confusion.

Use the final PivotTable wizard dialog box to designate where you want the PivotTable placed.

10. Click **Finish**, and the new, empty PivotTable opens (see the next figure).

Changing Field Names

If too many of your fields are named similarly, you can change their names in the PivotTable. Right-click over the field and choose **Field Settings** from the shortcut menu. Enter a new name in the **Name** text box and click **OK**.

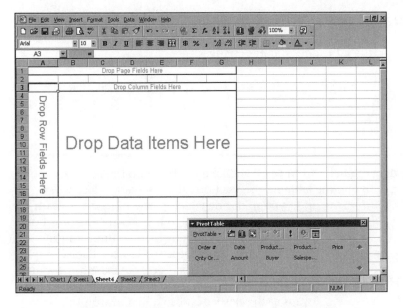

Wow, a brand-spanking-new PivotTable. What do you suppose you can do with this?

Analyzing with Your PivotTable

Now the real creating starts. Dragging and dropping are the primary actions used in making a PivotTable. You drag fields off the PivotTable toolbar and drop them on the table where you want them to go. The PivotTable toolbar has quite a few tools you can use, as explained in Table 21.1.

Table 21.1   PivotTable Toolbar Buttons

Button	Description
PivotTable ▾	Reveals a list of PivotTable commands.
	Formats your table. Click it to open an AutoFormat box and then choose a table format.
	Opens Excel's Chart Wizard feature and turns the table into a chart.
	Reopens the PivotTable Wizard so you can make changes to your original settings.
	Hides the selected field's data.
	Displays the hidden data.
	Refreshes the table and updates changes.
	Opens the PivotTable Fields dialog box, where you can change the summary function.
	Hides the fields.

To build your table, drag the fields from the PivotTable toolbar onto the table. As you can see in the following figure, the table has instructions about what to place where. It's up to you to decide which pieces of data you want to analyze. Just because all your fields are columns doesn't mean they have to remain as columns in the PivotTable. You can choose to view the data as rows. For example, in my sales orders database list, I want to see how much each salesperson sold to each buyer. I want each salesperson listed in a row on the PivotTable, so I'm going to use the Saleperson field from the PivotTable toolbar as my row field on the PivotTable. I want to see each buyer in a column, so I'm using the Buyer field as the column field. The quantity of sales (Amount field) will appear in the middle (data area) of the PivotTable. To do create the PivotTable described, here's the steps I would follow:

AutoFormats?

If AutoFormats sound familiar to you, we covered them back in Chapter 11, "Formatting for Fun or Profit." Flip back to Chapter 11 to learn more about AutoFormats.

1. I drag the **Salesperson** field over to the **Drop Row Fields Here** area of the table and drop it in place. The following figure shows what the table looks like after this action.

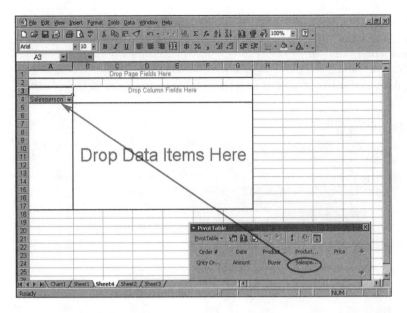

To build your own PivotTable, drag and drop fields onto the table where you want them to contribute to the analysis.

Drag and drop.

2. I drag the **Buyer** field over to the **Drop Column Fields Here** area and drop it in place. The next figure shows what the table looks like after I drop the field in place.

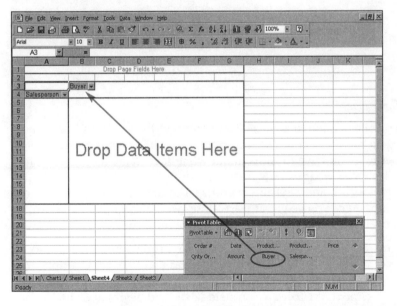

You can drag and drop as many fields as you want to analyze.

Drag and drop.

3. I drag the **Amount** field over to the **Drop Data Items Here** area (in the middle of the table) and drop it in place. As soon as I drop it in place, my PivotTable is instantly calculated, showing how much each salesperson has sold to each buyer.

303

As you can see from the figure, the instant table includes grand totals, and the summary function used is SUM. Your table won't work unless you drag at least one field to summarize into the data area (the middle of the PivotTable). Once you drag a field to the data area, that's when the PivotTable's calculations kick in. The SUM function is the default calculation, but you can choose other functions as well. You learn how later in this section.

A table is instantly calculated based on the field you drag over to the data area.

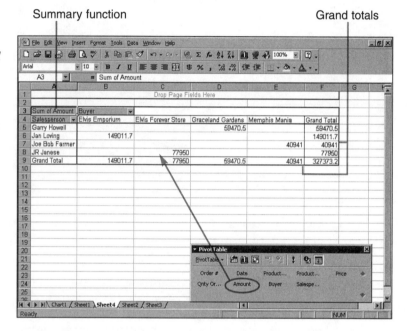

Drag and drop.

Changing the Analysis

The trick to using your PivotTable to analyze data is simply this—drag and drop the fields you want to analyze. That doesn't sound so bad, does it? Of course, there's a little more involved because you have to think about what data elements you want to see in the table and how you want to view them. Anything you drag and drop to the row fields area becomes a row, and anything you drag and drop to the column fields area becomes a column. Once you've got at least those two fields in place, you can then drag and drop exactly what you want to summarize onto the data area.

It takes some experimentation to figure out how your data is plugging in, but once you've got the hang of it, you can change your analysis as you like. For example, to remove a field, drag it off the table. In my new PivotTable shown in the previous figure, for instance, I can remove the Salesperson field label by dragging it right off the table. To add more fields, just drag them from the PivotTable toolbar to the table. As you add and subtract fields and change their position on the table, the data you're looking at "pivots," hence the name *PivotTable*.

You can use the control buttons (remember, when you drag a field onto the table and place it in the row or column area, it becomes a button) to change the data display. For example, you can click the **Salesperson** control button, as shown in the next figure, to reveal a list of salespeople. You can then select which salespeople you want to view or hide in the table display (click the check box next to the name, and then click **OK**). You can do the same with the **Buyer** control button. (Of course, your own control buttons will vary, based on your own database fields.)

If I don't want to see Jan's sales, I can deselect her name in this list.

Click here.

Click a PivotTable control button to specify which field data is displayed.

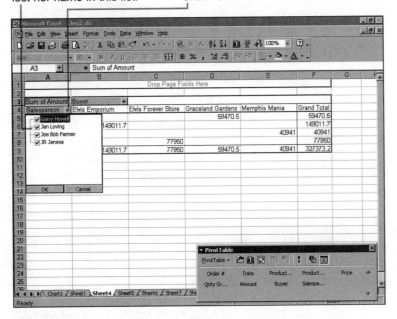

Changing the Summary Function

Now let's play with the data. How about using another summary function? In the previous figure, I totaled sales amounts. But what if I want to average the amount instead? That's easy; click the **Field Settings** button on the PivotTable toolbar. This opens the Field Dialog box, as shown in the next figure.

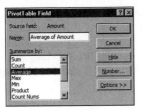

Use the PivotTable Field dialog box to change the summary function.

Use the **Summarize By** list box to choose another function (such as AVERAGE) and then click **OK** to exit the dialog box and apply the calculation to the PivotTable. The following figure shows the AVERAGE function applied. The figure after that shows the COUNT function applied.

The data area changes to reflect the new function.

Average function

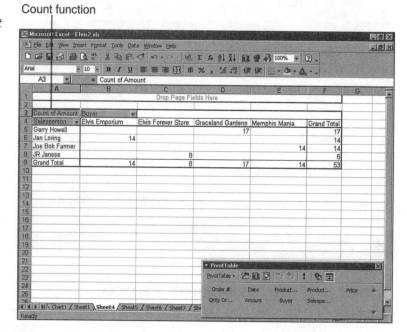

Here, the data area shows how many product items each salesperson sold.

Count function

Using Page Fields

As you're analyzing your data, you'll probably want to break it out sometimes to view separate PivotTables for various records. Use page fields to do just that. If you drag a field up to the **Drop Page Fields Here** area of the PivotTable, the field becomes a control button that you can then use to change the view of the PivotTable.

306

For example, the next figure shows a PivotTable that indicates which products each buyer has ordered. I want to look at each individual sales order in the PivotTable, so I dragged the **Order #** field up to the page fields area and dropped it in place. A click on the page field's drop-down button reveals a list of every order number (see the following figure). To view a particular number in the table, I select it from the list box and click **OK**.

Function Quick Change

To quickly change the summary function, double-click the summary function control to open the PivotTable Field dialog box and select a new function.

Page field   Click here to display the list.

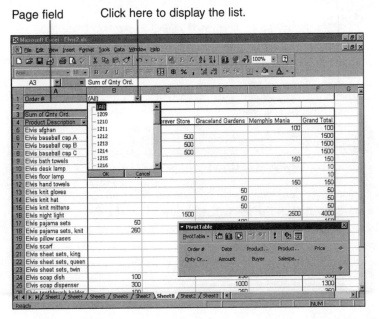

Use page fields to view specific records.

The next figure shows what happens when I select order number 1210. I quickly see that the Memphis Mania buyer has ordered 50 Elvis bath towels. Pretty cool, huh? To display all the records again, open the page field list and choose **All**.

Now I can see what the Memphis Mania buyer purchased in order #1210.

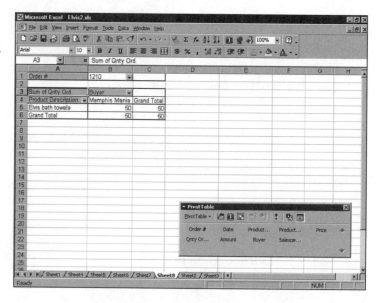

Use Separate Worksheets

To copy a page field view so each record appears on its own separate worksheet, click the **PivotTable** button on the PivotTable toolbar, choose **Show Pages**, and then click **OK**. This places each record's PivotTable on a worksheet; to view the table, click the appropriate worksheet tab. If you have 50 records, you'll add 50 worksheets to the workbook, so be warned.

Grouping PivotTable Items

Another tool to help you view your PivotTable is *groups*. You can group your records or fields to tidy up the PivotTable display. For example, the following figure shows a list of products and buyers and how much of each product was ordered. There's a lot of products to look through.

Now what would happen if I tidy up the product list and group related items in the list? The next figure shows just such an organizational technique applied. This time, you can clearly see the related products and the quantities in which the buyers are purchasing them.

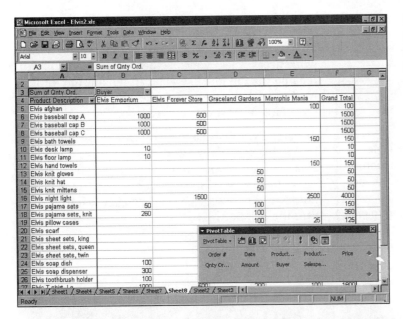

Here's a long list of products that could be organized into meaningful groups.

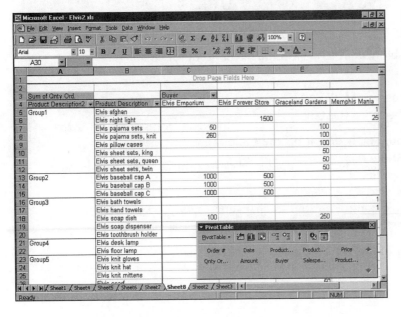

Here's a long list of products now grouped so that related items are together in the table.

To group your own data, select it on the table and then right-click and choose **Group and Outline**, **Group**. To ungroup a group, select it, right-click, and then choose **Group and Outline**, **Ungroup**.

Format It!

To format your PivotTable and print it out as a report, use the AutoFormat tool. Click the **Format Report** button and choose an AutoFormat. Learn more about AutoFormats in Chapter 11, "Formatting for Fun or Profit."

Leaving It All Behind

When you create a PivotTable, it appears on its own worksheet (unless you specified otherwise). You can rename the tab just like you can rename any other worksheet. When you save the workbook, the PivotTable worksheet is saved, too.

As part of your workbook, you can revisit the PivotTable at any time and make changes to your data analysis. If you want to delete the PivotTable, right-click the worksheet tab on which the table resides and choose **Delete**; then click **OK** to confirm the deletion.

The Least You Need to Know

➤ PivotTables are great for examining your data in different ways.

➤ Use the PivotTable Wizard to walk through the steps for creating a PivotTable.

➤ To build and change your PivotTable, drag the field buttons from the PivotTable toolbar onto the table.

➤ To remove a field, simply drag it off the table.

➤ To change the summary function, double-click its control button and choose another function.

➤ Use the PivotTable control buttons to change the way you view your data.

Chapter 22

Seeking with Goal Seek

In This Chapter

➤ Find out what Goal Seek is and whether it can help you find your lost car keys

➤ Learn how to make your worksheet reveal the answer you were looking for

➤ Discover tips for using Excel's scenario tools

Have you ever wanted to figure out how to make Excel show you the answer you want to see? Guess what—you can. Excel's Goal Seek tool helps you figure out how to reach the value you're looking for.

Perhaps you always wanted to know what would happen if you changed a few values here or there? You can utilize Excel's Scenario Manager to help you project what-if scenarios on your data. In this chapter, I explain the secret of using both these tools to analyze your data.

What's Goal Seek?

Goal Seek is exactly what its name implies: a tool to help you find the goal you're looking for. No, I'm not talking about finding your fortune or car keys, or anything like that. Rather, Goal Seek helps you find your way to a specific value in your worksheet.

Goal Seek actually lets you work backward to find where you need to change your input to produce the answer you're looking for. For example, perhaps you're getting ready to buy a car. You know how much you can afford to spend each month on a car payment, but maybe you're not too clear on how much your loan should be for. Goal Seek can help you determine the answer.

Take a look at the following figure. Here's an example of a very simple worksheet with a formula for figuring a monthly car payment using the PMT (payment) function (check out the Formula bar to see the formula). In this figure, I'm thinking about taking out a loan for $10,000 (obviously, I'm buying a used car here). When I run the formula, Excel tells me I can expect a monthly car payment of $243.66.

Here's a formula projecting a monthly car payment.

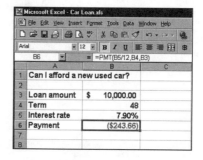

But what if I can't afford that? What if I wanted to pay only $200 a month? The following figure shows what happens when I tell Goal Seek I want to spend only $200 a month. To make this happen, my loan amount must change to $8,208.16. That's apparently all I can afford in a used car. Notice that the formula hasn't changed a bit, but the values in cell B3 and in cell B6 have been altered.

Here's an example of Goal Seek at work, projecting a different loan amount to meet my target payment value of $200 per month.

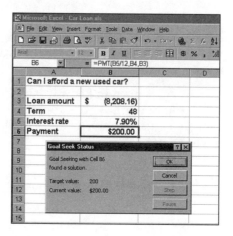

This is just one example. You can use Goal Seek to help you figure how much you need to sell to reach a sales goal, how many units you have to sell before you break even, and so on.

Going One-on-One with Goal Seek

In order to use Goal Seek, you have to have at least one input cell that affects the value of the cell containing your goal.

To use Goal Seek, follow these steps:

1. Select the cell containing the goal you want to change.

2. Open the **Tools** menu and select **Goal Seek**. This opens the Goal Seek dialog box, as shown in the following figure.

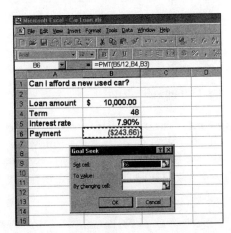

The unassuming Goal Seek dialog box.

3. The cell you selected in step 1 is referenced in the **Set Cell** text box. If you selected the wrong cell, now is the time to fix it before you move on (in other words, you should make any reference corrections now).

4. Click inside the **To Value** text box and enter your goal value, as shown in the next figure.

The next step is to enter your goal.

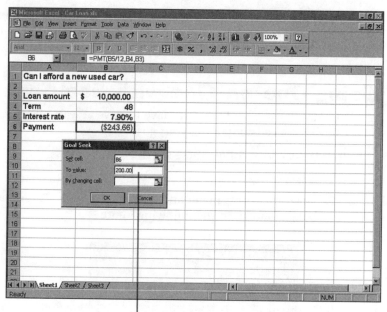

Enter your goal value here.

5. Click inside the **By Changing Cell** text box and enter the cell reference you want to change in order to reach your goal value (see the following figure). You can also click the cell directly on the worksheet. If the Goal Seek box is in the way, drag it out of the way or click the collapse button and then choose the worksheet cell.

Tell Goal Seek which cell value to change in order to reach your goal.

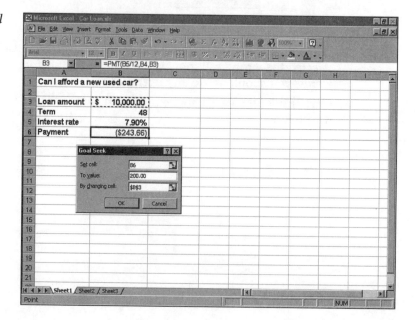

6. Click **OK**. Goal Seek produces a value change to meet your goal (see the following figure).

Here's my answer.

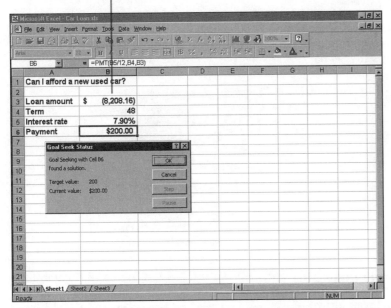

Goal Seek adjusts the worksheet value to help you meet your goal.

Getting Complex with Solver

If you want to figure out more complex answers, use Excel's Solver tool. It works a lot like Goal Seek but uses multiple variables. Solver is an add-in application, so you'll find it under **Add-Ins** in the **Tools** menu. Give it a try. If you need help, tap into the Help system.

The Scenario Scene

Excel's Scenario Manager can help you juggle all kinds of scenarios. You can save your scenarios and recall them when you want to make more changes. A *scenario*, in case you're new to the Excel scene, is a "what-if" speculation you perform on your data. You speculate what would happen to your data if you changed values here or there, or if you introduced a new value. For example, in a sales or inventory report worksheet, you might run a scenario that examines what would happen if you raised product prices or increased shipping and handling. In an employee database, you might speculate on the effects of raises. Get the idea?

To start a scenario, take your existing data and start making changes. Don't worry about messing up your data; the changes won't affect the underlying worksheet. When you've finished creating a scenario, open the **Tools** menu and choose **Scenarios**. This opens the Scenario Manager dialog box, shown in the next figure.

The Scenario Manager dialog box is empty the first time you create a scenario.

To add the new scenario, click the **Add** button. This opens the Add Scenario dialog box, shown in the following figure. Click inside the **Scenario Name** text box and type in a name for the scenario you just created. Use the **Changing Cells** text box to remind yourself which cells you changed to create the scenario.

*Fill out the Add Scenario dialog box and click **OK**.*

By default, the **Comment** text box enters your name and the data you created for the scenario. You can edit or add to the text as needed.

To protect your scenario from any changes, make sure the **Prevent Changes** check box is marked. Click **OK** to exit the Add Scenario box and return to the Scenario Manager dialog box. Notice that your new scenario has been added to the list (see the following figure). The next time you want to speculate with this scenario, open this dialog box, select the scenario name, and click the **Show** button. Now you can speculate all you want.

The scenario is now added to the list of scenarios.

Removing Old Scenarios

To delete a scenario you no longer want to keep, select it in the Scenario Manager dialog box and click the **Delete** button.

The Least You Need to Know

➤ Goal Seek works backward to help you change a value to meet a specific goal.

➤ To speculate how changes affect your data without destroying your data, use a scenario. You can save changes as a scenario and revisit the scenario again and again.

➤ The Scenario Manager dialog box keeps a list of all the scenarios you've saved.

Part 6

Nothing but Net

Ladies and gentlemen, we'll be landing in just a few moments. We hope you've enjoyed our book and will choose to read us again. In these final few chapters, we'll be covering Excel's net-worthy qualities for today's data-sharing world. You'll learn how to share data between programs, use Excel's Internet features, and turn your worksheets into Web pages. Please remain seated with your safety belts on until the chapters have come to a complete stop. Thank you again for flying The Complete Idiot's Guide to Microsoft Excel 2000.

Chapter 23

Integrating Excel with Other Applications

In This Chapter

➤ Learn how to use the new-and-improved Excel 2000 Clipboard feature

➤ Find out the difference between linking and embedding

➤ Learn how to import and export data

➤ Unearth Excel's emailing tools and learn to send your worksheets around the globe

No computer program stands alone these days; they're all built to share data. Excel is no exception. In fact, Excel has always allowed users to share data in all kinds of ways. In this chapter, you learn how to link and embed data and how to import and export data to swap between programs. You can use the knowledge you gain here to share data via email, a network, or just by copying files to disks.

Exploring the New and Exciting Clipboard Toolbar

We touched on moving and copying data way back in Chapter 12, "Rearranging Your Worksheet Data," but it's such an important part of Excel that the topic has popped up again. However, this time, we're going to dive in a bit deeper. I hope you can swim (I have some inflatable water wings you can borrow, if needed).

The fundamental concept of moving and copying data revolves around the ever-familiar Cut, Copy, and Paste commands. These commands are an essential part of every program today. When you move or copy data, you're placing it in a temporary holding area, called the Windows *Clipboard*. In past incarnations of Windows, the Clipboard was a bit limited; you had to immediately paste your cut or copied data or else you risked losing it if you closed the program and turned off the computer. Of particular annoyance was when you accidentally overwrote data on the Clipboard with new data, forgetting you had already cut or copied some data there that you still wanted to use.

Today's Clipboard toolbar (a new feature that's part of all Office 2000 programs, including Excel) can hold up to 12 cut or copied items, and you can choose when to paste each one. I'll show you an example. In the following figure, I'm getting ready to paste some data from one worksheet to another. As soon as you copy (or cut) more than one item, the Clipboard toolbar immediately opens onscreen. As you can see in the figure below, I copied various pieces of data to the Clipboard, which show up as icons in the floating Clipboard toolbar. To find out which icon represents which data, hover your mouse pointer over the icon. A ScreenTip will appear that identifies the data by the first few words or numbers of the data item. To paste the data, click the icon representing the data you want to paste.

It's Still There!

To close the Clipboard toolbar when you're through with it, click its **Close** (x) button.

The Clipboard toolbar tells you how many pieces of data are waiting to be pasted.

Clipboard toolbar   Each icon represents cut or copied data.

Using the Clipboard Toolbar Buttons

The Clipboard toolbar has three buttons you can use when managing items on the Clipboard. Hover your mouse pointer over a button to display a ScreenTip revealing the button's name. The first button, **Copy**, can be used to copy items to the Clipboard, just like the Copy button on the Standard toolbar. The **Paste All** button lets you paste every cut or copied item in the Clipboard into your worksheet all at once. The **Clear Clipboard** button clears every item on the Clipboard toolbar.

I know you're probably already familiar with using the Cut, Copy, and Paste commands, but here's a recap:

➤ To move data from one location to another—whether it's in the current worksheet, a different sheet, another workbook, or another file in another program—first cut the data using the Cut command. Click the **Cut** button on the Standard toolbar.

➤ To copy data, click the **Copy** button on the Standard toolbar.

➤ To paste the data, open the file or worksheet where you want the data pasted, click the cursor where you want the data inserted, and then click the **Paste** button.

➤ If you're pasting one of several items you've cut or copied to the Clipboard, you'll need to pick which item to paste from the Clipboard toolbar (see the previous figure).

Remember, just about every program under the sun uses the Cut, Copy, and Paste commands (if they're not on a toolbar, you usually find them in the **Edit** menu). Therefore, you can easily paste Excel data into other programs.

Clipboard Toolbar Not Showing?

To summon the Clipboard toolbar at any time, right-click over any other toolbar and choose **Clipboard** from the menu list of toolbar names.

Or Use the Shortcut Menu

You can also right-click selected data in Excel and other Microsoft programs and choose the **Cut**, **Copy**, or **Paste** commands from the shortcut menu that appears.

Pasting Excel Items into Excel Sheets

Don't forget you can also paste more than just data when you're cutting or copying in Excel. Use the Paste Special dialog box to paste specific aspects of your data, such as formatting only or just formulas. For more information about this technique, revisit the section "Using the Paste Special Command" in Chapter 12.

To Link or to Embed? That Is the Question

When you cut or copy data from one spot to another, it's a one-time thing. The data doesn't retain any connection to its source. But what if you want it to retain a connection? In that case, what you want is a little OLE.

OLE stands for *object linking and embedding*. OLE (pronounced *oh-lay*) is a feature that enables Windows programs to share data more dynamically. OLE lets you share data, and it retains a connection to its source, which is an improvement over ordinary cutting, copying, and pasting.

OLE

OLE, short for *object linking and embedding,* is a technology for sharing data from different programs.

How about an example? Let's say you've created a report in a word processing program, such as Word, and you want to insert a table of data from Excel. You might be inclined to just copy and paste the data into the document file. But what if it's a weekly report and the Excel information changes each week? Do you really want to keep copying and pasting the data each time it changes? OLE to the rescue.

With OLE technology, you can choose to link or embed the data. If you link it, for example, any changes made to the original data in Excel are immediately reflected in the table you inserted into the Word document. You don't have to lift a finger. If you embed the data instead, it's not updated automatically, but it does retain a connection to its source. You can make edits directly to the object without leaving the Word window; just double-click the embedded data, and the Excel tools pop up for you to make your changes.

OLE Lingo

The file in which you create the data you're linking or embedding is called the *source* file, or sometimes referred to as the *server*. The file to which you link or embed the data is called the *destination* file, or the *client*, or *target*. The actual data you link or embed is considered an *object*. Not all applications fully support OLE. Some can act only as the OLE client; others can take only the role of OLE server. For example, WordPad (an application that comes with Windows) can be a client but not a server. Thankfully, most of your major programs (such as any of the Microsoft Office programs) support OLE.

Which Is Better: Linking or Embedding?

Both linking and embedding are great, but to help you know exactly which operation is best for the job, Table 23.1 lists some considerations.

Table 23.1 Considerations for Linking and Embedding

Linking	Embedding
When you link an object, information about the object is stored in the source file, which means you have to save the original file you used to create the object.	When you embed an object, the information about the object (such as the program used to create it) is stored in the destination file. This means you don't have to save the original file you used to create the object.
If you link an object, you must be careful not to delete or move the source file.	If you embed the object, you don't have to worry about a source file.
When you link objects, there isn't any impact on the destination file's size.	When you embed objects, the destination file increases in size.

continues

Table 23.1 Considerations for Linking and Embedding
CONTINUED

Linking	Embedding
If you link an object and email the destination file to someone else, you may need to send along the source file, too, in case the other person wants to edit any part of the object.	If you embed an object and email it to someone else, you don't have to worry about sending along any additional files.
If you link an object and the original data changes, the linked data will automatically reflect the latest changes.	If you embed an object, you have to update it yourself. There's no direct connection to the source file.

The bottom line in determining whether to link or embed data is this: Do you want the data to reflect the most recent changes or not? If you do, then link the data. If you don't, then consider embedding.

How to Link Data

To link data in an Excel file, use these steps:

1. Open the file or worksheet containing the data you want to link and the file or worksheet to which you want to link the data.

2. In the source file, select the data you want to link and then click the **Copy** button or open the **Edit** menu and choose **Copy**.

3. Switch to the destination file and click where you want the linked data placed.

4. Open the **Edit** menu and choose **Paste Special**. This opens the Paste Special dialog box, as shown in the following figure.

Use the Paste Special dialog box to set links.

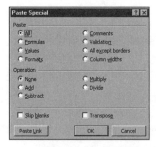

5. Click the **Paste Link** button. The data is inserted into the destination file.

The data is now part of your Excel worksheet. If it changes in its source location, the linked data will reflect those changes the next time you open this file.

You can also link entire files into your Excel worksheets. For example, you might link a database table from another file to your current worksheet, or you can link a Word report or a graphic. Use these steps to link an entire file, not just a single data object:

1. Click where you want the data to appear in the worksheet; then open the **Insert** menu and choose **Object**. This opens the Object dialog box, shown in the figure below.

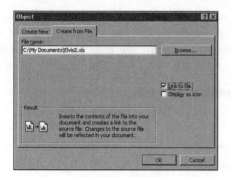

Use the Object dialog box to link entire files.

2. Click the **Create from File** tab and enter the filename and path of the file you want to link, or you can use the **Browse** button to locate the file.

3. Click the **Link to File** check box. (If you leave this check box unselected, the file will be embedded instead of linked.)

4. Click **OK**. The file is inserted and linked.

How to Embed Data

To embed a new data object in your worksheet, first click where you want the embedded data to appear and then follow these steps:

1. Open the **Insert** menu and choose **Object**. This opens the Object dialog box (see the next figure).

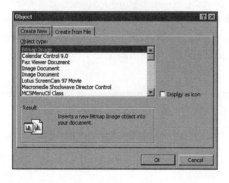

You can also use the Object dialog box to embed objects.

2. Click the **Create New** tab.

Embedding Existing Objects

If you've already got an object, such as a graphic, created in another file, you can embed it into your worksheet. Click the **Create from File** tab in the Object dialog box, and then enter the path to the file containing the object you want to embed or use the **Browse** button to locate the file. Click **OK**.

3. From the **Object Type** list, choose the object type you want to create.
4. Click **OK**. The object is embedded, and the source file's controls open onscreen so that you can create the new object.
5. When you're finished creating the object, click anywhere outside the object frame, and the Excel worksheet controls appear again.

Remember that the new object is now part of your Excel worksheet. To edit the object, just double-click it to reopen the source controls for making changes to the object.

What's with the Control Changes?

When you embed a new object or edit an embedded object, the Excel toolbar buttons and menus change to the source program's buttons and menus. Don't panic—you've not left Excel. Just make your edits using the proper tools and then click anywhere outside the object to redisplay the normal Excel program window elements.

Excel's Import/Export Business

Another way to share data is to import or export it. No, I'm not talking about foreign trade and commerce; I'm talking about working with different file formats. When you convert a file to another file format, you're indulging in the import/export business as far as computer files are concerned.

Perhaps your colleague uses Lotus 1-2-3 as his spreadsheet program. Well, he won't be able to read your Excel files unless you convert them by saving them in the WK4 (1-2-3) file format. When you save a file, you can specify another file format in the **Save As Type** drop-down list in the Save As dialog box (to open the Save As dialog box, display the **File** menu and select **Save As**).

Downgrading

If your friend or colleague uses an older version of Excel, you'll be happy to know you can save your file in a format suited for earlier versions of Excel. Some of your character or background formatting may be lost, but the data should convert unscathed by the difference in file formats.

In some instances, a colleague may give you a text file that contains data you want to use in Excel. When this happens, you can convert the text data into Excel data using the Text Import Wizard. First, display the Open dialog box (see Chapter 2, "File Fundamentals," to learn all about working with this dialog box). Next, click the **Files of Type** drop-down arrow, choose **Text Files** from the list, and then locate and select the file you want to convert. Click **Open** and the Text Import Wizard appears, as shown in the following figure. The wizard will walk you through the steps for converting the text into something Excel can recognize.

You have three text file formats you can work with using Excel:

➤ Formatted text (space-delimited), which creates a fixed-width text file

Exporting to a Text File

To save your Excel data as a text file for someone else, use the **Save As Type** drop-down list in the Save As dialog box to save the data as a text file.

The Text Import Wizard can help you convert text files.

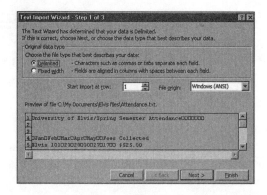

➤ Regular text (tab-delimited), which creates columns delimited by tabs

➤ CSV (comma-delimited), which creates columns separated by commas

The Text Import Wizard will generally recognize the file type you're trying to work with. Just follow the wizard's instructions to turn the data into something you can work with in Excel.

Sharing via Email

One more way you can tell Excel to share data is to do so via email. You can use the **E-mail** button on the Standard toolbar, or you can use the **Send To** command on the **File** menu. You can send your workbook as an attached file to an email message, or you can send the worksheet contents as part of your email message.

Before you get all excited about this aspect of Excel, I need to tell you about some system requirements. In order to email a message or workbook from the Excel window, you need Outlook 2000, a program for managing your schedule, email, and newsgroup participation. Outlook 2000 comes with Office 2000, in case you're using Excel as part of this particular suite of programs.

Don't Have Outlook 2000?

Don't worry; you can still attach Excel workbook files to your email messages using your regular email program. You just won't be able to email a worksheet as an email message directly from the Excel program window.

To send a worksheet as your email message's contents, open the **File** menu, choose **Send To**, and then **Mail Recipient** (or just click the **E-mail** button on the Standard toolbar). This opens Outlook 2000's message form below the toolbars, as shown in the following figure. From here, you can click inside the **To** text box and enter the email address of the person (or persons) you want to send the email to, or you can use the Address Book icon (to the left of the To text box) and choose a recipient from your address book. You can include additional recipients to Cc to, if needed.

E-mail form   Click here to send the worksheet as an email message.

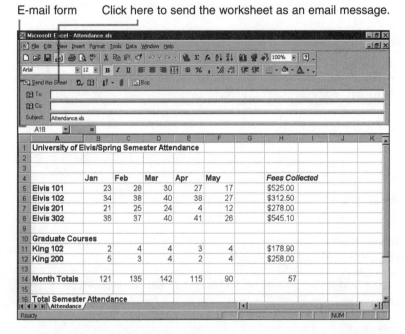

You can send your worksheet contents as an email message using Excel's email feature.

By default, the **Subject** text box includes the name of the workbook, but you can enter something more meaningful if you want. To actually send the message, click the **Send this Sheet** button (you need to be logged on to your Internet account, of course). As soon as you click the button, the message is sent, and the Excel program window returns to normal.

To send your Excel workbook as a file attachment instead of a message, open the **File** menu, choose **Send To**, and then **Mail Recipient (as Attachment)**. This opens the Outlook 2000 message form in its entirety, as shown in the next figure. Enter the recipient's email address in the **To** text box, and enter a more descriptive subject in the **Subject** text box, if needed. Click inside the message area and type your email message. Notice that the Excel workbook appears as an icon at the bottom of the message window, indicating that it's an attached file. As soon as you click the **Send** button (you need to be logged on to your Internet account if that's how you normally send email), the message is sent along with the workbook file.

You can also send the workbook as a file attachment to an email message.

Click here to send the message.

Enter the recipient's email address.

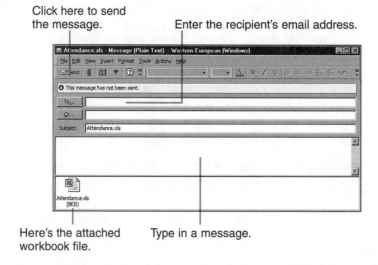

Here's the attached workbook file.

Type in a message.

The Least You Need to Know

➤ The Windows Cut, Copy, and Paste commands are fairly universal and provide an easy way to move and copy data between files.

➤ The new Clipboard toolbar allows you to copy up to 12 different items and then paste them in whichever order you want.

➤ When you link data, any changes you make to the original data are reflected in the linked data.

➤ You can quickly edit an embedded object by double-clicking the object.

➤ To share your files with other users who don't have Excel, convert the files to a compatible file format.

➤ Use Excel's email tools to send your worksheets as email messages or as attached files.

Chapter 24

Creating Excel Web Pages

In This Chapter

➤ Learn what it takes to become a bona fide Web surfer

➤ Check out the various ways you can surf Web pages and Excel workbooks

➤ Discover tips on performing a Web search

➤ Find out how to download files

➤ Learn how to run a Web query to grab data off the Internet

Unless you've been hibernating in a cave for the past four years or so, you're probably well aware of the impact the Internet is having on computer users around the globe. The Internet is a happenin' place, and you wouldn't want to miss out. Your Excel software doesn't want you to miss out either, so it comes equipped with several Internet tools to help you get the most out of the Internet. In this chapter, you learn how to use several of these tools to access the Internet, some of which you can use without leaving the comfort of your Excel program window.

Excel and the Internet

The Microsoft programmers have steadily added new Internet features to each version of Excel over the past few years. This latest rendition of Excel has the most Internet features ever. That's the good news. The bad news is you have to have your own Internet connection in order to use some of these features. If you're using Excel on an intranet (an internal corporate version of the Internet), you can use the Internet features to share Excel data with others in your office without necessarily needing an Internet account. However, if you're using Excel at home or in an office environment that doesn't offer an Internet connection, you'll have to scare up an Internet connection yourself, particularly if you're going to be using the Web. It all depends on your situation.

You may be wondering what sort of Internet features Excel has to offer. For starters, you can save and read HTML files as easily as workbook files. HTML, for those of you who are newbies to the Internet, is the file format for Web pages. Excel 2000 lets you save workbooks as HTML files which can be published on the Internet or an intranet. (Learn all about turning Excel workbooks into HTML files in the Chapter 25, "Using Excel on the Web.")

Got an Intranet?

If you're really, really lucky, your company might have an internal network, called an *intranet*, that works like the Internet but on a smaller scale. You can post and view Web pages found on the intranet, send email, and more.

Excel's Web tools also allow you to browse through workbooks and other Office documents that have links (or *hyperlinks*). For example, a link in an inventory spreadsheet might take you to a spreadsheet detailing manufacturing information. Links are typically underlined text in a worksheet that, when clicked, open another workbook or worksheet. A link might also take you to a Web page. For example, a link on the spreadsheet detailing manufacturing information might take you to the manufacturer's Web site. Regardless of where a link takes you, Excel is always ready to help you find your way.

Differences in Link Terms

Hyperlinks are not the same as the type of linking and embedding you learned about in Chapter 23, "Integrating Excel with Other Applications." Hyperlinks, called links for short, are shortcuts to viewing other Web pages or spreadsheets.

Getting Started with the Internet

If you're new to the Internet, you need to know that you must meet a few requirements before you can begin surfing the Web with everyone else. First of all, you need a modem. This shouldn't be a problem, because most new computers sold today come with modems.

Wait, I'm Really New!

If you've never used the Internet before, all you really have to know is that it's a gigantic international network of interconnected computers. The World Wide Web is just one aspect of the entire Internet. The Web is a collection of linked pages ranging widely in topics and intent. You can use the Web for business or leisure, going from page to page to learn more about a subject, company, product, or whatever.

Second, you need to establish an Internet account. If you're lucky, your company already has an Internet connection, and you're already hooked up and using it. If you're using your computer in a home environment or in an office that doesn't have an Internet connection, you'll have to set up an account with an Internet service provider, a company that lets you jump onto the Internet using its connection (for a monthly fee, of course).

How to Find a Service Provider

If you don't have an Internet account yet, you have plenty of service providers out there to choose from. Start by checking your city or town to see what's available. Look through your local Yellow Pages, check newspaper ads, or ask a local computer store employee for a recommendation. You can also find numerous providers advertising in computer magazines. Also, don't forget to ask your friends who they use.

Finally, you need a browser program, particularly if you're going to tap into the World Wide Web (or *Web* for short). No doubt you're already aware of the popularity of the Web, an incredibly vast collection of connected "pages" with all kinds of information. A Web browser is a program designed specifically for viewing and connecting to Web pages. If you bought Microsoft Office 2000 (of which Excel is a part), the program suite comes with the latest version of Microsoft's Web browser, Internet Explorer 5.0. If you bought a computer in the last two years or so, it probably came with an earlier version of Internet Explorer.

With those three requirements met (a modem, a service provider, and a Web browser), Excel users can surf the Internet using several of Excel's Web features.

Need Help Connecting?

Use the Internet Connection Wizard, a feature of Internet Explorer, to help you get started with your Internet account and Internet Explorer. Open the **Start** menu and select **Programs, Internet Explorer, Connection Wizard**. Now just follow the wizard prompts to walk you through setting up Internet Explorer to work with your Internet account.

Using the Web Toolbar

Excel's Web toolbar is common in each Office 2000 program, if you happen to be using Excel as part of the Office suite. Use the toolbar to link to other Office files, including Excel workbooks, or as a shortcut for opening Internet Explorer and viewing Web pages. Because the toolbar contains most of the commands you need to access the Internet, I'm going to introduce you to it right up front.

To display the toolbar, open the **View** menu, choose **Toolbars**, and then **Web**. You can also right-click a blank area of any toolbar and choose **Web** from the menu. Either method displays the Web toolbar, as shown in the following figure.

Table 24.1 explains what each Web toolbar button does. You'll see a great deal of similarity between this toolbar and the one found in Internet Explorer.

Web toolbar

The Web toolbar has familiar Web browsing icons and text boxes that look and act just like the tools in Internet Explorer.

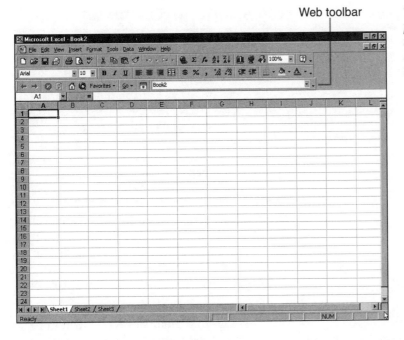

Table 24.1 Web Toolbar Buttons

Button	Description
⇐	Click the Back button to go back to the previous page you were viewing.
⇒	Click the Forward button to move forward to the page you were viewing before you clicked the **Back** button.
⊗	Click the Stop button to stop the current Web page from loading.
🔃	Click the Refresh button to refresh the current page and redisplay it again.
🏠	Click the Home button to view your browser's start page (also called a *home page*).
🔍	Click the Search the Web button to open a search tool for searching the Web.
Favorites ▼	Click the Favorites button to display a list of your favorite Web pages or workbook files or add new ones to the list. To view a page or file, select it from the list.
Go ▼	The Go button opens a menu of commands for visiting Web pages. Many of the commands are duplicates of commands already available as toolbar buttons.

continues

Table 24.1   Web Toolbar Buttons CONTINUED

Button	Description
	The Show Only Web Toolbar button turns off all the other toolbars except for the Web toolbar. Click it again to turn the other toolbars back on.
http://www.mcp.com	Use this text box to enter URLs (Web pages) you want to visit or Excel workbooks you want to open. You can also click the drop-down arrow and select pages you've previously viewed.

Finding Web Help

You can use the Excel Help menu to open your Web browser and find help on using Excel via Microsoft's Web site. Open the **Help** menu and choose **Office on the Web**.

Not Logged On?

If you're not logged on to your Internet account and you select an Internet tool in Excel, the Connection dialog box may appear for you to log on to your account. Click **Connect** and away you go.

The Web toolbar buttons work the same way as the other Excel toolbar buttons—you click a button to select it, but with a little twist. Depending on the button, a click may open your Web browser and display a Web page instead of activating an Excel command.

I don't expect you to remember each button I just showed you, but don't forget to flip back to this table in the paragraphs to come if you ever get confused about what a particular Web toolbar button does.

Wandering the Web

There are a couple of ways to access the Web using Excel's Web tools. You can click a link that takes you to a Web page, or you can enter an address for a specific page you want to visit. In either case, your browser window will open and display the appropriate page. Let's talk about links first.

As I mentioned earlier in this chapter, links are what makes the Web go 'round. Links, also called *hyperlinks*, are commonly displayed as underlined text, but you'll also find graphics and icons used to represent links on Web pages, too. To follow a link, simply click it. Links aren't exclusive to Web pages, though. You can also link to Excel worksheets, or even other Office 2000 files. As far as Excel is concerned, the only real difference in links is whether the link takes you to a Web page or to another Excel (or Office) file. If the link is to a Web page, your browser opens; if the link is to another Excel file, the workbook opens. Because we're focusing on the Web at the moment, take a look at an example of Web page links shown in the next figure.

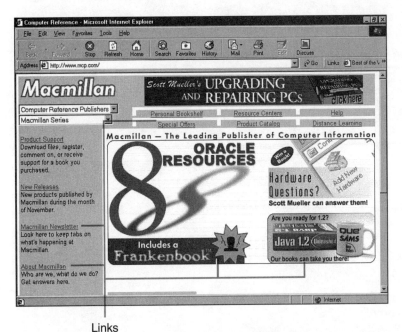

Web page links typically appear as underlined text on the page, but they can also be graphics or other visual objects.

Links

Following links allows you to wander the Web randomly, based on what interests you. Another way to go is to enter the exact address of the page or file you want to view. Every Web page has an address, called an *URL* (pronounced "Earl"). You'll find URLs everywhere, in advertising, on TV, in your local paper, or your friend or colleague may even include them in email messages. Once you know the URL you want to visit, you can do so from the Excel program window. Simply click inside the **Address** box on the Web toolbar in Excel and type the URL. A typical URL reference looks like this:

http://www.mcp.com

Is It a Link or Isn't It?

If you're not sure what's a link on a Web page, just hover your mouse pointer over the text or object. If the pointer takes the shape of a pointing hand, you've found a link. If not, it's not a link.

The next figure shows what an URL looks like entered into the **Address** text box. After you enter the URL, press **Enter**. Your Web browser opens and displays the requested Web page.

Use the Address text box on the Web toolbar to enter the URL you want to visit.

Click here and enter the URL.

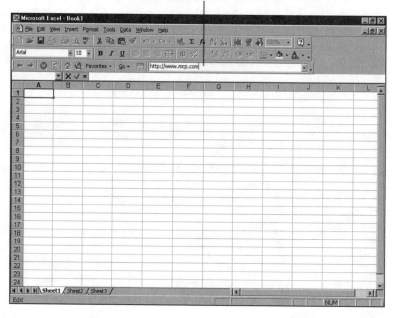

Check This Out

Marking Your Favorite Pages

When you come across a Web page you like and want to revisit, mark it as a favorite. Click the **Favorites** button on the Web toolbar and select **Add to Favorites**. This opens the Add to Favorites dialog box. Enter a name for the page (if you don't like the default entry) and click **Add**. The next time you want to view the page, click the **Favorites** button and choose the page from the list.

URLs aren't the only thing you can enter into the **Address** text box on Excel's Web toolbar. You can also use the **Address** text box to enter the paths of any computer files on your hard drive you want to view, whether it's an Excel workbook file, another Office file, or an HTML file. Of course, you have to remember exactly where the file is and enter the exact path to get to it. Because most users don't memorize the exact locations of their files, it's just as easy to use the Open dialog box to browse for and open files. However, if you've got other Web page files stored on your computer and want to view them when you're not logged on to the Internet, you can enter them in the **Address** text box (you can do this even when you're logged on).

Searching the Web from Excel

One of the most frustrating aspects of using the Web is searching for information. If following links won't take you to the information you need, try a search engine instead. Search engines are specially designed to frequently catalog and index Web pages. When you enter a keyword or phrase, the search engine looks through its catalog and returns a list of URLs where it found matches to your search criteria. Then you can explore each match and hopefully narrow down your search.

Techno Talk

URL

Short for Uniform Resource Locator, a URL is an address for an Internet site.

To use a search engine from Excel, click the **Search the Web** button on the Web toolbar. This opens the browser window and displays a page of search engines. Click the one you want to use to open the Search pane shown in the following figure. The Search pane displays the engine you chose, along with a text box for entering your key word or words. Click inside the text box and enter the word or phrase you want to search for, then click the **Search** button. Depending on which search engine you use, the button may be labeled differently (such as **Go** or **Start**).

Enter search text here.　　　Click here to start the search.　　　Choose a search engine.

Use the Search tool to look for specific topics or information on the Web.

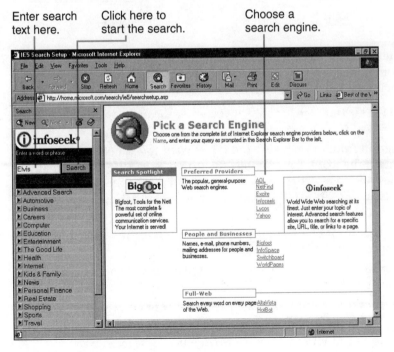

After a moment, the search engine displays a page of matching results (see the next figure). Depending on the text you entered, you may see thousands of matches or only a few. To follow a link, simply click it.

Here are the search results for the keyword "Elvis" (not that I'm fixated with this subject or anything).

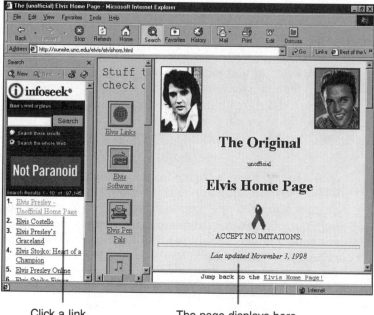

Click a link.

The page displays here.

Depending on the text you entered, your search may not have revealed the results you were looking for. In fact, with some search engines, it takes a little practice to get the hang of it. To help you narrow your search even further, here are a few tips:

➤ Be specific. You get better search results if you enter the exact words you're looking for.

➤ Enter a plus sign in front of each keyword if you want the search results to absolutely contain the word. For example, the search term **rose** results in anything using the word *rose*—whether it's flowers, Axl Rose, or the Rose Bowl parade. If you type **+garden +rose**, you find only pages that use both these terms.

➤ Use a minus sign in front of a word if you don't want to see pages with the term. For example, **+rose –hybrid –florist**.

➤ Use an **AND** operator if you want the search result to include both occurrences of the words, such as **garden AND rose**.

➤ Use an **OR** operator if you want to locate pages that contain at least one of the words, such as **rose OR flower**.

➤ It's a good idea to use all lowercase letters when entering search text.

Downloading Files

Gazillions of files are out there on the Internet that you can download right onto your own computer, and some of them are even Excel workbook files. The hardest part of downloading a file is finding the right file to download. Once you've located the file, the rest is a breeze. Click the file's download link to start the process. The File Download dialog box appears onscreen (see the following figure). Click the **Save This Program to Disk** option and then click **OK**.

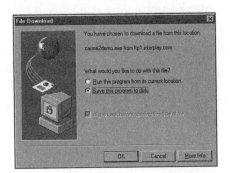

The File Download dialog box asks you what you want to do with the file.

Virus Alert!

Be aware that any file you obtain from the Internet can contain a computer virus. To keep your computer protected, be sure to run an antivirus program, such as Norton Anti-Virus or McAfee VirusScan, to check any files you download before you do anything with the file. Many virus-protection programs offer monthly updates you can download as well. Check your own program for more details.

Next, indicate where you want the downloaded file to be saved. It's a good idea to save downloaded files in a temporary folder. (Create a folder called 'Temp' on your C drive for this purpose.) Once you decide where to save the file, click the **Save** button. The download starts in earnest.

Depending on the size of the file and the speed of your modem, the download may take only a moment or several hours (be warned). If you're downloading particularly large files, you might want to schedule the download during off-peak hours (in the

343

evening or early morning, for example). If, after starting the download, you decide you can't spend three hours downloading a huge, honking program file, just click **Cancel** to put a stop to it all.

Running a Web Query

Here's a feature that's really cool. You can grab information you see on a Web page and pull it into your Excel worksheet. For example, you can download information such as stock quotes or corporate financial information and place it into your worksheet. You can do all this using Excel's Web Query feature.

When you install Excel, several Web Queries are installed for you. You can see these listed in the Run Query dialog box, as the steps below will show. These are static queries, which mean they retrieve the same data every time you run them. You can also create dynamic queries in which you specify what data to retrieve. We'll concentrate on static queries.

To run a static query, use these steps:

1. Open a new worksheet (click the **New** button on the Standard toolbar).
2. Click the first cell, open the **Data** menu, choose **Get External Data** and then **Run Saved Query**. This opens the Run Query dialog box, shown in the next figure.

The Run Query dialog box lists the queries that come with Excel.

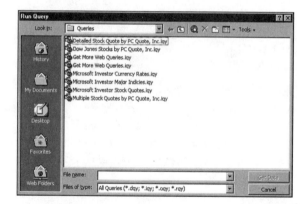

3. Choose a query from the list (such as **Dow Jones Stocks by PC Quote, Inc.**) and then click **Get Data**.
4. The Returning External Data to Microsoft Excel dialog box appears (see the next figure). Click **OK** to continue.
5. The Dial-Up Connection dialog box appears for you to log on to your Internet account if you aren't already connected. Click **Connect**.

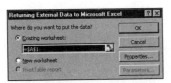

This dialog box lets you determine where the downloaded data is to appear.

6. After a moment or two (well, actually a minute or more, depending on the speed of your connection), the stock quotes download into your worksheet, as shown in the following figure.

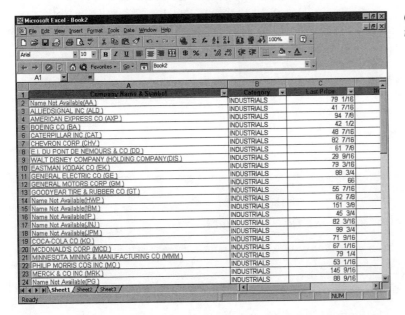

Get a load of this—an instant stock report!

You can now use the data as you see fit, or you can save it as a file. You can also click the company name, which happens to be a link, to visit its Web site.

To run a dynamic query, click the second sheet in the worksheet and then open the **Data** menu and choose **Get External Data**, **Run Saved Query**. This opens the Run Query dialog box again. This time, select **Detailed Stock Quote by PC Quote, Inc.** and click **Get Data**. Click **OK** in the Returning External Data to Microsoft Excel dialog box. The Enter Parameter Value dialog box now opens, as shown in the next figure. Here, you can specify exactly which ticker symbol you want to download information on (for example, enter **MSFT** for Microsoft). Click **OK** to log on to your Internet account again (that is, if you logged off after step 6 in the previous list) and download the information. Pretty cool tool, huh?

Enter your ticker symbol in the Enter Parameter Value dialog box and click OK.

Log Off!

When you're done running Web queries, don't forget to log off your Internet connection.

As you can see, if stocks and such are your game, then Excel's got plenty of up-to-the-minute data sources you can tap into on the Internet. Be sure to check out the other available Web queries in the Run Query dialog box. Check out the Get More Web Queries options, too.

The Least You Need to Know

➤ Use the Web toolbar to tap into Excel's Internet features.

➤ You can quickly open your Web browser from within Excel and view Web pages.

➤ Use the search tools to find the information you're looking for on the Web.

➤ You can download all kinds of files from the Web, including Excel workbook files.

➤ Download financial information, including stock reports, using Excel's Web Query tool.

Chapter 25

Using Excel on the Web

In This Chapter

➤ Find out what a Web page really is

➤ Learn how to save Excel worksheets as Web pages

➤ Discover tips on inserting your own hyperlinks

Web pages are exceedingly popular these days, and anybody can create one. You'll find a wide range of Web pages out there—for fun as well as for business. Just about everybody has a Web page on the Internet today, so you might as well join the crowd if you haven't already. In this chapter, you learn how to turn your Excel worksheets into Web pages. You can then post these pages on the Internet or on a company intranet. For example, you might want to post your company's year-end earnings, or your department's softball scores. You can turn any Excel worksheet item into a Web page, including charts, graphics, and more. We touch on a few of these things in this chapter, but be sure to explore all the possibilities on your own.

Creating a Web Page in Excel

In case you've been wondering all this time, let me explain exactly what a Web page is. It's actually just a simple text-based document, but when you open it in a Web browser, such as Internet Explorer, the simple text becomes headings, bulleted lists, links, graphics, multimedia clips, and more. How the heck does it do that? It's all in the coding.

HTML

HTML stands for *Hypertext Markup Language*, the special coding that's used to build Web pages.

The simple text isn't quite as simple as you might think. Web pages are written in HTML, which stands for *Hypertext Markup Language*. HTML is a special text code that Web browsers can read. Special coding (known as *tags*) tells where each Web page element starts and stops. Thankfully, you don't have to know this code if you want to make a Web page. However, it's pretty interesting stuff, if you care to explore it. Many fine books are available on writing HTML code. We just won't cover it in this one.

Web Pages with Word

Microsoft Word is a far better tool than Excel for building Web pages. If you've got Word, check out Word's Web Page Wizard. It walks you through all the steps for creating your own dynamic Web pages, including fancy–schmancy backgrounds. You can then fill the page with your text, or even data from an Excel workbook.

Rather than mess with HTML code, you can convert an existing Excel worksheet into a Web page by opening the **File** menu and choosing the **Save As Web Page** command. When you select this command, the Save As dialog box opens, as shown in the following figure. However, unlike the ordinary Save As dialog box, this one has options for dealing with Web pages.

Use the Save As dialog box to save your worksheets as Web pages.

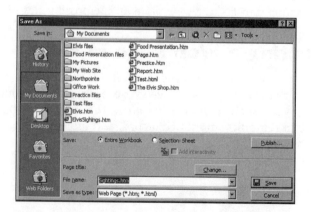

First, you need to specify exactly what part of the workbook you're saving as a Web page—click either **Entire Workbook** or **Selection: *data*** (*data* standing for whatever you've currently selected in the worksheet).

Next, enter a name for the file. Click inside the **File Name** text box and type one in. No need to worry about file type, because the Web page file format (HTML) is selected automatically. To give the page a title, click the **Change** button and enter a Web page title; then click **OK**. To save the file "as is," click **Save**. The Excel title bar now reflects the Web page format; notice that .htm is added to the filename. HTM and HTML are both recognized as Web page file formats.

If your worksheet has several different elements, such as a chart or graphic as well as data, you can specify which item to include on a Web page. For example, you can put PivotTables, text, shapes, WordArt objects, and other such items on your Web page. Excel's publishing features let you save any part of a workbook as an HTML item. To choose exactly which item to publish, such as a chart or the entire sheet's contents, click the **Publish** button to open the Publish as Web Page dialog box (see the next figure). Click the **Choose** drop-down list and select the item you want to publish; you can only publish one item at a time.

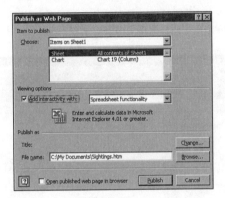

Sometimes I don't think you're reading these captions. I'm being paranoid, right? Here's the Publish as Web Page dialog box; use it to select which item to include on the page.

You can also choose to save the item as interactive or noninteractive. If you choose to save the item with interactive functionality, others who view the item can work with it and make changes to it (if they have Excel 2000 or the Office 2000 Web components). If you don't select this option, others can only view the item. To add interactive functionality to an item you've selected in the **Choose** list box, click the **Add interactivity with** check box, and then use the drop-down list to select **Spreadsheet functionality** or **PivotTable functionality**.

After you've made all the selections you want to make in the Publish As Web Page dialog box, click the **Publish** button.

Preview First

To see how the item looks on a Web page before exiting the Publish as Web Page dialog box, click the **Open Published Web Page in Browser** check box. This opens your browser window so you can view the worksheet in Web page format.

After you've saved your Excel data as a Web page using the Save As dialog box, you can make changes to it. For example, you might change the formatting or layout of the page or move items around. Before you do, take a moment to preview how the page looks. Open the **File** menu and select **Web Page Preview**. This opens your browser window, and the Web page is displayed. In the following figure, I've turned the data about Elvis sightings into a Web page, including a chart.

Here's my newly created Web page displayed in the Internet Explorer window. Isn't it lovely?

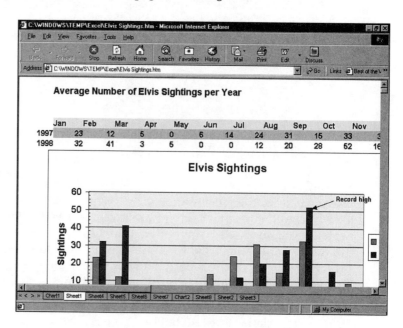

To return to Excel, click the **Close** button in the upper-right corner of the Internet Explorer window. If you make changes to the page, just click the **Save** button on the Standard toolbar, and the changes are saved to the Web page file.

Inserting Links

Without links, Web pages wouldn't be so darned popular. Links, also called *hyperlinks*, are the driving force behind the Web's phenomenal use. Quite simply, links are shortcuts to other pages or files. Links jump you from one page to the next, whether it's on the same Web site or on a completely different computer on a completely different continent.

Not the Same As Linking and Embedding

Hyperlinks you insert into Web pages or worksheets are not the same as linking and embedding data. Back in Chapter 23, "Integrating Excel with Other Applications," you learned how to make Excel share data between files using Object Linking and Embedding (OLE for short). Hyperlinks are quite different. Hyperlinks, or links for short, are simply shortcuts to viewing other Web pages or spreadsheets.

You can easily add links to your Web pages or to your regular Excel worksheets, and you can add as many as you like. The links can be to another Excel workbook file stored on your computer or to a Web page out on the Internet. For example, if you create a Web page out of an Excel worksheet that details your department's softball scores, you might add a link to the page that takes you to the division league Web site, or to another worksheet on your computer that details your team's players and game highlights. Or how about links to both places? As I said, you can add as many links as you like.

Linking Worksheets

Remember, links aren't just for Web pages. You can add links to worksheets, to other Excel workbook files, or to other Web pages.

Linking Tip

If you're linking two Excel files, it's a good idea to save them both in the same folder. That way you won't inadvertently move one and break the link.

To insert a link, use these steps:

1. Click in the worksheet cell where you want a link inserted. (Remember, you can add a link to an Excel Web page or to a worksheet.)

2. Open the **Insert** menu and choose **Hyperlink**, or you can click the **Insert Hyperlink** button on the Standard toolbar. This opens the Insert Hyperlink dialog box, as shown in the following figure.

3. In the **Link To** bar, click the **Existing File or Web Page** icon.

Use the Insert Hyperlink dialog box to insert a link into your Web page or worksheet.

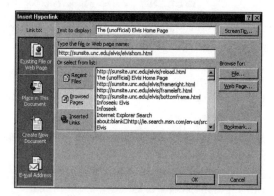

4. In the **Text to Display** box, enter the text you want to use as the link text. This is the text other users will see as the link.

ScreenTip Alert!

If you're using newer versions of Internet Explorer (version 4 on up), you can hover your mouse pointer over a link and see a text description of the link. To add such a thing to your own inserted link, click the **ScreenTip** button and enter the link text. Click **OK** to return to the Insert Hyperlink dialog box.

5. In the **Type the File or Web Page Name** box or the **Or Select from List** box, indicate the file or page you're linking to. If it's a Web page and you know the URL, type it into the text box. If it's a URL of a page you've recently visited, you can select it from the list box. Notice the list box has options for listing **Recent Files, Browsed Pages**, and **Inserted Links**. Click a button to reveal its associated list.

6. If you don't know the file location or URL, use the **File** button to locate the file to which you want to link; then click **OK** to return to the Insert Hyperlink dialog box.

Right-Click!

You can also right-click the cell in which you want to insert a link and then choose **Hyperlink** from the shortcut menu.

7. If it's a Web page you're linking to and you want to verify the page first (always a good idea), click the **Web Page** button to open your browser window and view the page.

8. Click **OK** to exit the dialog box and insert the link. The following figure shows a link in a worksheet cell.

Link

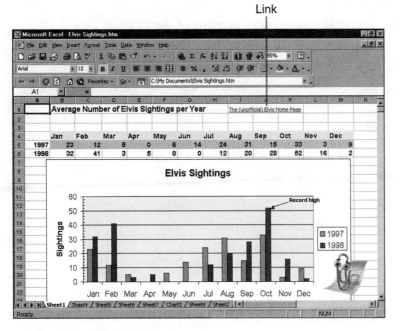

Here's a link added to my worksheet.

Links are blue and underlined on your worksheet. To test the link, click it. If the link is to a Web page, your browser window opens (you may have to connect to your Internet service provider first) and displays the page.

If it's a link to another worksheet or file, the appropriate file opens along with the entire application for viewing the file. When linking to other spreadsheets, use Excel's Web toolbar to navigate back and forth between linked sheets; it's fast and fun. Click the **Back** button to move to the previous sheet or click the **Forward** button to move to the next sheet (after you've clicked the **Back** button, of course).

To edit a link, first select the cell. Then right-click and choose **Hyperlink**, and then **Edit Hyperlink**. This reopens the Hyperlink dialog box (only this time it's called the Edit Hyperlink dialog box). From here, you can make changes to the link or edit the link text. To get rid of the link altogether, right-click it, choose **Hyperlink** and then **Remove Hyperlink**.

The Least You Need to Know

➤ HTML coding is the backbone of every Web page, but thankfully you don't have to know anything about it.

➤ You can turn existing Excel worksheets into Web pages.

➤ You can choose exactly which worksheet item to include on a Web page, whether it's a range of cells, a chart, or an entire sheet.

➤ Hyperlinks are shortcuts that take you to other Web pages or other Excel workbooks.

➤ You can add links to your Web page or to your worksheet.

Windows 98 in a Flash

In This Appendix

➤ Control the computer using the mouse

➤ Start and handle programs using Windows 95 or Windows 98

➤ Use buttons and menus to give commands

➤ Complain about your computer using the right words

This appendix is about *Windows*, the program that handles how you control all the other programs. There are a number of different versions of Windows around, but you are probably using Windows 95, Windows 98, or Windows NT. These all work pretty much the same.

Maybe this is the first time you have used your computer, or maybe it's not. If you have used a computer before, you probably know most of the stuff in this appendix—but read it over anyway so that you're comfortable with what we're calling things in the rest of the book. (Did you know, for example, that we are no longer calling the W key "the W key?" Instead, we are calling it the *Harold Stassen Memorial Digital Wuh-Sound Input Device*.)

A Mouse in the Hand

Attached to your computer is probably a white lump of plastic with two or three buttons on it. You use this device to control the computer. The Geeks in Charge of Naming Computer Things (GICONCT) decided that because you would be spending so much time with your hand on it, they should name it after something you would never put your hand on. It's called a *mouse*. You use the mouse by putting your hand on it and sliding it across a flat surface (usually a *mouse pad* made for just such usage).

Try sliding your mouse around. When you slide it, you should see something move on your computer screen. When you slide the mouse side to side, something on your screen also moves side to side. When you slide the mouse forward, it moves up the screen, and when you move the mouse back, it moves down the screen. This thing is called a *pointer*, and it's subject to your every command. It will follow you to the edge of the Earth—or at least the edge of the screen.

Missing a Mouse?

If your computer doesn't have a mouse, it probably has a *trackball* (push your hand across the top of the ball, and the pointer is pushed in the same direction), a *pad* (drag your finger across this flat rectangle, and the pointer is dragged similarly), or a similar pointing device.

The Point of the Pointer

The pointer is used to point to different things on the screen. When you want to give the computer a command pertaining to an onscreen item, you use the pointer to tell the computer which item.

The pointer takes on different shapes at different times. Usually, it's an arrow, which makes a very clear pointer. When you are pointing to an area of text, the pointer might turn into something that looks like a thin, tall capital *I*. This is sometimes called an *I-bar* or *I-beam*, and it's handy because you can put the thin vertical bar between two letters.

Sometimes the pointer turns into a picture of an hourglass. This means that the computer is busy doing something, and you have to wait until it's done. If you get sick and tired of seeing the hourglass, it's either time to get a faster computer, or time to go do something else, like take a snack break.

Clicking's a Snap!

It's not enough to point to something to give a command. After all, the pointer is always pointing to something. You have to have a way of letting the computer know that it's time to act on what you are pointing at, and that's what the mouse buttons are for.

The mouse has two buttons. The left one is the one that you use most of the time. When we talk about *clicking* something, we mean that you *point* to it with the pointer and then press the left mouse button. Don't hold it down, just push down and then let up on it quickly. To *double-click* something, you point at it and, instead of clicking once, you click twice.

Right-clicking is just like *clicking*, except that you use the right mouse button rather than the left one. You don't do this nearly as often.

Lefties Are All Right!

If you have a mouse that's set up for left-handed use, you use the right button for normal clicking, and the left button when we tell you to right-click.

My Mouse Has a Wheel in the Middle!

Some of you may be using the Microsoft IntelliMouse, a mouse with an extra wheel button in the middle of it. You can use the wheel to move up and down a document page, for example. You simply move the wheel forward or backward with your finger.

Clicking a Button

On your screen is a rectangle with a little colorful Windows symbol in it and the word **Start**. It's probably in the lower-left corner of the screen. (If you don't see it, try pointing to the very bottom of the screen; a gray bar should appear with **Start** at the left end.) This is a *button*, a rectangular area on screen that, when you click it, issues a command to the computer. At this point, the **Start** button is probably the only button on your screen, but soon you will have more buttons on your screen than there are on a dry cleaner's floor!

Notice how the button looks as if it is pushed out from the gray bar that it is on. Click the button, and you see two things. One is that the button looks pushed in. That means that the button is currently *active*, that it is having an effect. The other is that a list of items appears above the button. This list, called the *Start menu*, shows a number of commands that you can give to the computer. Pushing the **Start** button tells the computer to show you the commands (see the following figure). Click the button again, and the list disappears, and the button appears pushed out again.

Pressing the Start button made the Start menu pop up.

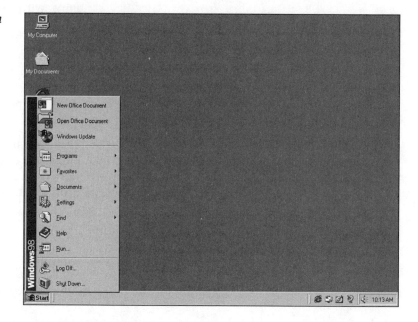

Try *right-clicking* the big open background area of the screen display (this is called the *desktop*). A short list of commands that you can choose pops up. This is called a *shortcut menu*. By right-clicking many things in Windows, you get a menu of commands that apply to what you clicked. For example, right-click the desktop, and you get a shortcut menu of commands that can change the desktop.

Dragging Ain't No Drag!

Sometimes, you have to move something from one part of the screen to another. This is called *dragging*, and it's quite easy. To take a swing at it, let's try dragging one of the *icons* around your desktop. (The icons are the little pictures with words underneath. Each one stands for a different program, file, or device on your computer.)

Find the icon with the picture of a computer on it (it probably says **My Computer** underneath it.) Point to that icon. While pointing to it, push down the left mouse button and hold it down. With the button pressed down, slide the mouse around. A transparent copy of the icon follows your pointer. It's the ghost of your My Computer icon!

Slide the pointer over to an area of the desktop where the ghost icon isn't overlapping any other icon. Let go of the mouse button, and one of two things happens:

➤ The icon disappears from where you dragged it, and reappears where you moved it to, or...

➤ The icons rearranged themselves in neat columns, with the icon appearing in a new spot.

If the second thing happened, it doesn't mean your dragging didn't work. Your copy of Windows is set up to keep the desktop tidy, and the moment it saw that something was out of the group, it tidied everything up. If your real desktop worked as well as your computer desktop, you would always be able to find a pencil when you needed one!

In either case, you can put things back to the way they were by dragging the icon you moved back from where you took it. If the rearranging icons covered up the place where the icon was before, drag it just a bit higher on the screen than the icon that took its place, again making certain that the ghost icon doesn't overlap any other icon.

When You Need a Menu

You have already seen how the Start menu and the shortcut menu can appear when you need them, hiding away like squirrelly, umm, squirrels the rest of the time. Menus provide access to tons of commands without taking up a lot of screen space when you don't need them.

Start Up the Start Menu, You Upstart!

Click the **Start** button again. Take a look at the Start menu. Each line has a picture and a word or phrase explaining what that command does. Some of the lines also have an arrowhead at the right edge, pointing toward the right. The arrowhead indicates that ancient native peoples used these menus, probably while running primitive versions of Windows.

Actually, the arrowhead means that that command brings up another menu. Slide your pointer up the menu. Notice how, as the pointer passes over each command, it changes color. This color change is called *highlighting*. Click the line marked **Programs**.

Programs had an arrowhead on it, so that means that another menu (often called a *submenu*) will appear next to this one. It may be just one column, but it may be several. Find the line marked **Windows Explorer** (it should be near the end of the last column), and click it. This starts a program that enables you to sort through the files on your computer's disk drives.

Why Don't You Drop Down and See Me Sometime?

If you followed my last instruction, a big rectangle appears onscreen, filled with all sorts of stuff. This is the Windows Explorer *window*, the area of the screen where the program displays controls and information (see the following figure).

359

Your Windows Explorer window may look different depending on your Windows version and settings.

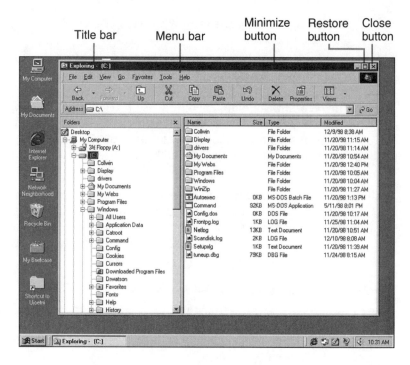

Title bar   Menu bar   Minimize button   Restore button   Close button

Managing Menu Mishaps

If you accidentally bring down the wrong menu, don't worry. Just click the menu name again, and that menu disappears!

At the top of a window are two bars. The first, called the *title bar*, has a name for the window. On the Windows Explorer window, it says **Exploring** followed by the name of your hard disk.

The second bar is called the *menu bar* (as opposed to, say, a *bar menu*, which lists drinks and other beverages that may include tiny paper umbrellas). It has a series of words on it. Each word is the name of a menu. Click the word **View**. A menu of commands appears below it—these are commands that have to do with the way that the program displays the list of what's on your disk. Click the command **Refresh**. This tells the program to recheck what's on the hard disk and to display the information again; you should be able to see when the display is being redone.

Keyboard Kwikies!

Sometimes you don't want to keep moving your hand to the mouse and then back to the keyboard; you just want to keep typing. Reaching your foot for the mouse is too much exercise after a while! Luckily, you have ways to give menu commands without clicking the menu.

If you click the **Edit** menu, you see some commands with things like **Ctrl+V** or **Ctrl+A** on the end of them. This tells you the shortcut for that command. The **Ctrl+V** on the end of the Paste command means that you can do a Paste command at any time by holding down the key marked **Ctrl** and pressing the key marked **V**, for example. Other keys you might see referred to include the **Shift** key and the **Alt** key. If a menu item is followed by **Shift+Alt+X**, for instance, that means that you can issue that command by holding down the Shift key and the Alt key, simultaneously, and tapping the X key. Of course, if you are new at typing, you might need both hands and your nose to do this.

On the menu bar, one letter of each word is underlined (for example, the **V** in **View** is underlined.) This means that you can bring the menu up by holding down the **Alt** key and pressing the underlined letter's key (such as **Alt+V**). On the menu that appears, one letter in each command is underlined; just press the key for that letter (such as the **R** in **Refresh**) to issue that command. So, in full, to get the refresh command, press **Alt+V**, and then let go of the Alt key and press the **R** key. It may sound like a lot of work—but if you think that's a lot of work, you should talk to your grandpa, who will tell you that real work is carrying 16 tons of rocks a mile up hill every day, just to earn your lunch (a rock sandwich). (Of course, your grandfather actually sold shirts for a living, but that's no reason why you should have it easy!)

Gray Means No Way

Most of the menu commands are in easy-to-read lettering, probably black. If you see one that's almost the same color as the background (probably gray), it means that you can't use this command now. (These are commands that only work under certain conditions.)

Windows Don't Have To Be a Pane!

If you're using several programs simultaneously, you can end up with a screen full of windows overlapping and even completely hiding each other. This can make your desktop as messy as that "stuff" drawer in your kitchen, where you *know* there's an almost-working 9-volt battery, if only you could find it! Luckily, there are tools that let you move windows around, change their sizes, and even hide them for a while (very handy if you're playing Space Bunny Attack and hear your boss coming.)

Wipe Away Your Window

At the right end of a window's title bar are three buttons. The first, which has a straight line in it, is the *Minimize* button. Click this, and the window disappears! Don't worry. It's not gone for good, so you can still help the Space Bunnies save the galaxy. If you look at the *taskbar* (the bar with the **Start** button on it), you see a button with the title of each window you are currently using. Click the button that has the title of the window you just minimized, and the window reappears, good as new, with each Space Bunny still intact.

Seize the Size!

The middle button has one of two pictures of it. If it has two overlapping rectangles, this window is currently in *Full-Screen* mode, so that it automatically takes up all the screen space available. When a window is in Full-Screen mode, you can't move it or change its size. It is seemingly invincible, but for one fatal flaw, its Achilles' heel (or, for those of us with more modern heroes, its Kryptonite): If you click this button (called the *Restore* button), it goes from Full-Screen mode to *Resizable* mode, and then you can do what you want with it! You have torn down all of its defenses!

If the middle button has just a single box on it, the window is already in Resizable mode. Clicking this button (called the *Maximize* button) puts the window into Full-Screen mode. This is good if you want to see as much of your Space Bunny Attack game as possible in the window.

Become a Mover and a Shaker... and a Resizer!

For you to move a window, it has to be in Resizable mode. Point to the window's title bar and then drag it. Depending on how your computer is set up, you may be dragging the whole window or just an outline of it. Drag it up, drag it down, drag it all around! When you let go of the mouse button, the window is where you dragged it!

If you want to change the size of a window, point to the lower-right corner of the window. The pointer turns into a slanted arrow with arrowheads in both directions (like a two-way street sign would look). Drag the corner, and you find that you are moving the corner of an outline of the window. Move it so that the outline is the size that you want the window to be, and then release the mouse button. The window now appears in the rectangle. With a little practice, you get so quick at dragging that you're ready for the drag races!

Wiping Out the Window

The button on the far right of the title bar, the one with an X in it, is the *Close* button. After you finish using a window, click this and the window disappears. This also tells the computer that you're done using the program that opened the window; so if you are running a program where you create a file (like a word processor), be sure you have saved the file before clicking it.

Let's Rap About Dialog!

Sometimes, a program asks you for information. To do that, it uses a *dialog box*, a type of miniaturized window. Most dialog boxes don't have a menu bar and can't be resized, but they can be moved around. More importantly, you use a dialog box to give the computer additional information to carry out a task. A dialog box is a basically a form. Just like paper forms can have blanks to fill in, boxes to check off, items to circle, and so on, computer forms have a lot of different ways of getting information. After all, filling out a form on a computer should be just as much fun as filling out a paper one!

To see some of these in action, click the **Start** button and select the **Find** command. When the second menu (sometimes called a *submenu*) appears, pick the **Files or Folders**... command. (The ... at the end of a command name lets you know that if you select that command, you get a dialog box (see the following figure). You can't complain that you weren't warned!)

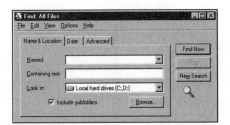

A dialog box.

Tab: It Isn't Just for Dieters Any More!

On the Find: All File dialog box, you can see a file folder shape with a form on it. At the top of it, in the tab where the name of the folder would go, are the words **Name & Location**. Next to it are two other tabs, just like a set of good file folders with the staggered tabs. Click one of those other tabs, and another form appears. By clicking a tab, you can easily choose which form you want to work on!

A Text Field Is the Type for Type

Check the **Advanced** tab and the **Name & Location** tab. On one of them (depending on which version of Windows you are running), you find a white area marked **Containing Text**. This is a *text field* (also called a *text box*), one that you can type into. To put some words into that field, click the field, and then type. You can use the cursor keys and the Backspace key to correct any typos you make. Or, you can leave your mistakes in and just confuse the computer!

Drop Down and Give Me 20!

On the **Advanced** tab is a field labeled **Of type**, which has a button at the end with a down arrow. This is a *drop-down list*—good for choosing one item from a list of items. Click the button (the *drop-down button*, which is a better name for it than *Mildred*), and a list of items appears under it. Click any item, the list goes away, and that item appears in the field.

What the Scroll Is That?

At the right side of the drop-down list, you will see a vertical bar with a box inside it. This is a *scrollbar*, which sounds like a Dead Sea tavern. Actually, it's Windows's way of telling you that it has more to show you than it can fit in the area it has to work in. The bar area represents the whole list. If the box is at the top of the bar, it means you are seeing the start of the list; if it's at the bottom of the bar, you are looking at the bottom of the list.

To see more of the list, just drag the box down the bar or click the arrows at the top or bottom of the bar. (If you see a sideways scrollbar, it means that what the computer is trying to show you is wider than the space it has. A sideways scrollbar works just like a regular one, but in a more horizontal fashion.

Check Out the Check Box!

Click the **Name & Location** tab. At the bottom of the form you see a little box marked **Include subfolders**. This is a *check box*. It either has a check mark in it, which means *yes*, or it's empty, which means *no*. To change a check box from checked to unchecked (or vice versa, or even the other way around), just click it!

Option Button, Option Button, Who's Got the Option Button?

Click the tab marked either **Date Modified** or just **Date**. At the left of the form, you see two columns of circles. These circles are called *option buttons*. These "buttons" are used to select one thing from a small list of choices; you use them to select one from a list of choices, and when you select one by clicking it, a dot appears in the circle. You can only have one button selected in each column at a time; when you click one, the dot disappears from the preceding selection.

Click the lowest option button. When you click it, the field next to that option turns white, but if you then select the button above that one, that field turns gray. That's because that field is only used if you use that option; when it turns gray, the computer is telling you that you don't have to fill it in.

The Least You Need to Know

➤ Sliding the mouse across your desk moves a pointer on the screen.

➤ *Clicking* means to point the pointer at something and press the left mouse button once.

➤ *Double-clicking* means to point at something and quickly press the left button twice. *Right-clicking* means to point at something and press the right button once.

➤ A *menu* enables you to select from a list of commands, by clicking the menu name to bring up the list and then clicking the command you want.

➤ A *dialog box* is a form that the computer displays, asking you for information.

Speak Like a Geek

absolute reference   A cell reference in a formula that always refers to a specific cell address or name and doesn't change even when copied or moved. Absolute references are always preceded by a dollar sign ($), such as $B$2.

active cell   The cell you're currently working in; the active cell is surrounded by a selector border.

active worksheet   The worksheet you're currently using.

address   The location of a cell or range on the worksheet grid, such as B4 or E25:K45.

add-ins   Additional miniprograms and features you can add to Excel, such as Web authoring tools, templates, and file converters.

arguments   The values in an equation that aren't operators (also see *operator*). An argument can include a constant, a cell reference, a range name, or a function.

block   A group of cells. Also known as a *range*. (Also see *range*.)

cell   The intersection of a column and a row in an Excel worksheet. Cells can contain data and formulas for calculations.

cell reference   The exact location of a cell in the worksheet, based on its column label and row number, such as B4. Cell references can be used in formulas.

Clipboard   A temporary storage area for data you cut or copy. The Windows Clipboard enables you to move or copy data from one area of the worksheet to another, from one file to another, or from one program to another.

Clipboard toolbar   A new feature in Excel 2000 that enables you to cut or copy multiple items, and then paste them into the worksheet in any order.

data points   Data that can be represented numerically on an Excel chart or graph.

data series   Any series of related information, such as the days of the week or number sequences.

database   An organized collection of data, such as an inventory or an address list. After it's entered, the database data can be sorted, filtered, and retrieved.

destination file   When you're linking or embedding data, the file where the data is contained is referred to as the *destination* or *container file*. The file where the data originates is called the *source file*.

equation   A calculation performed on a series of values using mathematical operators or functions. Also called a *formula*. (Also see *formula*.)

external reference   A reference to a cell or range found in another workbook.

field   When you're using Excel as a database, a *field* is any column in the database that holds a certain kind of data. For example, in an address database, each part of an address record (such as name, address, and zip code) is considered a field.

field buttons   When you're using Excel PivotTables, column labels in the data list are displayed as buttons.

file   When you save a worksheet you create in Excel, it's saved as a file on your computer's hard disk drive, or to another storage device (such as a floppy disk). You can reopen and reuse files when you save them, and you can also share them with other users.

folder   Used to organize and store files on your computer's hard disk drive. Called *directories* in previous incarnations of Windows.

format   To change the appearance of Excel data. For example, you can format all the totals in your spreadsheet as bold or italic.

formula   Calculations that can be performed on spreadsheet values.

formula bar   The bar above the worksheet area where you can enter formulas and functions.

frame   When you're working with objects such as graphics, a frame appears around an object when the object is selected. You can resize and move frames to alter the appearance or placement of the object on the worksheet.

function   A prebuilt formula. Excel has over 300 functions you can use to perform numerous kinds of calculations on your spreadsheet values.

graphic   Any electronic image you can add to a worksheet, such as a picture, clip art, a shape you draw with Excel's drawing tools, a chart, or a graph. A graphic object can be resized and moved anywhere on the worksheet

graphic report   Data represented by a chart, graph, or table on a worksheet.

gridlines   The lines that appear on a worksheet to separate the columns and rows of cells. Gridlines don't ordinarily print unless you choose to print them.

HTML   Hypertext Markup Language; the underlying coding for all Web documents, including any Excel files you convert to Web pages.

hyperlink   A shortcut to another file or Web page. Also called a *link*.

label   Worksheet data that's treated as text and cannot be calculated.

legend box   A box on a chart or graph that tells what each chart or graph element represents.

link   When referring to Web pages, a link (also called a *hyperlink*) is a shortcut to another Web page or to another file. Links are typically identified by colored, under-lined text; however, links can also be graphic images. Click a link to follow it to another Web page or file.

linking   An OLE (object linking and embedding) feature that lets you copy data from one program or file to another, yet still maintain an active connection to the source data. Any time the source data changes, the linked data is also updated.

list   Information in a database arranged in columns and rows.

macro   Prerecorded keystrokes or mouse movements that enable you to quickly perform a computer task or command.

name box   The area on the formula bar identifying the active cell or range. Also called the *reference box*.

object   A picture, drawing, or shape placed on a worksheet. An object can be resized and moved.

online   To be connected to another computer or network of computers, such as the Internet.

operator   A mathematical symbol used to calculate values on your spreadsheet. Operators include + (add), – (subtract), * (multiply), / (divide), = (equal), > (greater than), and < (less than).

page field   Another worksheet page that contains fields used in a PivotTable.

PivotTable   A table that shows interactive relationships between data.

print area   A selected cell or group of cells in a worksheet that you want to print.

range   A group of related cells in a worksheet defined by a cell reference or name.

range name   A name given to a block of cells in a worksheet to better identify the data they contain.

record   An entry in a database, typically a row in the worksheet. For example, a person's name, address, and zip code qualifies as a record.

reference   A name or address of a cell or range in a worksheet.

relative reference   By default, cell references are relative to their location on the worksheet. When you move or copy a cell reference to another location, the reference

369

reflects the new surroundings. For example, if you have a formula in cell A3 that adds cells A1 and A2 (A1+A2) and you then copy the formula to cell B3, the cells' references in the formula change to B1+B2. This is called *relative referencing*. (Also see *absolute reference*.)

result   The answer to an Excel calculation.

scenario   Suppositions you make about your data, such as predicting future results based on variances in the data. For example, you might create a scenario that calculates an auto loan based on several different interest rates.

selection handles   The tiny black boxes that appear around a selected object, such as a graphic image or shape.

sheet   Short for *worksheet*.

source data   The data you move or copy from the originating file or program and place in the destination file or program.

spreadsheet   A program made to imitate a ledger's rows and columns and used to organize and display data. You can use spreadsheets to perform complex mathematical functions on the values entered.

syntax   Excel's rules about where to place parentheses and other punctuation used in formulas.

template   A predesigned spreadsheet that already has formatting applied. All you have to do is add your own data.

value   A number in an Excel worksheet that can be calculated.

wizard   An automated process for completing a computer task, such as creating an Excel chart. A wizard walks you through each step, enabling you to customize the results as needed.

workbook   A collection of worksheets. Also called a *file*.

worksheet   A single Excel spreadsheet used to enter data. Also called a *sheet*, for short.

Index

Get FREE books and more...when you register this book online for our Personal Bookshelf Program

http://register.quecorp.com/

 Register online and you can sign up for our *FREE Personal Bookshelf Program...*unlimited access to the electronic version of more than 200 complete computer books—immediately! That means you'll have 100,000 pages of valuable information onscreen, at your fingertips!

 Plus, you can access product support, including complimentary downloads, technical support files, book-focused links, companion Web sites, author sites, and more!

 And, don't miss out on the opportunity to sign up for a *FREE subscription to a weekly email newsletter* to help you stay current with news, announcements, sample book chapters, and special events including sweepstakes, contests, and various product giveaways.

 We value your comments! Best of all, the entire registration process takes only a few minutes to complete...so go online and get the greatest value going—absolutely FREE!

Don't Miss Out on This Great Opportunity!

QUE®is a product of Macmillan Computer Publishing USA—for more information, visit: *www.mcp.com*